EDGEFIELD COUNTY, SOUTH CAROLINA

MINUTES OF THE COUNTY COURT

1785—1795

Probate Judge Office

Compiled by:

Brent H. Holcomb, C. A. L. S.

Please direct all correspondence and orders to:

www.southernhistoricalpress.com
or
SOUTHERN HISTORICAL PRESS, Inc.
PO BOX 1267
375 West Broad Street
Greenville, SC   29601
southernhistoricalpress@gmail.com

ISBN #0-89308-158-2

Printed in the United States of America

INTRODUCTION

Edgefield was formed in 1785 in Ninety Six District and was one of the largest counties formed in South Carolina. By the County Court Act of 1785, the county court of Edgefield was to sit beginning on the second Monday of January, April, July and October. With the alteration of the county court system in 1791, this intermediate court was to sit on the first Monday of June and November and the county court to sit the 11th of March and 1st of September.

Unfortunately some years of the County Court Minutes for Edgefield are missing: 1791-93 and 1796-99. However, the most valuable records (from 1785 to 1790) are extant. In any county, records prior to the 1790 census are valuable, but particularly in the case of Edgefield. This is due to the fact that Edgefield has lost one or two early deed books. Over 175 deeds proved or acknowledged in open court in 1786 and 1787 cannot be found. (Furthermore, upon examination of the deed books and upon comparison with the court minutes, Deed Book 2 dates from an earlier time than Deed Book 1.).

By the County Court Act of 1785, the county courts were to record deeds, try small cases, take bastardy bonds, grant tavern licenses, etc. By an act of 28 March 1787, these courts were also made courts of ordinary: proving wills, granting letters of administration, appointing guardians, etc. Probates before this date can be found in records of Ninety Six District back to 1781. Proving deeds became quite a problem--finding two witnesses to come to court or sending a dedimus to any county to take testimony of a witness--and took a great amount of court time. By an act of 29 January 1788, a deed could be proved by any one witness before a magistrate (not in open court) or acknowledged in open court by grantor. The matter of dedimi sent to other counties is one of the best ways to determine emigration. Notice the number of these from Edgefield sent to Georgia. In 1800 the county court system in South Carolina was abolished, and all counties became known as districts.

The court minutes abstracted here are found in two original volumes, now lamenated and housed in the Edgefield Office of Probate Judge. Original pagination is given in the left margin.

Brent H. Holcomb, C. A. L. S.
Box 21766
Columbia, S. C. 29221
February 19, 1979

Cover Drawing of Edgefield Probate Judge Office; Courtesy of Lynn Hendrix

[Pages 1-5 are missing in the original]

6 William Shaw & Daniel Brown Esquires having [produced] from
the Judges of the Court of the Common Please of this   appointed to plead in the Superior Court in this   approved
of by this court.

Ordered that the Petit Jury be dismissed.

William Dobey & John Herndon two of the subscribing witnesses
--- and release from Bryan Green to David Boswell for three
hundred ---- land made oath that they did see Bryan Green convey to ----- Boswell the aforesaid land in manner aforesaid
which ---- to be recorded.

Mrs. Rachael Rambo the wife of Banaja Rambo being ----- examined
by Benj. Tutt Esquire relinquished her rights -- and thirds to
the land conveyed by her husband Benaja Rambo to William Dobey
which is ordered to be recorded.

Ordered that the Clerk receive the presentments of the Grand
---- which being read and ordered to be recorded are as follows.

We present James Hollingsworth for retailing sprituous liquors
contrary to law.

We present Duggin McDugal for the same offence.

We present John Gibson for assaulting Jacob Smith.

We present John Watkins for assaulting of William Abney.

                              Jacob Smith, Foreman.

Ordered that prosecutions be commenced against the several
persons above present.

Ordered that the Court be adjourned untill tomorrow morning.

                              Leroy Hammond
                              Arthur Simkins
                              John Purvis
                              Benj. Tutt
                              John Moore

The Court met according to adjournment the 10th January 1786.
Present the Worshipful Leroy Hammond, Arthur Simkins, John
Purvis, Benj. Tutt, John Moore, William Anderson

Robert Lang and David Boswell two of the subscribing witnesses
to a lease and release from Banaja Rambo for three hundred acres
land to William Dobey made oath that they did see Banaja Rambo
convey to the said Dobey the aforesaid in manner aforesaid which
was ordered to be recorded.

7 - Lease and release from Henry Parkman to Henry Parkman, Jr. --
hundred & seventy five acres land was proved by the oaths of --
& Henry Rody which was ordered to be recorded -- lease & release
from Lacon Ryan to Benjamin Darby for -- acres land was proved
by the oaths of Samuel Walker & -- Berry which was ordered to
be recorded.

-- of lease & release from Matthew Gayle Jr to Matthew Gayle

1

--hundred acres land was proved by the oaths of John Gayle &
-- Davis which was ordered to be recorded. -- Stark came into
court and acknowledged his deed of lease & release -- hundred
acres land to Nicholas Eveleigh Esquire which was -- to be
recorded.

-- Stark came into court and acknowledged his deed of lease &
release to Benj. Bell for two hundred acres land which was ordered to be recorded.

John Purvis came into court and acknowledged his Deeds of lease
& release for three hundred and seventy six acres land to Nicholas Eveligh Esquire which was ordered to be recorded.

Rosannah Gunnels came into court and acknolwedged her Deed of
gift to Daniel Gunnels, Sarah Gunnels, Dicy Gunnels, Moses
Gunnels & Saunders Gunnels, which was ordered to be recorded.

Deeds of lease & release from Peter Day to Joshua Hammond for
one hundred acres land was proved by the oaths of same, Christopher & Joseph Hightower which was ordered to be recorded.

Henry Parkman came into court and acknowledged his deeds of
lease & release for one hundred & fifty acres land to Henry
Parkman Jr. which was ordered to be recorded.

The Opinion of the Justices of Edgefield County respecting the
regulations invested on them by the County Court Law in the
following matters, 1st with regard to the regulating Taverns.

That Jamaica or West India Rum be sold by the pint or smaller
quantity at the rate of one shilling & expence per pint.
Rum distilled on the Continent or Taffia at the rate of nine
pence the pint.
French brandy at the same tates as Jamacia or good West India
Rum
Peach Brandy at one shilling the pint.
Whiskey at ten pence the pint.
Geneva at one shilling and six pence the pint.
Madeira wine if good at four shillings per quart or bottle, if
ordinary at two shillings and four pence per quart or bottle
For Dinner if hot one shilling & six pence- if cold one shilling.
Supper or breakfast one shilling.
Clean lodging four pence.
Stabling and fodder for horses each a night one shilling.
Corn pt. quart three pence.

8   Ordered that the following persons be appointed overseers for
the different roads under mentioned.

Van Swearingen Sr for that part of the Publick road from the
county line to the Spring on Horns Creek.

Van Swearingen Jr. from the spring on Horns Creek to the Island
ford road near Harris.

Angus McDaniel from that part of the said road to Turkey.

-- Bailey from the said creek to Cyper Creek.

William Carson from the said creek to Cuffetown creek.

2

Samuel Stalnaker from Cuffetown to Brannons --- for the road leading from Ninety Six to the Ferry -- to Augusta D

William Lipscomb for that part of the road from Ninety Six to Horse Pen Branch.

Jonathan Dawson from the said branch to the old road.

William Dawson from that road to Turkey Creek.

James Coursey from Turkey Creek to Gunnels branch.

George Martin from Gunnels branch to Horns Creek.

John Hancock from Horns Creek to Sweet Water.

Abraham Richardson & Fields Purdiew from Snowhill and Augusta Ferry
For the road leading from Augusta Ferry to the Island Ford on Saludy River.

Thomas Lamar Jr from that part of the road beginning at the said Ferry to the upper Cherokee pond

Thomas Carter from the Cherokee pond to Chevous Creek

Benjamin Cook from Chevous creek to Horns creek

John Gray from Horns Creek to Log Creek

Thomas McGinnis from long creek to where said road crosses the road from Long Cane to Charleston

Benjamin Lewis from the said cross road to Jefferson branch

Reuben Holloway & Frederick Ward from Jefferis branch to the Island ford on Saludy river

For that part of the road leading from Augusta Ferry to Anderson Ferry on Saludy River viz

Benjamin Ryan for that part beginnin- at the Cherokee pond to the Piny Wood House

John Swearingen from the Piny Wood House to John Jones

John Jones from John Jones to Amos Richardson

Amos Richardson & William Abney from Amos Richardsons to Saludy river at Andersons Ferry.

9 Arthur Watson from the county line to Dry Creek

Frederick Sesson from Dry Creek to Amos Richardson

Dudley Pruet from Amos Richardsons to Burtons old place

William Matthews from Burtons old place to county line at Ninety Six.

For the road leading from near Fort Charlotte to the Charleston road near the white pond

Jacob Hill from the county line to Horse Creek; John Carter from Horse Creek to Stevens Creek; William Farrar from Stevens to the Old Meeting House; Edward Prince from the old meeting house to the Rockey Pond; Drury Pace from the Rocky ponds to Elliots Cabin; James Mays from Elliots cabin to the county line near the mouth of Little River.

For the road leading from Ninety Six towards the Junipet Ouzts; Thomas Anderson from the county line to halfway swamp; William Hill from halfway swamp to where the road intersects Carsons road; Nathaniel Abney from Carsons Ferry road to Little Saludy River; Andrew Lee from Little Saludy to the county line including the road from Lees Ferry untill it intersects the above road.

Ordered that the docket be called over.

Fields Perdiew vs John Spencer. Case. Judged by default.

The same vs. James Buckelew. Case.

The Same vs James Vessels. Case.
This day came the parties by their attorney & the Defendant comes & denies the promises in the Declaration supposed and prays it may be inquired into by the County, therefore the tryal of the Issue is referred untill next court.

10 The same vs Van Swearingen. Case. Judt. by default.

John Herndon vs Leonard Nobles. Case. Judt. by default.

The same vs the Same. Assault & Battery. The same.

George Garbet vs Rolly Roebuck. Debt. This day came the parties by their attorney & the defendant comes and defends the debt in the declaration supposed and prays it may be inquired into by the County therefore the tryal of the issue is referred untill next court.

Obiah Clay vs Bartlet Martin. Debt. This day came the parties by their Attorney & the defendant comes and defends in the declaration supposed and prays it may be inquired by the county therefore the tryal of the Issue is referred untill next court.

Shields Marsh vs Jenkin Harris. Tresspass assault & battery. This day came the parties by their attorney & the defendant comes and defends the force & injury etc. when & say that the assault & battery in the declaration were of the plaintiff proper assault & the plaintiff says was of the Defendants own wrong without any such cause & this he prays may be inquired of by the Country and the defendant likewise the same therefore the tryal of the issue is referred until next court.

James Thompson vs Rolly Roebuck. Debt. Judgement confessed according specialty.

George Brewer vs Joseph Read & Others. Case. Judt. by default against John Morris. the writ not served on Read.

John Harris vs Shields Marsh. Slander. This day came the parties by their attorney and the defendant comes and defends

the injurious words in the Declaration supposed & prays it
may be inquired into by the County before the tryal of the
issue is referred until next court.

11 Burgess White vs Edward Couch. Case. Judt. by default.

Frances Settles vs Abraham Heath. Case. Judt. by default.

Frances Settles vs Richard Johnson. Case continued

Fields Perdiew vs George Miller. Debt. Judt. by default.

George Nee vs John Crawford. Debt petition. This day came
the plaintiff and withdraws the action and pays the cost.

William Brown & Harmon Galman admrs. of Joseph Reed vs John
Purvis Esq. Debt. This day came the defendant and the plaintiff tho solemnly called made default nor did his suit further
prosecute therefore on motion of the defendant aforesaid it
is considered by the court that the defendant recover against
the said Plaintiff five shillings besides his costs....

Broughton & Read vs Hester Fields. Case Petition. This day
came the plaintiff & the defendant by her attorney wherefore
upon debating the matter it is considered by the court that
the action be dismissed and the plaintiff to pay all cost.

Jeremiah Webb vs James Carson. Case. Continued.

Stephen Mallet vs James Christopher. Case Petition   continued.

12 Broughton & Read vs James Anderson Case. Petition. Ordered
that the Plaintiffs produce their book of. account-

William Jeter vs Banajah Rambo. Debt. This day came the
parties by their Attorneys and the defendant comes and defends
the debt in the Declaration supposed and prays it may be
inquired of by the country and therefore the tryal of the
Issue is referred until next court.

John Rainsford vs George Miller & James Booth. Debt. continued.

John Davison vs James Gray. Case. Judt. by default.

John Gray vs Francis More. Assault & battery. This day came
the parties by their attorneys and the defendant comes and
defends the assault in the Declaration supposed were of the
Plaintiffs proper assault and the plaintiff says it was of
the defendants own rong without any such case and this he
prays may be inquired of by the country and the defendant
likewise the same and therefore the tryal of the issue is
referred untill next court.

James Martin vs Thomas Broughton. Debt. This day came the
parties by their attorneys and the defendant comes and defends
the debt in the declaration supposed and prays it may be inquired of by the country therefore the tryal of the issues
referred untill the next court.

Samuel Mishat vs Adam Brewnar. Debt. This day came the de-

5

fendant by William Shaw Esq. his attorney and the plaintiff
tho solemnly called made default nor did his search further
prosecute therefore on motion of the defendant by his attorney
it is considered by the court that the defendant recover
against the said plainitff s 5 besides his cost....

John Watson indorse of Wm. Nicholas vs Edward Couch & John
Ryan. Debt. This day came the Plaintiff by William Shaw
Esq. and withdraws his action and pays his cost.

13 James Vessels vs Morris Calaham. Case. Petition. On the
plaintiff making oath that the sum of Ƚ 3 12.10½ the amount
of his acct on which his action was founded was fully due
to him whereon it is considered by the court that the Plaintiff recover by debt aforesaid with his cost....

James Vessels vs Francis Nicholas Debt. continued.

John Randol vs John McCreles. Debt. This day came the parties by their Attorneys and the defendant comes and defends
the debt in the declaration supposed and prays it may be inquired of by the country therefore the tryal of the issue is
referred until next court.

Ordered that the Sheriff return the Attachments.

Benjamin Tutt Esq. vs John Harrison. On original attacht.
Judt. by default.

Leroy Hammond vs James Scott. attachment. John Martin being
summoned as a Garnashee and not appearing it is ordered that
he appear on the first day of next court on the default thereof that execution shall issue against the property attached
in his hands.

Abraham Richardson vs Daniel Elum. Attachment. dismissed.

Robert Davis vs Thomas Rees. Attachment dismissed.

Jacob Odom vs Thomas Adams. Attachment dismissed.

The court then adjourned till tomorrow morning nine O'Clock.
Leroy Hammond, Arthur Simkins, John Purvis, Benj. Tutt, John
Moore, Wm. Anderson.

14 The court met according to adjournment 11th January. Present
the worshipful Leroy Hammond, Arthur Simkins, John Purvis,
Benjamin Tutt, John Moore, Wm. Anderson, Esquires.

Deeds of lease and release from Samuel Gardner to John Rainsford for 350 acres land was proved by the oaths of Philip
Johnson and Alexander Oden which was ordered to be recorded.

Deeds of lease and release from Joseph Williams to John Jones
for 300 acres land was proved by the oaths of William Clark
and William Rice Clerk, which was ordered to be recorded.

James Harris came into court and acknowledged his Deeds of
lease and release fro 50 acres land to Samuel Marsh which was
ordered to be recorded.

Lewis Tilman came into court and acknowledged his Deeds of
lease and release for 225 acres land to Stephen Tilman which

was ordered to be recorded.

On application of Bartlet Martin he is admitted to keep Tavern for one year from the date hereof whereupon he the said Bart-let together with Jones Rivers & George Cowen entered into and acknowledged their bond according to law.

As did the following persons in form aforesaid, vizt.

Andrew Lee securities Jacob Smith & William Butler.
Frederick Ward securities John Moore & Joseph Burton
John Jones securities William Clerk & Isaac Lewis
Joseph Burton securities John Norwood & Frederick Glover.
Enoch Grigsby securities William Butler & Andrew Lee.
Robert Stark securities Bartlett Martin & Jones Rivers.
Benjamin Cook securities Robert Lang & Frances Moore
John Harris securities James Harris & Moses Harris.
Thomas Chappel securities William Abner & Morris Gwin.

Arthur Simkins esquires came into court and acknolwedged his Deeds of lease and release for 238 acres land to Samuel Lan-crum which was ordered to be recorded.

The Court proceeded to the assignement of the taxable inhab-itants for the purpose of making payment for the public buil-ding.

Ordered that the sheriff do collect one eighth part from each taxable inhabitant of the tax such person was liable to pay year 1784 for the above mentioned.

15 [torn] that each person that has been admitted to keep Tavern at thy court   unto the court, previous to their receiving a license for that purpose   of £ 3 sterling agreeable to law

Ordered that each of the overseers of the roads appointed by the court be served with a copy of the order of court and instructions for their guide

Ordered that the jurors defaulters be fined according to law and that the clerk do furnish them with a copy of this order

Ordered that this court be adjourned to the second Monday in April next to meet at the plantation of John Harris. Leroy Hammond, Arthur Simkins, John Purvis, Benj. Tutt, John Moore, Wm. Anderson.

At a court adjourned over to the second Monday in April which met according to adjournment the 10th at the plantation of John Harris 1786. Present the worshipful Arthur Simkins, Hugh Middleton, Benjamin Tutt, John Moore & Wm. Anderson, Esquires.

Peter Carns Esquire having produced a certificate from the Judges of the court of common pleas of the State of his being regularly appointed to plead in the Superior Courts of this State was approved of by this court.

William Jeter being returned to serve as a grand juror last court made default, it was ordered that unless that he made a satisfactory excuse to the court he should be fined which he did to the satisfaction of the court.

John Swearingen being excused from being overseer over a road
Thomas Cotton was appointed in his room.

Ordered that the sheriff return the writ of Venire for the
Grand Jury the names of the Grand Jury that appeared

Bartlet Martin	Isaac Lewis	Richard Moore
James Martin	John Thomas	Mat Martin
Joseph Collier	Frances Moore	William Spraggins

Upon motion of Charles Goodwyn Esquire ordered that he be admitted an attorney of this Court being an attorney of the
court of common pleas.

Ordered that this court be adjourned untill tomorrow morning
10 o'clock. Arthur Simkins, Benjamin Tutt, John Moore, Wm.
Anderson.

16 The court met according to adjournment 11th. Present the
Worshipful Arthur Simkins, William Anderson, John Moore &
Russel Wilson, Esq.

Samuel Stalnecker came into court and acknowledged his Deed
of lease & release from 250 acres land to James Tutt which
was ordered to be recorded.

Arthur Watson came into court and acknowledged his deeds of
lease & release for 133 acres of land which was ordered to
be recorded.

John Crow came into court and acknowledged his deeds of lease
& release to William Dawson for 547 acres land which was ordered to be recorded.

Arthur Watson came into court and acknowledged his deeds of
lease & release for 130 acres of land to Ezekiah Watson which
was ordered to be recorded.

Deeds of lease & release from Moses Prescot to Frederick Williams for 200 acres land was proved by the oaths of   which
was ordered to be recorded.

Deeds of lease & release from John Reed to James Tutt for 100
acres land was proved by the oaths of John Crow & Samuel Stal-
nicker which was ordered to be recorded.

Robert Stark came into court and acknowledged his Deeds of
lease & release for 700 acres land to James & John Martin
which was ordered to be recorded.

Deeds of lease & release from John Caroway Smith to Charles
Goodwin 309½ acres land was proved by the oaths of Benjamin
Tutt & John Purvis Esquires which was ordered to be recorded.

James & John Martin came into court and acknowledged their
Deeds of lease & release for 700 acres land to Hugh Middleton
which was ordered to be recorded.

John Chaney came into court and acknowledged his Deeds of
lease & release for 200 acres land to Thomas Berry which was
ordered to be recorded.

Robert Melton came into court and acknowledged his Deeds of
lease & release for 50 acres land to Peter Hilliard which was

8

ordered to be recorded.

Deeds of lease & release from Elizabeth Blakely to Hugh Middleton for 100 acres land was proved by the oaths of Edmond Martin & James Harrison which was ordered to be recorded.

17 -- Martin came into court and acknowledged his Deeds of lease & release to Philip King for 250 acres land which was ordered to be recorded.

Deeds of lease & release from Isaac Crowder to Joel Lipscomb for 100 acres land was proved by the oaths of David Cunningham and Julius Nicholas which was ordered to be recorded.

Deeds of lease & release from Thomas Ray ·to Drury Mims for 100 acres land was proved by the oaths of Thomas Hagin & Nicholas Dillard which was ordered to be recorded.

Deeds of lease & release from Isaac Kirkland to James Walker for 200 acres land was proved by the oaths of Samuel Walker and Conrad Galman which was ordered to be recorded.

John Harkins came into court and acknowledged his Deeds of lease & release for 450 acres land to Samuel Ramsey which was ordered to be recorded.

Deeds of lease & release from Thomas Adams for 100 acres land to Thomas Palmer was proved by the oaths of William Jeter & William Jeter Jr. which was ordered to be recorded.

Robert Melton came into court and acknowledged his Deeds of lease & release to Samuel Satcher for 100 acres land which was ordered to be recorded.

Mrs. Hannah Melton being prively examined by Hugh Middleton Esq. one of the Justices relinquished her right of dower & thirds to the land conveyed by her husband Robert Melton to Samuel Satcher which was ordered to be recorded.

William Jeter Sr.'came into court and acknowledged his deeds of lease and release to Philip Johnson for 80 acres land which was ordered to be recorded.

Deeds of lease & release from John Barkley to Obediah Henderson for 300 acres land was proved by the oaths of Andrew Thompson & James Cook which was ordered to be recorded.

James Coursey came into court and acknowledged his Deeds of lease and release John McPatrick for 125 acres land which was ordered to be recorded.

Ordered that the Grand Jury be drawn to serve next court

18 The names of the Grand Jurors drawn
Abner Perin, David Zubly, Samuel Ramsay, John Jones, Richard Allison, James Lyon, Aquilla Miles, John Ryan, Thomas Wilson, Matthew Gale, Fields Perdiew, Andrew Lee, Thomas Lamare, John Williams, John Martin, Jacob Brooks, Frederick Glover, John Hammond, Richard Johnson, Drury Adams.

Ordered that the petit jury be drawn to serve next court.
The names of the Petit Jurors drawn

Thomas Baker	William Maples	Henly Webb
Thomas Cotton	James Henderson	Caleb Holloway
Isaac Lewis	James Brooks	Richard Dean
Peter Rappy	Robert Anderson	Joseph Nun
Joseph Culbreath	Matthew Devour	Thomas Deloach
Thomas Youngblood	William Holloday	Anguish McDonald
John Garret	Thomas Carter	Robert Thompson
William Rotten	William Walker	Peter Zimmerman
Ezeriah Lewis	Shadrick Henderson	Thomas Chappel
		Philip May
		Edward Mitchel

Present Hugh Middleton and Benjamin Tutt, Esquires.
Ordered that the Sheriff return the venire for the Petit Jury.

The names of the Petit Jury that appeared
John Hancock, Micajah Cowley, Seth Howard, Solomon Duglish,
Frederick Tilman Sr., Ogdon Cockcroff, Michael Deloach,
Robert Deshaso, James Carson, William Stalsworth, Wright
Nicoson, Frederick Tilman Jr.

Ordered that the Grand Jurors that was summoned and made default should make a sufficient excuse upon oath for their
non attendance by sitting of the next court otherwise they
will be fined

Ordered that James Hollingsworth and Dugal McDugal been presented by the Grand Jury for retaling spirituous liquors appearing in court and no evidence appearing against them be
discharged from their further attendance on this court

On a Petition from Sundry Inhabitants of this county to have
a road opened from Masons Ferry on Savannah River tne hearest
and best way to the road leading from Fort Moore Bluff to
Charleston and to cross Horns Creek at Ravens Bridge

19   Ordered that the said Petition be granted and that Nathaniel
Bacon and Benjamin Bowers be appointed overseers to lay off
and open the said road and that all inhabitants liable to
work on roads and living within six miles of said road be
compelled to work on the same

Ordered on the Petition of a number of inhabitants of the
county living at the head of the waters of Cuffeetown on
Beaver dam creek that a new road be opened from Jesse Harris'
Mill to fall unto the Charleston road near the Widow Williams
and that Nathaniel Henderson, William Stalworth and John Cooke
be appointed overseers for the purpose of effecting it and
that the said road be cut twenty five feet wide

Ordered that the appearance docket be called over in future by
the clerk twice and the parties either Plaintiff or Defendant
shall not be bound to try their suits on the first calling but
the second shall be defenitive and the causes taken in course
as they stand upon the docket and that Petitions and summons
shall stand first on the Docket

Deeds of lease and release for 3 acres land to Arthur Simkins
Esq. & others Commissioners & C was proved by the oaths of
James Harris and Harmon Galman which was ordered to be recorded.

Deeds of lease & release from John Sally to John Pounds was
proved by the oaths of Butler Williams and Elisha Walker for

10

200 acres land which was ordered to be recorded.

Joshua Hammond came into court and acknowledged his Deeds of lease & release to Frances Settles for 752 acres of land which was ordered to be recorded.

Deeds of lease & release from John Russell to Samuel Gardner for 300 acres land was proved by the oaths of John Hater and John Rainsford which was ordered to be recorded.

A Bill of sale from Daniel Jones to Hugh Middleton Esquire was proved by the oaths of John Rainsford and Frederick Tilman which was ordered to be recorded.

Benjamin Ryan came into court and acknowledged his Deeds of lease & release for 150 acres land to Nathan White which was ordered to be recorded.

20 David Thompson vs James Mays. Ordered on motino of Mr. Goodwyn and by consent of parties that a commission dedemus Potestation be issued from the court directed to John George Esq., Justice of Wilks County State of Georgia and such other Magistrates as he chooses to take of this position of Thomas Mitchel a witness in this case and that they return the same by the next court and that due notice be given to the defendant when and where the said examination is to take place

James Mays vs Ezekiel Harlin. Ordered that a commission Dedemus Potestatem be issued from this court directed to Col. Cleveland and George Walton Esquires Justices of the peace for Franklin County State Georgia to take the disposition of Susannah Ward & Charlotte Mays on the second week in June next in behalf of the defendant and that due notice be given the plaintiff to cross examine the witnesses.

Ordered that the court be adjourned 'till tomorrow Morning nine O'Clock. Arthur Simkins, Hugh Middleton, John Moore, William Anderson.

The court met according to adjournment with Present the Worshipful Arthur Simkins, Hugh Middleton, Benj. Tutt, John Moore, William Anderson, Russel Wilson, Esq.

John Davidson vs James Gray Case. Judt. confessed according to specialty.

Deeds of lease & release acknowledged in open court by John Witzel to William Shaw for 1½ acre land which was ordered to be recorded.

Ordered that a commission Dedimus Potestation issue from this court directed to John & William Moore & William Anderson Esquires or any two of them to receive the renunciation of Mrs. Eleanor Witzel wife of John Witzel her right of Dower and thirds to the land conveyed by her husband to Wm. Shaw and report to next court

On application of John Galman permission was granted him to keep Tavern Securities James Carson & Samuel Mays

On application of William Day at the Island ford Saluda permission was granted him to keep Tavern Securities William Anderson & John Galman.

On application of Seth Howard permission was granted him to
keep Tavern Securities William Anderson & John Galman.

Ordered that the Sheriff amke a return to the court on the
second Monday in July next of the money he has collected
agreeable to an order of last court

William Jeter Jr. vs Banaja Rambo. Debt. Judt. confessed
according to specialty staying execution six months

Ordered on the petition of a number of Inhabitants that a road
should be opened from Mill Creek crossing a branch below John
Hancocks race paths to the Cherokee pond by Thomas Lamar and
John Hardy is appointed overseer of the said road

On motion of Mrs. Shaw that a Dedimus Potestation issue to
take the examination of John Aikens directed to John Jones
State of Georgia or any other Magistrate on the behalf of
Timothy McKenney at the suit of Frederick Glover.

Ordered that the Petit jurors defaulters should make a sufficient excuse upon oath for their non attendance at this
court on the second Monday in July next otherwise they will
be fined.

It is the opinion of the court that a constable should be
appointed to attend during the sitting of this court and that
James King and William Frazier be appoined for that purpose
and sworn

Solomon Duglish one of the Petit Jury on account of sickness
was excused attending the court and Frederick Williams was
appointed to serve in his room

Fields Perdiew & Co. vs John Spencer. Case. This day came
the Plaintiffs by Brown their attorney and the defendant tho
solemnly called made default and thereupon came a jury to
wit John Hancock, Seth Howard, Frederick Tilman Junr., Michael
Deloach, James Carson,Wright Nicholson, Ogdon Cockroft, Robert Deshazo, William Stalsworth, Frederick Tilman Jr., Frederick Williams & Norris Gwin...the defendant is guilty of the
debt...the plaintiffs damages Ŀ 7 s 3 d 3½...John Hancock,
foreman.

22 Fields Perdiew & Co. vs Van Swearingen. Case. This day came
the Plaintiffs by Brown their attorney and the defendant tho
solemnly called made default and thereupon came also a jury
(same as preceding)...the defendant is justly owing the Debt
in the declaration...Ŀ 11 s 1 d 1...John Hancock, foreman.

Fields Perdiew & Co. vs Simon Gentry. Case. This day came
the Plaintiffs by Brown their attorney and the defendant
who solemnly called made default...they do asses the Plaintiffs
damage Ŀ 5 s 15 d 9...John Hancock, foreman.

Fields Perdiew & Co. vs George Miller. Case. This day came
the plaintiffs by Brown their attorney and the Defendant tho
solemnly called made default and ther came also a Jury(same
as preceding)...the defendant is justly owing the debt...Ŀ 8
s 9 besides costs...John Hancock, foreman.

Jeremiah Webb vs James Carson. Case. Continued by consent
of parties.

Fields Perdiew & Co. vs James Vessels. Case. on application
of the parties this cause is referred to the decision of
Leroy Hammond Esq. and Harmon Boseman with power...and umpire
and their report to be made a rule of court

John Herndon vs Leonard Nobles. Assault & Battery. This day
came the Plaintiff by his attorney and withdraws his action
and pays his cost

The same vs The Same. Case. The same rule as above.

George Garbet vs Rolley Roebuck. Debt. This day came the
plaintiff by his attorney and withdraws his action and pays
his costs.

Shields Marsh vs Jenkin Harris. Assault & battery. This day
came the plainttiff by his attorney and withdrawns his action
and pays his cost

John Harris vs Shields Marsh. Slander. This day came the
Plaintiff by his attorney and withdraws his action and pays
his cost.

George Brewer vs Joseph Read & John Marsh. Case. This day
came the plaintiff by Brown his attorney and   thos solemnly called made default and thereupon came a jury to wit (same
as before)...the defendant is justly owing Ŀ 40...John Hancock,
foreman.

Burgess White vs Edward Couch. Debt. Judgement confessed according to specialty.

James Mays vs Ezekiel Harlin. Trover. Ordered that a commission Dedimus Potestation issue from this court to take the
deposition of John Ward on behalf of the Plaintiff before Col.
Cleveland Justice of the Peace Franklin County State Georgia
to give the defendant 15 days notice to attend and cross
examine

Stephen Mallet vs James Christopher. Debt Petition. This
day came the Defendant by William Shaw Esquire his attorney
and the Plaintiff tho solemnly called made default therefore
on motion of the Defendant by his Attorney aforesaid it was
considered by the court that the deft. recover against the
Plaintiff his cost by him about his defence in this behalf
expended

Hameter Foy vs Amos Richardson. Case. Petition. This day
came the plaintiff Peter Carnes her attorney and his defendant by   Goodwyn his attorney she withdraws her action
and pays her cost.

Frances Setles vs Richard Johnson. Case. This day came the
Plaintiff by Peter Carnes his attorney the defendant by
Brown his attorney and thereupon came a jury to wit (same as
before)...the Defendant is guilty of the assumptions in the
declaration mentioned and they do assess the Plaintiff damages
Ŀ 25 besides his costs.... John Hancock, foreman.
From which aforesaid judgment the Defendant prays an appeal
and to him it is granted to the court of   to be held at
Ninety Six on 26 Nov next on his complying with the laws

13

Deeds of lease & release from Isaac Methel to Samuel Stalnecker for 250 acres land proved by the oaths of Benjamin Tutt and James Tutt which was ordered to be recorded

Deeds of lease & release from James Moorehead to James Tutt for 125 acres land was proved by the oaths of Samuel Deloach & Samuel Stalnaker which was ordered to be recorded

Benjamin Tutt Esquire came into court and acknowledged Mortgage for negroes to Hugh Middleton & John Purivs Esquires which was ordered to be recorded

The Court adjourned untill tomorrow Morning 9 O'Clock. Arthur Simkins, Hugh Middleton, Benj. Tutt, John Moore, Wm. Anderson, Russel Wilson.

The Court met accoridng to adjournment 13th. Present the Worshipful Arthur Simkins, Hugh Middleton, Benjamin Tutt, William Anderson & Russel Wilson.

Deeds of lease & release from Robert Mosely, John Rainsford for 57 acres land was proved by the oaths of David Burk & Richard Tutt which was ordered to be recorded

Benjamin Tutt Esquire came into court and acknowledged his deeds of lease & release for 65 acres land to Samuel Gardner which was ordered to be recorded

Benjamin Tutt Esquire came into Court and acknowledged his Deeds of lease & release for 612 acres land to William Dawson which was ordered to be recorded

Deeds of lease & release from Harmon Galman, William Brown, Joseph Addison & Lucretia Galman for 150 acres land was proved by the oaths of James Gunnel & John Gray which was ordered to be recorded

Frances Setles vs Abraham Heath. Case. This action dismissed by consent of parties

Jeremiah Webb vs James Carson. Case. Continued by consent of parties

Broughton & Read vs James Anderson. Debt. Petition. This day came the Plaintiff by their attorney Brown and the defendant by William Shaw his attorney, wherefore upon debating the matter it is considered by the court that the Plaintiff take nothing by their bill but for their false clamour be in mercy....

John Rainsford vs George Miller and James Booth. Debt. This day came the Plaintiff by Charles Goodwyn his attorneys and withdraws his action and pays his cost.

26 John Davidson vs James Gray. Case. Judgment confessed.

John Gray vs Frances Moore. Assault & battery. This day came the plaintiff by Brown his attorney and the Defendant by William Shaw his attorney and thereupon came a Jury to wit (same as before)...the defendant is guilty of the assault... the Plaintiff damages for Ł 2 s 5 besides his costs....

14

John Kennedy came into Court and acknowledged his Deeds of lease & release for 116 acres land which was ordered to be recorded

James Martin vs Thomas Broughton. Debt. The plaintiff came into court and confessed judgment for Ł 54 s 7 d 6 with interest on staying executive untill 1 December next.

James Vessels vs Frances Nicholas & Others. Continued.

John Randol vs John McCrelis. Debt. continued

John Gray vs Francis Moore. Assault & Battery. Henry Ware was allowed 4 days attendance as a witness in this action in behalf of the Plaintiff.

27 Benjamin Tutt Esq. vs John Harrison. Debt on Attacht. This day came the Plaintiff by Daniel Brown his attorney and his defendant tho solemnly called made default and thereupon came a jury to wit (same as before)...the defendant is guilty of the debt...the plaintiff damages Ł 100 besides his cost....

Leroy Hammond Esq. vs James Scott. Debt. on attacht. continued by order plaintiff

Alexander Alexander vs John Sharpton & George Crim. Judicial attacht. ordered

John Ryan vs John Richardson. Dismissed at Pltfs cost

Jones Rivers vs Henry Key. Continued.

The same vs Thomas Key. Continued.

The Same vs Elizabeth King. Continued.

Frances Brooks Adminiss. vs Robert Thompson. Judgment by default.

28 John Hammond vs Isaac Davis. Capias ordered

John Williams vs Thomas Bizzel. Judgement by default.

Robert Moseley vs John Rainsford. Continued.

Frederick Glover vs Timothy McKenney. Continued.

John Randol vs James Gray. Continued.

Richard Johnson Junr. vs Francis Setles. Continued.

The same vs the Same. The same order.

John Duglish vs John Williams. Continued.

Solomon Edwards vs William Footwine. Continued.

Robert Stark asse. vs Sarah Harris Ex. Continued.

29 James Moore vs Arthur Warson & Robert Stark Executors of Michael Watson. Debt. Dismissed by order of Plaintiff.

William Fairchild vs Howel Johnson. Judgement by default.

John Randol vs Rolley Reobuck. Case. Judgment by default.

Wm. Brown & Harmon Galman vs John Purvis Esq. Dismissed by order of Plaintiff

James Masy vs Ezekiel Harlen. Continued.

David Thompson assee vs James Mays. Continued.

Fields Perdiew & Co. vs John Cannon. Judicial attachment ordered in this case.

William Cook vs Jones Rivers & wife. Continued.

William Jeter vs John Hammond. Continued.

John Williams vs John Crawford. Continued.

30 John Mims vs Thomas Lamar Continued.

Abemeleck Hawkins vs Thomas Lamar   Continued.

Drury Glover vs Van Swearingen. Continued.

William Footwine vs Abner Harrel. Petition Dismissed at Plaintiffs cost.

John Williams vs Lewis Clark. Referred to Samuel Marsh & Frederick Sesson

William Nicholas vs Edward Couch & John Ryan. Continued.

Edward Couch vs William Nicholas Judgment on default.

Charles Goodwyn vs Edward Couch. Judgment confessed on staying execution three months.

John Copp vs Thomas Sheriff. Judgment confessed by Defendant on staying execution till 1st Oct. next

31 John Rainsford vs Garret Buckelew. Petition. Dismissed at Plaintiffs cost.

Frederick Session vs William Butler. Petition Dismissed each paying his cost

James Robinson vs Edward Couch. Dismissed by order of court.

Ulyses Rogers vs John Pounds. Dismissed by order of Plaintiff Defendant paying cost

The same vs the same   The same order.

Robert Stark Junr. vs Banaja Rambo. Continued.

John Williams vs Thomas Bezzil. Dismissed at Plaintiffs cost.

Benjamin Tutt Esq. vs John Norris. Judgment by default.

The Court adjourned until the second Monday in July next to meet at the plantation of John Harris. Arthur Simkins, Hugh

Middleton, Russel Wilson.

Court adjourned over to the second Monday in July which met according to adjournment at the plantation of John Harris the 10th July 1786. Present the Worshipful Leroy Hammond, Hugh Middleton, John Purvis & John Moore, Esquires.

Jacob Cleveland came unto court and acknowledged his Deeds of lease & release to John Ryan & Benjamin Ryan for 100 acres land which was ordered to be recorded.

Frederick Tilman came into court and acknowledged his deeds of lease & release to Robert Speer for 100 acres land which was ordered to be recorded.

Mrs. Milla Tilman being privately examined by John Moore Esquire one of the Justices relinquished her right of dower & thirds to the land conveyed by Jacob Cleveland her husband to John & Benjamin Ryan which was ordered to be recorded.

Benjamin Arrinton made his excuse on oath for his non attendance as a Juror last court which was received and ordered to be recorded.

Present Arthur Simkins Esq.

The Rev. Charles Bussey made his excuse by affidavit for his non attendance last court as a juror which was received and ordered to be recorded.

Philip Lamar made his excuse by affidavit for his non attendance as a juror last court which was recieved and ordered to be recorded.

William Frazier made his excuse for his non attendance last court as a juror which was recieved and ordered to be recorded

James King came into court and acknowledged his deeds of lease & release for 100 acres land to Robert Speir which was ordered to be recorded

Mrs. Sarah King being privately examined by John Moore Esquire one of the justices relinquished her right of Dower & thirds to the land conveyed by her to Robert Spier which was ordered to be recorded

Drury Adams came into court and acknowledged his deeds of lease & release to John Olliver for 200 acres land which was ordered to be recorded

Richard Lowry came into court and acknowledged his Deeds of lease to George Bussey for 200 acres land which was ordered to be recorded

John Williams S. D. made his excuse for his non attendance as a Grand Juror which was received and ordered to be recorded

Thomas Spraggins made his excuse for his non attendance as a Grand Juror which was recieved and ordered to be recorded

33 Jacob Brooks made his excuse for his non attendance as a Juror was received and ordered to be recorded

Thomas Franklin came into court and acknowledged his Deeds of lease & release for 200 acres land to Edmund Franklin which was ordered to be recorded

Ward Taylor came into court and acknowledged his Deeds of lease & release to Neri Taylor for 100 acres land which was ordered to be recorded

John Purcel came into Court and acknowledged his Deeds of lease & release to Samuel Gardner for 25 acres land which was ordered to be recorded

Present Russel Wilson Esquire.

Henry Somerall came into court and acknowledged his Deeds of lease & release for 150 acres land to John Martin which was ordered to be recorded

Samuel Gardner came into court and acknowledged his deeds of lease & release to John Purcel for 100 acres land which was ordered to be recorded

Deeds of lease & release from Thomas Roberts to John Roberts for 100 acres land was proved by the oaths of John Cannada & John Purcell which was ordered to be recorded

On motion of Samuel Gardner ordered that a Commession Dedimus Potestatem issue directed to Hugh Middleton Esquire to privately examine Mary Ann Gardner wife of the aforesaid Samuel Gardner whether or not she did relinquish her right of Dower and thirds to the land conveyed to her husband containing 175 acres to Shirly Whatley

On Motion of Mr. Prince ordered that Commission Dedimus Potestation issue directed to Robert Harper a justice in Wilks County State Georgia to examine Whalton Whartley he being a witness to a tract of land conveyed by Frederick Stallions to Robert Middleton and report to next court

William Thomas made his excuse for his non attendance as a juror which was received and ordered to be recorded

Richard Johnson Junr came into court and acknowledged his Deeds of lease & release for 463 acres land to John Eldirdge which was ordered to be recorded

34   Ordered that the Grand Jury be drawn to serve next court. The names of Grand Jurors drawn

Alexander Newman	John Bullock
Thomas Galpin	James Coursey
William Jeter Senr	Thomas Lamar H. C.
Thomas Mayberry	George Cowen
Philip Johnson	Nathaniel Howel
James Hargrove	Richard Johnson
Arthur Watson	Henry Key
Robert Lamar	George Martin
Jacob Smith	Jones Rivers
Fields Perdiew	Robert Samuel

Ordered that the Petit Jury be drawn to serve next court. the names of the Petit Jurors drawn

John Buckhalter	Edward Hampton	James Kitcherside
Robert Christie	Joseph McDonald	Howel Johnson

George Mock	James Tutt	George Gibson
Thomas Lamar, B. M.	James Lavingston	William Little
Richard Laner	Edward Coe	John McFatrick
Hugh CArson	Joseph Day	David Nichoson
Frederick Tilman	Marshal Martin	John Griffith
David Bowery	Burgess White	Mishack Wright
William Wallace	Alexander McDugal	Lot Warren
Allen Bean	Edmund Franklin	

Philip May having made his excuse upon oath he was not able to attend this court as a juror was excused any further attendance at court

On motion of Captain George Cowen ordered that a commission Dedimus Potestatem issue directed to Henry Grabel a justice of the Peace State Georgia privately to examine Mrs. Sarah Dupus whether or not she relinquished her right of dower & thirds to the lands conveyed by her husband to Capt. George Cowen containing 450 acres and report upon it to the next court

Deeds of lease & release from John Curry to Peter Day for 95 acres land was proved by the oaths of John Hancock & William Covington which was ordered to be recorded

Captain John Ryan made excuse upon oath that he was not able to attend last court as a Grand Juror which was received and ordered to be recorded

Captain George Martin made an excuse upon oath that he was not able to attend last court as a Grand Juror which was received and ordered to be recorded

David Burke came into court and acknowledged his Deeds of lease & release for 22 acres also for 14 acres land to John Hammond Sr. which was ordered to be recorded

On Motion of Mr. Hancock & others ordered that John Martin Aquilla Miles, Thomas Carter, William Covington & Shirley Whatley or any three of them do view the ground from Gunnels Creek to Adams Ferry on Savannah River and mark out the convenince unconvenience of opening a road to the said Ferry and report to the next court

Ordered that the Sheriff return the writ of Venire for the Grand Jury. The names of the grand jury that appeared Aquilla Miles, Jacob Brooks, Abner Perrin, Drury Adams, Thomas Wilson, Samuel Ramsey, John Martin, James Lyon, John Jones, Richard Jones, Andrew Lee, John Ryan, John Williams, Frederick Glover, David Zubly.

The Court appointed Aquilla Miles, foreman.

Cornelius Roe made his excuse by affidavit for his non attendance as a juror last court which was recieved and ordered to be recorded.

John Cowley made his excuse upon oath for his non attendance last court as a juror which was redeived and ordered to be recorded.

Ordered that the Sheriff return the writ of venire for the Petit Jury. The names of the Petit Jury that appeared

Thomas Baker	James Henderson	Henly Webb
Thomas Cotton	Robert Anderson	Caleb Holloway
Isaac Lewis	Mathew Devour	Richard Dean
Joseph Culbreath	William Holloway	Thomas Deloch
Thomas Youngblood	Thomas Carter	Robert Thompson
Ezeriah Lewis	Shadrick Henderson	Peter Timmerman
		Edward Mitchel

Ordered that the appointment of Charles Goodwyn Esq. to be County Attorney be confirmed and recorded

Ordered that the Clerk do furnish the County Attorney with a list of the names of such persons that have obtained permission to retail spirituous liquors that have not complied with the law

36   On application of Shadrick Roger permission was granted him to keep Tavern he having entered into bond with William Covington and John Hancock according to law

Ordered this Court be adjourned untill tomorrow morning 9 O'clock   Leroy Hammond, Arthur Simkins, Hugh Middleton, John Purvis, John Moore, Russel Wilson.

The Court met according to adjournment 11th July 1786

Present the worshipful Leroy Hammond, Arthur Simkins, Hugh Middleton, John Moore, Esquires.

Ordered that Benjamin Harris & James Lamar be appointed overseers of the road leading from Masons Ferry on Savannah River to the road leading from Fort Moore Bluff thence to the road leading to Charleston

James Yancey Esquire having produced his license to practice as an attorney in this State was approved of bythis court and ordered to be recorded

Daniel Rogers came into court and acknowledged his deeds of lease & release for 22 acres land to John Frazier which was ordered to be recorded

Deeds of lease & release from John Varnor to Thomas Cotton for 150 acres land was proved by the oaths of Samuel Marsh & John Frazer which was ordered to be recorded

Ordered that Frederick Session whew cause on the first day of next court why he suffered the road to be turned over which he was appointed overseer

Ordered that Barret Travis shew cause on the first day of next court why he turned the Public road near mine creek contrary to law

Ordered that the Clerk receive the Commission Dedimus Potestatum returned by William Anderson & John Moore Esquires who were commissioned privately to examine Eleanor Witzel report that she did relinquish her right of Dower and thirds to the land conveyed by John Whitzel her husband to William Shaw Esquire which was ordered to be recorded

John Pounds came into Court and acknowledged his Deeds of lease and release for 150 acres land to Robert White which was ordered. to be recorded

Frances Brooks vs Robert Thompson. Case. On Judgment by
default. Referred to John Moore Esq. & William Matthew with
power of Umpirage and report to the Clerk in one month by
consent of parties

Ordered on the Petition of a number of Inhabitants that Lewis
Tilman, John Chany, Aquilla Miles, Charles Martin & Captn
Cowen do view the ground from the County Court House the
best way to Wards Ford on Stevens Creek thence along Major
Middleton Old Ferry Road untill it falls into the road, leading from Long Cane to Hitts Ford near Thomas Clarks and report to the next court

Present Benjamin Tutt Esquire

Edward Couch vs William Nicholas. Trover. Ordered to be
referred to Capt. John Ryan & Capt. John Fairchild with
power of umperage and report the first day of next court

Ordered that the sheriff return all proceeds at least two
days before the sitting of the court at the clerks office,
and that the clerks not receive any returns contrary to this
order

Deeds of lease & release from John Norris to John Purcel for
55 acres land was proved by the oaths of John Henderson &
Samuel Gardner which was ordered to be recorded

William Cook vs Jones Rivers. Case. Ordered that all matters
and disputes between the Parties be referred to Major Middleton and Aquilla Miles with power of umpirage and report the
next court and their award to be final

Thomas Anderson made his excuse upon oath for his non attendance as a Grand Juror which was ordered to be recorded

Major Fields Perdiew made his excuse upon oath for his non
attendance at this court as a grand juror which was recieved
and ordered to be recorded

Mathew Gale Junr made his excuse upon oath for his non attendance as a grand juror which was received and ordered to be
recorded

Ordered that the appearance Docket be called over

Felix Gilbert vs Charles Bruce. Case. Petition dismissed

The State vs Fields Perdiew. Assault on Indictment. On
this case being referred to the Grand Jury to wit Aquilla
Miles, ABner Perrin, Thomas Wilson, John Martin,John Jones,
Andrew Lee, John Williams, Jacob Brooks, Drury Adams, Samuel
Ramsey, James Lyon, Richard Jones, John Ryan, Frederick Glover & David Zubley do on their oaths say that the defendant
is not guilty....

38   On motion of Major Fields Perdiew permission was granted to
      Morris Perdiew to keep Tavern on Savannah river on his giving
      bond according to law, Major Fields Perdiew and Captain
      Richard Johnson agreed to be his security

Richard Johnson vs Frances Settles. Case. on appeal.
Ordered that the bond be delivered to the appellant the suit
being comprimissed.

The same vs The Same. Debt. Ordered that this cause be referred to Abraham Richardson and James Vessels, with power
of umpirage and report to next court.

On motion of John Martin in behalf of Edward Wade deceased
ordered that a bond given by Abraham Frits to make a conveyance to 250 acres land situate on hard Labor Creek to Isaac
Ramsey 9 Feb 1772 be admitted to the records of this court
The hand writing of Robert Wallace one of the subscribing
witnesses thereto being proved by the oaths of Benjamin Tutt
Esq. Samuel Howard & John Wallace. Also the assignment of
the said bond was proved by the oath of James Martin.

On Motion of John Chany ordered that a bond bearing date 1781
from Joseph Rees to the aforesaid Chaney to make a conveyance
to a tract of land containing 200 acres situate on Cedar Creek
be admitted to the records of the Court House. the hand writing of the said Rees being proved by the oaths of Thomas
Hagins.

Ordered that the sheriff to the comissioners what money he
has collected for the use of the Public Buildings

Isaac Davis vs William Hitower. Attachment. The service of
this attachment was proved by Shadrick Rozier lawful constable

Ordered that Jacob Brooks be admitted a security for John
Gorman for Tavern License in the room of Philip Mays

Ordered that this court be adjourned untill tomorrow morning
9 O'Clock. Leroy Hammond, Arthur Simkins, Hugh Middleton,
Benj. Tutt & John Moore.

The court met according to adjournment 12th. Present the
Worshipful Arthur Simkins, John Moore & Russel Wilson, Esq.

39   James West came into court and acknowledged his deeds of
lease & release for 12 acres land to John Hammond which was
ordered to be recorded

Ordered that the appearance Docket be called over

Samuel Muchet vs Adam Brewner. Petition   dismissed

Richard Johnson & wife vs Arthur Watson & RobertStark. Petition. This day came the Plaintiff by Charles Goodwyn their
attorney and the defendants by Peter Carnes their attorney
wherefore upon debating the matter its considered by the court
that the plaintiff take nothing by his will, but for his
false clamour be in mercy, and the defendant....recover his
cost and s 4 lawful money.

Present John Purvis Esquire:

James Robinson vs Edward Couch. Petition. Ordered to be
referred John Fairchild & Christopher Hicks with power of
umpirage and report the first day of next court

22

Benjamin Arrington vs John Watson. Petition dismissed

John Garret vs William Jeter. Petition. dismissed at defendants cost

Thomas Swearingen vs Peter Hilliard. Petition. This day came the parteis and the Plaintiff says that the sum of ⅃ 5 the amount of his account on which his action is founded was justly due to him whereon its considered by the court that the plaintiff recover against the said defendant his debt aforesaid together with his cost by him in and about him in this behalf expended and the said defendant in mercy etc.

Levi Jester vs James West. Petition dismissed at defendants cost

William Jeter vs Lawrence Rambo. Petition dismissed

Robert Stark vs Dempsy Tyner Petition dismissed

40   Amity Hubbs vs Joseph Towles Assault dismissed

James Moore vs Arthur Watson & Robert Starks. Debt. Continued. Richard Johnson entered security for cost.

David Zubly vs John Tobler. Debt continued.

The same vs Mary Dick Exec of John Dick. Continued.

Joseph Hightower vs John Harris. Debt. Dismissed

Robert Deshazo vs Frederick Holmes. Case continued

John Hammond Junr vs Richard Johnson Junr. Assault dismissed at Defendants cost

John Cole vs William Carson. Assault. This day came the Defendants in three actions brought by John Cole the Plaintiff who being solemnly called made default nor did his suit further prosecute...the defendants recover s 5 besides their costs...
The same vs John Wallace.
The same vs Isaac Howard.

41   William Langmire vs Benjamin McCary. Slander. Continued

William Clerk vs John Catlet Garret. Trover. Continued.

John Garret vs Judith Clerk. Case. Dismissed

The same vs James Murry. Case. Judgment by default

John Goff vs John Kirkland. Debt. continued

Robert Stark vs Rolley Roebuck. Case continued

The same vs Banajah Rambo   Case continued

The same vs William Harris. Case. The plaintiff agrees to stay execution until Nov. on the defendants confessing judgment for ⅃ 5 5. 6 and cost

23

The same vs James Harris. Case. continued.

The same vs Jenkin Harris. Case. Continued.

Alexander Alexander vs John Sharpton & Others. Debt. on attcht. settled

Isaac Davis vs William Hightower. On attcht. John Hightower garnisher be called and not appearing, ordered that he shew cause why judgment should not go against him first day of next court

42   John Carget vs John Spencer. Trover. Continued.

Richard Johnson vs Arthur Watson & Robert Stark, Exrs. of Michael Watson. Trover. Continued.

Pricillar Watkins vs Jane West. Trover. The plaintiff in this action made default nor did his suit further prosecute therefore it is considered by the court that he be nominated

Ordered that the Issue Docket be called over

Jeremiah Webb vs James Carson. Case. This action is referred to Edward Couch, John Salter, Joseph Towles & William Covington with power of umpirage & report first day of next court

James Vessles vs Francis Nicholas & Others. Case continued by consent of parties.

John Randal vs John McCreles. Debt. Dismissed

Leroy Hammond Esq. vs James Scott. On attacht. continued

Jones Rivers vs Henry Key. Debt. dismissed

The same vs Thomas Key. Debt. dismissed

The same vs Elizabeth King. Debt dismissed.

Absent John Purvis Esquire.

43   John Hammond Senr. vs Isaac Davis & Mathew Finly. Trespass dismissed the plaintiff to pay all cost but the defendants lawyer fee.

John Williams vs Thomas Bizzil. Case. continued.

Present John Purvis Esq.

Robert Mosely vs John Rainsford. Case continued. The defendant in this action having pleaded to the jurisdiction of the court its ordered that this case stand over for the opinion of a full court

Frederick Glover vs Timothy McKenny. Case. This day came the plaintiff by Daniel Brown his attorney and the Defendant by William Shaw his attorney, wherefore upon debating the mat=ter it is considered by the court that the plaintiff take nothing by his bill but for his false clamour be in mercy and the Defendant...recover his cost and s 5....

John Randal vs James Gray. Trover. This day came the Plaintiff by Peter Carnes his attorney, and the Defendant by Charles Goodwin his Attorney, wherefore upon debating the matter, it is considered by the Court that the Plaintiff recover nothing, but ofr his false Clamour be in mercy and the Defendant...recover his cost and s 5....

Richard Johnson vs Frances Settles. Case. Continued.

The same vs The same. Debt Dismissed

John Duglass vs John Williams   Debt Dismissed

Solomon Edwards vs William Footwine. Case. continued.

44   Robert Stark assee vs Sarah Harris & Others. Case. continued.

William Fairchild vs Howel Johnson. Assault. dismissed at the defendants cost.

John Randal vs Rolley Roebuck. Case. Continued.

James Mays vs Ezekiel Harlen. Trover. dismissed.

David Thompson Assignee of Mrs. Oden, assnee of George Dooly vs James Mays. Debt. This day came the Plaintiff by Charles Goodwin his Attorney and the Defendant by William Shaw his attorney, and thereupon came also a jury to wit, Thomas Baker, Thomas Cotton, Isaac Lewis, Joseph Culbreath, Thomas Youngblood, Ezeriah Lewis, James Henderson, Robert Anderson, Mathew Devour, William Holliday, Thomas Carter, Shadrick Henderson who being sworn the truth to speak...the defendant does not owe the debt...Thomas Cotton, foreman.

Richard Johnson & wife vs Arthur Watson & Robert Stark Exec. of Michael Watson. On motion of the Plaintiff by Yancey his attorney that a new tryal should be granted on this action. rejected.

James Moore vs Arthur Watson & Robert Stark, Exec. of Michael Watson. Debt. Dismissed.

On motion of Samuel Evans by Charles Goodwyn his attorney it being proved by the oaths of John Harris his ear was bit off in an affray. Ordered that this proof be admitted to the records of this Court.

Deeds of lease and release from John Miller to George Chaney for 200 acres land was proved by the oaths of Thomas Hagins and John Mimms which was ordered to be recorded.

45   On motion of Robert Moseley he was allowed his attendance on this court as a witness at the suit of John Mims against Thomas Lamar which was ordered to be recorded

Ordered that all cases not called over should stand over until next court by consent of parties that is on the Issue Docket and not now called.

Ordered that this court be adjourned until the second Monday in October next. Arthur Simkins, John Moore, Russel Wilson.

The court met according to adjournment at the plantation of
John Harris the 9th October 1786. Present the Worshipful
Arthur Simkins, John Purvis, Benjamin Tutt, Esquires.

Ordered that this court be adjourned to the house of Drury
Mims near the county goal. Arthur Simkins, John Purvis, Ben-
jamin Tutt. The Court met according to adjournment at the
house of Drury Mims near the County Goal 9th of October 1786.
Present the Worshipful Arthur Simkins, Benjamin Tutt, Russel
Wilson, Esquires.

Ordered that the grand jury be drawn to serve next court.

Present Leroy Hammond & John Purvis Esqs.

The names of the Grand jury drawn.
Lud Williams, John Sturzenaker, Lud Williams, William Green,
Thomas Wilson, William Abney, Thomas Key, Isham Green, Wil-
liam Butler, John Childs, John Herndon, Abner Perrin, Samuel
Crafton, James Anderson, Solomon Pope, Philip Lamar, Mathew
McMillan, Caleb Holloway, Joseph Collier, William Spraggins,
John Clerk.

46   Ordered that the Petit Jury be drawn to serve next court
The names of the Petit Jury

William Hill	Matt Martin	James Mays
Nathan Fort	Jacob Pope	Sammuel Messer
William Talbot	James Allen	Moses Harris
Andrew Mock	Frederick Session	Charles Partin
Frederick Ward	John Hardy	James Gray
George Foreman	Leleston Perdiew	John Hogg
Shirly Whatly	Robert Pow	Moses Prescot
John Savage	Ezeriah Lewis	Robert Russel
George Bussey	Mathew Gale Sr.	Peter Chasteen
Joseph Cunningham	Joshua Jacobs	Hilory Philips

Mrs. Mary Ann Gardner being privately examined by Russel
Wilson Esquire one of the Justices relinquished her right
of Dower & thirds to the land conveyed by her husband to
Shirley Whatley which was ordered to be recorded

Thomas Peter Carns having produced his commission to practice
as an Attorney and Solicitor in this State was approved of
and admitted to the records of this court

Present William Anderson Esq.

Ordered that the Sheriff return the writ of Venire for the
Grand Jury

John Bulloch	James Coursey
Thomas Mawberry	Thomas Lamar
Philip Johnson	Nathaniel Howell
James Hargrove	Henry Key
Arthur Watson	George Martin
Thomas Lamar	George Cowen
Jacob Smith	Jones Rivers
Fields Perdieu	William Jeter

The Court appointed John Bullock Foreman.

Ordered that the Sheriff return the Writ of Venire for the
Petit Jury
The names of the Petit Jury that appeared

John Buckhalter, Edward Cox, Thomas Lamar, B. M., Howell
Johnson, Hugh Carson, John McPatrick, Frederick Tilman Sr.,
John Girffith, William Wallace, Meshack Wright, James Laving-
ston, Hugh Carson, Joseph Day, James Tutt, Marshal Martin.

On motion of Drury Mims permission was granted him to keep
Tavern securities Thomas Hagins & Edward Mitchel on his complying with the law

On motion of Robert Melton permission was granted him to keep
Tavern on his bond according to law Seucrities William Humphries & James Tutt

Absent Russel Wilson Esquire.

Isaac Foreman came into court and made oath that he did see
James McCoy sign & seal a bill of sale for several negroes
whose names were therein mentioned to Thomas Holley which
was ordered to be recorded

William Rodes came into court and acknowledged his Deeds of
lease & release for 190 acres land Uleses Rogers which was
ordered to be recorded

Mrs. Frances Rodes being privately examined by William Anderson Esquire one of the Justices relinquished her right of
dower & thirds to the lands conveyed by her husband to Ulesses
Rogers which was ordered to be recorded

Isaac Foreman came into court and acknowledged his deeds of
lease & release for 150 acres land to Lewis Nobles which was
ordered to be recorded

Jacob Fudge came into court and acknowledged his deeds of
lease & release to Benjamin Cook for 162 acres land which
was ordered to be recorded

Mrs. Margaret Fudge being privately examined by William Anderson Esq. one of the Justices relinquished her right of
Dower & thirds to the land conveyed by her husband to Benjamin Cook which was ordered to be recorded

William Anderson came into court and acknowledged his deeds
of lease & release for 50 acres land to Joseph Deck which was
ordered to be recorded

Benajah Rambo came into court and acknowledged his Deeds of
lease & release to Samuel Doolittle for 73 acres of land which
was ordered to be recorded

Mrs. Rachel Rambo being privately examined byWilliam Anderson
one of the Justices relinquished her right of dower and thirds
to the land conveyed by her husband to Samuel Doolittle which
was ordered to be recorded

Joshua Dean came into court and acknowledged his Deeds of
lease and release to Jabish Hendricks for 200 acres land which
was ordered to be recorded

48   Deeds of lease & release from George Goggins to William Dean
for 100 acres land was proved by the oaths of Joshua Hammond
and William Abney which was ordered to be recorded

Deeds of lease & release from Joseph Towles to William Dean was proved by the oaths of William Abney & Samuel Mays for 200 acres land which was ordered to be recorded

Bargain and sale from Joseph Towles to William Dean for 25 acres land was proved by the oaths of William Abney & Samuel Marsh which was ordered to be recorded

Ordered that the court be adjourned untill tomorrow morning 9 O'Clock. Leroy Hammond, Arthur Simkins, John Purvis, Benj. Tutt.

The Court met according to adjournment the 10th. Present the Worshipful John Purvis, Benjamin Tutt, William Anderson.

Deeds of lease & release from Jacob Holly to Richard Bush for 100 acres land was proved by the oaths of Richard Bush Jr. and Prescott Bush which was ordered to be recorded

Deeds of lease & release from Jacob Holly to Richard Bush for 100 acres land was proved by the oaths of Richard Bush and Prescot Bush which was ordered to be recorded

Bill of Sale from Isaac Munden to Richard Bush for one Negro Boy was proved by the oaths of Richard Bush Jr. & Prescott Bush which was ordered to be recorded

Deeds of lease & release from Oliver Martin to Lucy Ellison for 100 acres land was proved by the oaths of Benjamin Moore and John Smith which was ordered to be recorded

Present Leroy Hammond, Arthur Simkins & Russel Wilson Esqs.

Mathew Gale & wife vs Jacob Smith & wife. Slander   Dismissed

Leroy Hammond in open court acknowledged his deeds of lease & release to Samuel Savage for 150 acres land which was ordered to be recorded

49   John Ryan came into court and acknowledged his deeds of lease & release for 119 acres land to John Lucas which was ordered to be recorded

Mrs. Martha Ryan being privately examined by William Anderson Esq. one of the Justices relinquished her right of Dower & thirds to the land conveyed by her husband John Ryan which was ordered to be recorded

Bill of Sale from Nathan Breed to Samuel Landrum for one negro was proved by the oaths of Silas Sellars which was ordered to be recorded

Deed of Gift from Leonard Noble to Saunders Noble for one Negro Woman and her increase was proved by the oath of Leroy Hammond Esq. which was ordered to be recorded

John Hancock came into court and acknowledged his Deeds of lease & release for 200 acres land to John Curry which was ordered to be recorded

Allen Hinton came into court and acknowledged his deeds of lease & release for 150 acres land to Alexander Frazier which was ordered to be recorded

Deeds of lease & release from John Currie to John Pierce for 1661 acres land was proved by the oaths of John Hancock and Abraham Pierce which was ordered to be recorded

On the Petition of Sundry Inhabitants that a road be opened from Perkinshes Ford to Big Saluda river the best and most direct way to the court house

Ordered that Arthur Simkins & Russel Wilson Esquires, Jacob Smtih, Amos Richardson & Nathan Melton or any three of them do view the ground and report to the next court

Ordered that the order bearing date the 11th of April for openeing a orad from Mill Creek to the Cherokee Pond be reversed

Ordered that a road be opened from the Court house to Lamars Ferry on Savannah River beginning at the Court House to John Chaneys thence to Drury Mims thence to Lewis Bodies Mill seat thence to Matt Martins near James Kings thence down the old road that leads to Henry Wares to Wares Ford on Stephens Creek thence to Lamars Ferry on Savannah River and that the following persons be appointed to open and keep in repair the same to wit Lewis Tilman from the court house to Tilmans old field, James King from thence to Matt Martins from thence Richard Lowry to Wares ford on Stephens Creek, from thence Henry Ware to Lamars Ferry on Savannah River

50   Absent John Purvis & Russel Wilson Esquires

Ordered that the Docket be called over beginning with the Petitions.

Francis Brooks vs Robert Thompson. Trover. Settled at defendants cost

Leroy Hammond Esq. vs James Scott. On attacht. dismissed at pltfs cost

John Mims vs Thomas Lamar. Assault & battery dismissed at Plaintiffs cost

Present John Purvis Esq.

Charles Powell vs Richard Pond. Summons & Petition dismisse

Thomas Mawberry vs Thomas Beckham. Sum & Pted. continued untill tomorrow

John Canada vs Soloman Bird. Case. Sumd. & Petn. This day came the plaintiff by Peter Carns his attorney and the Defendant by Charles Goodwyn his attorney wherefore upon debating the matters, its considered by the court that the plaintiff take nothing by his Bill but for his false clamour be in mercy and the defendant...recover his cost....

The State vs James Richard. Assault. The grand jury having found a true bill Ordered that Capias Issue to take the body of James Richards

Ordered that the clerk receive the Presentments of the Grand Jury.

Thomas Dunn proved his attendance of 2 days 5s on the suit Cannada against Bird

Benjamin Arrinton vs John Watson. Case sumd. & Petn. Ordered to be referred to Edward Couch & Arthur Watson with Powerof Umpirage and report to next court

51   Ordered that the Clerk pay Mr. Robert Burton Eight dollars for making a Jury Box for the use of the County out of what Public money he has in his hands

Ordered that this court be adjourned untill tomorrow Morning 9 O'Clock. Leroy Hammond, Arthur Simkins, Wm. Anderson

The Court met according to adjournment 11th. Present the Worshipful Leroy Hammond, Arthur Simkins, William Anderson, Russel Wilson, Esquires.

Deeds of lease & release from Elijah Pajeat to Joab Trivil= lian for 60 acres land was proved by the oaths of Robert Deshazo and Lewis Deshazo which was ordered to be recorded

Deeds of lease & release from Thomas Harrison to Jefferry Hill for 200 acres land was proved by teh oaths of Thomas Shelson and William Cox which was ordered to be recorded

Thomas Mauberry vs Thomas Beckham. Debt. Sumd. Petn. Judgment according to specialty.

The State vs John Rainsford. Assault.

Ordered that the Sheriff take into Custody John Rainsford

John Rainsford acknowledged in open court to owe Ь 50 and Frederick Tilman Senr. Ь 25 by his securities to the County Lawful Money and that the said John do not depart this county untill he be discharged by order thereof

52   Ordered that Joseph Nun be appointed overseer over the road in the room of Benjamin Ryan excused

Ordered that all the causes referred last court be continued be referred untill next court and should no report then be made they shall stand on the Docket as before referred this order to be observed as a general rule in future

Deeds of lease & release from Daniel Hartley to Robert Stark was proved by the Oaths of James Gunnel and Robert Stark Jr. for 250 acres land which was ordered to be recorded

The State vs John Rainsford. Assault. Ordered that John Rainsford be fined in the sum of Ь 5 lawful money and that he be continued in Custody untill paid

David Zubly vs John Tobler. Continued.

David Zubly vs Mary Dick Exr. of John Dick.

Absent William Anderson Esq.

Frederick Glover came into Court and made oath that at the time of Hugh Terpins illness and on his death bed then he sent to the said deponent and James Edwards and requested of

them to be particular and remember that he had made use of
£ 600 of Mrs. Sarah Terrys money in Charleston for the use
to the best of his knwoledge and had not given her credit
for it and further he said Turpin said in their presence that
the monies in the said right hand bottom drawer of the leaf
part of the desk belonged to the said Mrs. Terry and further
this deponent sayeth not

David Zubly vs Mary Deck Ex. of Jno Deck. Case.

Ordered that the Court be adjourned till tomorrow 9 O'Clock.
Leroy Hammond, Arthur Simkins, John Purvis, William Anderson,
Russel Wilson.

The court met according to adjournment the 12th day of Oct
1786. Present the worshipful Leroy Hammond, Arthur Simkins,
John Purvis, Russel Wilson, Esq.

54 On motion a Number of Inhabitants Ordered that William Moseley,
John Herndon and Drury Murphey be appointed to view the
ground leading from Seth Howards the nearest and best way
to the new road leading from Meltons to Charles Martins and
make report to next court

Relinquishment of Right in a tract of land from John Stewart
to Esther Stewart was proved by the oaths of Thomas McGinnis
and Eva Whiteman which was ordered to be recorded

Ordered that Benjamin Cook be cited to appear on the first
day of next court to shew cause why he did not keep the road
in repair of which he was overseer agreed to a presentment
of the grand jury.

Ordered that the legislature be furnished with a copy of the
third and fifth presentment of the grand jury of the county
court of Edgefield

Ordered that Robert Stark, Rowland Williams and James Barrentine be appointed commissioners to open a road the nearest
and best way from the ridge to Adams Ferry on Savannah River
& report to next court

Robert Deshazo vs Fredrick Holmes. Case. Refer'd to Henry
King and William Sesson with power of Umpirage and report to
next court

William Longmire vs Benjamin McCary. Slander continued at
defendants cost

55 Drury Glover vs Vann Swearingen. Dismissed for want the
Defendant being served with a copy of the accompt.

Francis Nichols vs Fields Pardue. Continued.

Samuel Evans vs Jones Rivers. Continued.

Mathew Gayle vs Jacob Smith. Slander dismissed at Deft. cost

Hamutel Foy vs John Berry. Judgment confessed by the Defendant.

Robert Pow vs Barrot Travis. Slander dismissed at Deft.
costs

William Meeler vs Christean Roundtree. Continued

Elijah Hubbard vs William B. Harvey. Judt. by Deft.

Fields Pardue vs John Cannon. judicial attmt. renewed

56   Edward Van vs Ann Sommerall.

John Herndon vs John Randol. Continued.

Martin Cloud vs Neri Taylor Continued.

Martin Cloud vs John Keneda. Continued.

Samuel Hammond vs Allen Henton. Continued.

Garret Buckelew vs Samuel Ramsey. Continued.

James Vessels vs James Christopher adm. of Wm. Davis. Continued.

William Evans vs James Richards. dismissed

Thomas Carter vs William Nichols and Seth Howard.

57   Dyer Frazer vs James Robinson   Contd.

John Mims vs George Miller. Contd.

William Evans vs Jesse Roundtree. Contd.

John Whitly vs John Gibson. Contd.

Joseph Morris vs William Longmire. Contd.

Jones Rivers & uxor vs Eliza King. Contd.

Robert Jaris vs Barkley Martin. Dismissed.

Nimrod Jones vs Banaja Rambo. Dismissd.

George Mee vs Stephen Bettice. Contd.

John Hoes vs Jesse Glover. Contd.

58   David Burk vs James Christopher Contd.

Morris Callaham vs Drury Murphey. Contd.

Elijah Warren vs William B. Harvey. Contd.

Michael Oadum vs Bryan Green. Contd.

Thomas Franklin vs Frederick Williams. Contd.

Robert Melton vs Laurence Bambo(sic). Contd.

Charls Franklin & Uxor vs Frederick Williams, Howell Holley
& John Watson. Contd.

John Garret vs Robert Mosely Contd.

Joshua Hammond vs James Christopher.   Contd.

59 William Coursey came into court and acknowledged his deeds
of lease & release to William Longmire for 150 acres land
which was ordered to be recorded

Ordered that the Issue Docket be called over

Benjamin Tutt vs John Morris.

On motion of Wm. Carns Esq. Ordered that Dedimus Potestetem
Issue directed to Robert Forsith and William Freeman two
Justices for the state of Georgia to examine Doctor Cornelius
Dysert in behalf of the Plaintiff William Evasn against Jesse
Roundtree and return it to next court, the plaintiff first
giving the Deft. lawful notice of ten days

John Ryan acknowledged a bill of sale to John Ryan for one
negro fellow which was ordered to be recorded

John Goff vs John Kirkland. Refered to Arthur Watson and
Edward Couch with power of umpirage and report to next court

60 William Clerk vs John C. Garret.
Neri Taylor made oath that he attended two days at the suit
of John Cannada vs Solomon Bird as a witness

Robert Stark vs Sarah Harris & Others. Refered to John
Rainsford and John Frazier with power of umpirage and report
to the next court

John Williams vs John Crawford. Christian Gomillion as
special bail in this action in liew of James Baringtine.

Ordered that this court be adjourned untill the second Monday
in January to the house of Drury Mims near the goal.
Leroy Hammond, Arthur Simkins, Russell Wilson.

The Court met according to adjournment at the house of Drury
Mims near the County Goal the 6th of January 1787. Present
the worshipful Arthur Simkins, Hugh Middleton, John Moore,
Esq.

Ordered that the Grand Jury be drawn the name of the grand
jury drawn to serve at April Court
1. James Lyon   11. Samuel Ramsey
2. Robert Lang   12. Michael Buckhalter
3. John Furman   13. John Gray
4. Richard Lowery   14. William Mathews
5. James Harrison C. T. 15. George Forest
6. William Childs   16. Samuel Burgess
7. Morris Gwin   17. Benjamin Cook
8. James McMelan   18. Isaac Lewis
9. Thomas Dozer   19. Charles Martin
10. Nathan Abney   20. Benjamin Harris

Ordered that the Petit Jury be drawn to serve at April Court
The names of the Petit Jury so drawn
1. Toliver Cox   14. Jacob Brown
2. James Thomas   15. Solomon Lucas
3. Robert Burton   16. James Carson
4. William Watson   17. Benjamin Blackley
5. Thomas Wooten   18. Butler Williams
6. James King   19. William Hayne
7. James Booth   20. Joshua Dean

33

8. Bryan Green	21. Edward Couch
9. Jeffery Hill	22. Peter Dust
10. William Carson	23. Laurence Rambo
11. Alexander Frazier	24. Van Swearingen Sr.
12. William Murphey	25. Ezekial Gentry
13. Andrew Corzier	26. Ezekiel McClandol
	27. Phil Ships
	28. John Cowley
	29. John Roebuck
	30. Alexander Downer

Deeds of lease & release from Morris Calliham to John Blalock was acknowledged and ordered to be recorded

62 Ordered that the Sheriff return the Writ of Venire for the Grand Jury the names of the Jurors that appeared

Philip Lamar foreman	John Sturgenaker
Lud Williams	William Butler
Thomas Wetson	John Herndon
Isham Green	Samuel Crafton
John Celos	Solomon Pope
James Anderson	Mathew McMillan
Caleb Holloway	John Clerke
William Spraggins	

Ordered that the grand jury be sworn which was accordingly done The court having first appointed Philip Lamar foreman

Edmond Martin came into court and acknowledged his lease and release for 200 acres land to James Harrison which was ordered to be recorded

Ordered that the Sheriff return the writ venire for the Petit Jury. The names of the Petit Jury that appeared William Hill, Ezeriah Lewis, Shirley Whatley, Moses Harris, John Savage, Charles Partin, George Bussey, James Gray, James Allen, John Hogg, John Hardy, Moses Prescot, Sileston Pardue, Robert Russel, Robert Pow

On application of Ben. Harris permission was granted him to keep tavern securities Isaac Harris, William Evans

On application of James King permission was granted him to keep Tavern Securities Barkley Martin, William Jeter

On application of Abriam Richardson permission was granted him to keep Tavern, Joseph Hightower & John Randol

63 On application of Andrew Lee permission was granted him to keep tavern, securities Ulesses Rogers and Solomon Pope

On application of Jenkins Harris permission was granted him to keep Tavern Securities Job Lyon & Van Swearingen

On application of Anguish McDonald overseer of road leading from Island ford road near Harris to Turkey Creek was excused on account of his indisposition and Capt. Coursey appointed in his room

Deeds of lease & release from William Davis to Mathew Wills for 175 acres was proved by Barkley Martin & William Hardy which was ordered to be recorded

John Moore Esq. came into court and acknowledged his deeds of lease & releas for 150 acres land to Joseph Collier which was ordered to be recorded

Robert Stark acknowledged his deed as late sheriff of the District to Evan Morgan for 300 acres land which was ordered to be recorded

William Humphrey came into court and acknowledged his deed of lease & release to Samuel Satcher for 100 acres land which was ordered to be recorded

Deeds of lease & release from John Clackler to Richard Quarles Sr. for 350 acres land was proved by the oath of Wm. Watson and Richard Quarles which was ordered to be recorded

Robert Spur came into court & ackd. his Deeds of lease & release to Sibeston Pardue for 50 acres land which was ordered to be recorded

Robert Spur came into court & acknowledged his Deeds of lease & release to Lewis Galman which was ordered to be recorded

64   Present Benjamin Tutt Esq.

Deeds of lease & release from John Clackler to Richard Quales for 50 acres was proved by the oaths of Seth Howard and William Watson which was ordered to be recorded

Neri Taylor came into Court and acknowledged his deeds of lease & release for hundred (sic) acres land to Coll Collins whcih was ordered to be recorded

Mrs. Jemima Taylor privately examined by John Moore Esq. one of the Justices relinquished her right of dowery of land conveyed by her husband to Coll Collins

James Harrison acknowledged his deed of lease and release Elizabeth Miller for 200 acres land which was ordered to be recorded

Mrs. Elizabeth Spurs was privately examined by John Moore Esq. one of the Justices relinquished her right of Dowery thirds of land conveyed by her husband to Lileston Pardue and land conveyed by her husband to Lewis Tilman

Mrs. Sarah Foreman was privately examined by John Moore one of the Justices relinquished her right of Dowery & thirds to the land conveyed by her husband to Lewis Nobles which was ordered to be recorded

Ordered that the court be adjourned untill tomorrow morning 9 O'clock. Arthur Simkins, Hugh Middleton, Benj. Tutt, John Moore.

The Court met according to adjournment January 9th 1787. Present the Worshipful Arthur Simkins, Hugh Middleton, John Moore, William Anderson, Esq.

65   The state vs Thomas Smith & Roddy Smith.

The State vs John Martin No bill Philip Lamar, foreman

The state vs James Tutt.

Absent Arthur Simkins Esq.

Ordered that the Clerk pay into the hands of the undertaker
of the public buildings to go in aid of the public buildings
all the money received by him this court for the duties
tavern lisence

Present Arthur Simkins, Benjamin Tutt, Esq.

Thomas Beckham came into court and acknowledged his deeds of
lease and release for 100 acres of land to Serard Whatley
which was ordered to be recorded

Mrs. Mary Beckham was privately examined by Wm. Anderson Esq.
one of the Justices reported that she did relinquish her
right of dower & thirds to the land conveyed by her husband
to Sherod Whatley which was ordered to be recorded

66 On application of James Frazier permission was granted him
to keep tavern securities Daniel Rogers & Thomas Cotten

On application of Joel Chandler permission was granted him
to keep tavern securities Richard Johnson & John Williams

On application of Enoch Grigsby permission was granted him
to keep tavern securities Russel Wilson & William Butler

On application of Robert Stake permission was granted him
to keep tavern securities Russel Wilson & Wm. Shaw

On application of William Baker permission was granted him
to keep tavern securities Morris Gwin & Wm. Anderson

On application of John Harris permission was granted him to
keep tavern securities John Hill, James Vessels

The Grand Jury having returned their presentment Ordered
that the legislature be furnished with a copy of them

Ordered that James Tutt give security to appear at next court
in two securities principal Ł 50 securities Ł 25 each

Ordered that Thomas Smith & Roddy Smith give securities
principal in Ł 50 securities Ł 25 each

Thomas Smith appears in Court by Benj. Cook his Security
and acknowledged to owe the County principal Ł 50 security
Ł 25 each

Bill of sale from Sanders Nobles to the children of Nancy
Jones was proved by the oaths of Benj. Cook, Robert Ling &
James Tutt by this security came into court and acknowledged
to owe the County Ł 50 his securities Daniel Bird &
James Coursey each Ł 25

67 On application of Shadrick Rozier permission was granted him
to keep tavern securities James Vessels, John Harris.

Ordered that Capt. Johnson, Benj. Cook and John Gray shall
value the timber provided by Arthur Simkins Esq. for the
Court House and not made use of for that purpose and report

the value next court

Ordered that the road be opened agreeable to the return of
of the commissioners from Augusta to Ridge and Abram Oadum,
Philip Snipès and George Mee are appointed overseers for
opening the same

John Crawford came into court and acknowledged his lease
and release to John Williams for 150 acres of land which
was ordered to be recorded

William Anderson came into court and acknowledged his Deeds
of lease and release for 784 acres of land to Nicholas
Eveliegh Esq. which was ordered to be recorded

On petition of Sundry Inhabitants order that Thomas Cotton,
Roland Williams & James Barrinton to view the ground from
the court house or Harrises Plantation to the old long cane
road at or near Roland Williams for the purpose of opening
a road and report next court

68   John Williams came into court and acknowledged his deeds
of lease and release to James Barrington for 100 acres of
land which was ordered to be recorded

Deeds of lease and release from John Parker to Isaac Parker
for 100 acres of land was proved by the oaths of Lud Williams
and Casper Neal which was ordered to be Recorded

On application of Mark Dick permission was granted her to
keep Tavern   Securities   Lud Williams, John Sturgenaker

Deeds of lease and release from Mathew Stoker to Nicholas
Minor for 50 acres of land was proved by the oaths of Richard
Quarles & Robert Stoker which was ordered to be recorded

Deeds of lease and release from John Salter to Thomas Sheriffs for 200 acres of land was proved by the oaths James
Robinson and Joseph Walker which was ordered to be recorded

Thomas Sheriff came into court and acknowledged his lease &
release to John Walker for 100 acres of land which was ordered to be recorded

On Motion of Sundry Inhabitants for a road from Halens Ferry
to Ninety Six, Ordered that Benjamin Blake, James Hagoo &
Thomas Freeman view the ground & report to next court

Ordered that Thomas Beckham, Jacob Wise and Jesse Roundtree
be appointed overseers to clear the road from Haters pond to
Adams Ferry

69   Ordered that Thomas Beckham, Robert Melton, John Lucas &
Charles Martin and Nicholas Minor be appointed overseers of
the orad leading from Blears ford on Stevens Creek to Hatchers pond, Thomas Beckham to begin at Hatchers pond to the
old wells, then Robert Melton to Horns creek thence Charles
Martin to Ninety Six road, thence to Stevens Creek Nicholas
Minors

Ordered that John McCoy be appointed overseer of road in the
room of James Mays moved

Ordered that William Brooks be appointed overseer of road in room of Peter Farrar moved

David Sibley vs Mary Deck. Ordered that James Asberry be allowed for 6 days attendance for the plaintiff in this case

Ordered that Isaac Lewis be appointed overseer on the road in room of John Jones excused

On petition of the Inhabitants, Ordered that John Mays, Lewis Watson, Thomas Butler be appointed to view ground from Harlins Ferry to the Rogue Shoals on Stevens Creek thence to Charleston road near Col. Purvis and report to next court

70   Bill of Sale from William Pardue to Morriss Pardue was proved and ordered to be recorded

Deeds of lease and release from Thomas Lemour to Andrew Pickens Esq. for 412 acres of land was proved by the oaths of William Evans and Fields Pardue which was ordered to be recorded

Absent Benj. Tutt & William Anderson Esqs.

Robert Stark vs Sarah Harris. Thomas Hagins proved his attendance in this action as a witness 12 days at 2/6

Ordered that Major Pardue be appointed overseer of road in room of Thomas Lamour for neglecting his duty

Ordered that Robert Burton be appointed overseer over the road leading from Log creek to John Jones on the road to Anderson Ferry

Ordered that the court be adjourned untill tomorrow morning nine o'clock. Arthur Simkins, Hugh Middleton,John Moore, William Anderson

The Court met according to adjournment the 10th of Jan 1787 Present Arthur Simkins, Hugh Middleton,John Moore, Esqs.

On application of John Lucas permission was granted him to keep Tavern Securities Lileston Pardue and Ben Cook

Ordered the appearance docket be called over the first time

71   Ordered the Issue Docket be called.
Benjamin Arrington vs John Wattman.

James Robinson vs Edward Couch.

Thomas Cambel vs John Armstrong.

On application of William Day permission was granted him to keep tavern John Cargill and John Caldwell securities

John Hill proved his attendance as witness two days
Thomas Cambel vs John Armstrong.
Benjamin Arrinton vs John Wattman.

72   William Hargrove vs Benjamin Cook.

William Hargrove vs William Nicholas

James Henan vs Leonard Nobles.

Doby Hunter vs Rufus Inman.

The same vs George Chaney.

William Hargrove vs William Nicholas.

Jesse Roundtree vs Joel Chandler

Daniel Parker vs James Tutt.

73   William Mealer vs James Vessels

Thomas Banks & wife vs Mary Sails.

Fields Pardue vs John Cannon

John Clark vs John Hicks.

Solomon Butts & wife vs James Green.

74   Thomas Banks & wife vs Catlet Cauley.

William Nichols vs James Hargrove.

John Anderson vs Henery Key.

Benj. Joyner vs John Herndon Admr. of Will Wm. Herndon.

James Johnston vs John Roberts.

Edward Couch vs Burgess White.

75   John Randolph vs Thomas Beckham.

The Same vs The Same.

Timothy Russell vs Isaac Lefeaver & wife.   Debt.

Samuel Carter vs Drury Glover.

Lewis Coody vs William Pardue. Attachment.

Ordered that Morris Pardue be examined as garnishee in the
above cause tomorrow.

The Court then adjourned untill tomorrow morning nine o'clock.
Arthur Simkins, Hugh Middleton, John Moore.

The court met according to adjournment. 11th. Present
worshipful Arthur Simkins, Hugh Middleton and John Moore, Esq.

76   Deeds of lease and release from James Livingston to Elizabeth
King for 50 acres of land was proved by Harry Ware and John
King which was ordered to be recorded

On application of John Loucas permission was granted him to
keep Tavern. Securities Isaac Foreman and Benjamin Rambo

Mary Wilson vs Thomas Murphey.

John Covington vs James Scott.

William Farrell vs James Massey.

John Handcock vs Robert Robinson.

Timothey Cooper vs Thomas Murphey. Attachment.

77 Henry Drummond vs Thomas Rogers.

Rolly Robuck vs Mark Lott Senr.

Richard Johnston vs Robert Stark & Arthur Watson Ex. of
Michael Watson.

Same Jury sworn and impannelled to try the Issue formed and
a true verdict...they find for the Plaintiff Ŀ 12 s 6 d 7
with intrest from 26 March 1784 to be recorded as the law
directs   William Hill, Foreman

Lewis Watson proved four days attendance as a witness in
this suit.

Ordered that this Court be adjourned untill the second Monday
in April next. Arthur Simkins, Hugh Middleton, John Moore.

78 The Court met according to adjournment at the Court House
the second Monday in April the 9th day, 1787. Present the
Worshipful Arthur Simkins, Hugh Middleton, Russell Wilson,
Esquires.

Ordered that the Grand Jury be drawn to serve the next court
The names of the Jury so drawn

1.	David Zubly	11.	Nathan Abney
2.	Thomas Anderson	12.	John Studsanaker
3.	Robert Belcher	13.	Alexander Newman
4.	John Hancock	14.	James Coursey
5.	William Longmire	15.	Samuel Crafton
6.	Joseph Burton	16.	James Harrison
7.	John Gawman	17.	Samuel Burgess
8.	James Brooks	18.	Isham Green
9.	Right Nicolson	19.	William Mathews
10.	Benjamin Cook	20.	Henry Key

Ordered that the Petit Jury be drawn

1.	David Zegler	16.	Jacob Fudge Sr.
2.	David Boswell	17.	Alexander Burnett (Burket?)
3.	Lewis Clark	18.	James Harrison R B
4.	James Cox	19.	Zackeriah James
5.	Aaron Etheredge	20.	James Christopher
6.	James Henderson	21.	James Ruston
7.	John Clackler Jr.	22.	Shaderick (sic)
8.	James Butler	23.	Christopher Gomillion
9.	Absolum Roberts	24.	Daniel Marcus
10.	Joab Chandler	25.	Samuel Deloach
11.	Richard Lundy	26.	Richard Henderson
12.	Drury Croft	27.	Peter Rampy
13.	Casper Neal Sr.	28.	Edmond Powel
15.	George Sawyer	30.	John Stuart

Ordered that the Sheriff return a writ of venire for the
grand jury
The names of the grand jury that appeared
James Harrison, James Lyon, Robert Long, William Childs,
Morris Gwin, James McMillian, Thomas Dozer, Richard Lowery,

John Grey, Samuel Burgess, Benj. Cook, Isaac Lewis, Charles Martin, Samuel Ramsey.

The Court having appointed James Harrison foreman ordered him to be sworn.

Ordered that the Sheriff return the writ of venire for the Petit Jury. The names of the Petit Jury that appeared

1. Toliver Cox
2. James Thomas
3. Robert Burton
4. William Watson
5. James King
6. James Booth
7. Bryan Green
8. Jeffery Hill
9. William Carson
10. William Murphey
11. Andrew Crozen
12. Jacob Brown
13. Solomon Lucas
14. Benjamin Blackly
15. Butler Williams
16. Joshua Dean
17. Edward Couch
18. Peter Durst
19. Lawrence Rambo
20. Philip Shipes

Deeds of lease and release from Timothy McKingo to Tommy Kelen Smith for 300 acres of land was proved by the oaths of James Harkins and Mary Eakins which was ordered to be recorded

Robert Moseley came into court and acknowledged his deeds of lease and release for 100 acres of land to George Tillery which was ordered to be recorded

Penelope Mossely was privately examined by Hugh Middleton Esq. one of the Justices relinquished her right of dower and thirds to the lands conveyed by her husband to George Tillery

Present Leroy Hammond Esq.

Deeds of lease and release from Isaac Ray to Richardson Bartley for 240 acres of land proved by the oaths of William Murphey and William Doby was ordered to be recorded

Deeds of lease and release from Patrick Jarvis to Wm. Dobey for 100 acres of land was proved by the oaths of Drury Murphey & James Hargrove which was ordered to be recorded

81 Absent Leroy Hammond Esq.

James Tomelin came unto court and acknowledged his deed of lease and release for 180 acres of land to Daniel Hern was ordered to be recorded

Absolom Roberts came into court and acknowledged his deeds of lease and release for 100 acres of land to Thomas Carter which was ordered to be recorded

Mrs. Nancy Roberts was privately examined by Arthur Simkins Esq. relinquished her right of dower and thirds to lands conveyed by her husband to Thomas Carter which was ordered to be recorded

Col. Collins came into court and acknowledged his deeds of lease and release for 250 acres of land to Charles Broadwaters which was ordered to be recorded

Mrs. Elizabeth Collins was privately examined by Arthur Simkins Esq. one of the Justices relinquished her right of dower

and thirds of lands conveyed by her husband to Charles Broadwater which was ordered to be recorded

Samuel Doolittle came into court and acknowledged his deeds
of lease and release for 200 acres of land to William Jeter
Jr. which was ordered to be recorded

Mrs. Nancy Doolittle was privately examined by Arthur Simkins
Esq. one of the Justices relinquished her right of Dower and
thirds of land conveyed by her husband to Wm. Jeter

82 Charles Broadwater came unto court and acknowledged his deeds
of lease and release for 50 acres land to Scarburgh Broadwater
which was ordered to be recorded

Thomas Lamar Sr came into court and acknowledged his deeds of
lease and release for 115 acres land to Jacob Fudge was ordered
to be recorded

Beneja Rambo came into court and acknowledged his deeds of
lease and release for 100 acres of land to Fielding Reynolds
which was ordered to be recorded

Daniel Hern came into Court and acknowledged his deeds of
lease and release for 100 acres of land to Churchel Gibson
which was ordered to be recorded

Deeds of lease and release for 150 acres of land from John
Chaney to Joshua Deen was proved by oaths of Wm. & John Abney
which was ordered to be recorded

Deeds of lease and release from Philip Harrell to John Clark
for 250 acres of land was proved by the oaths of William &
John Abney which was ordered to be recorded

Amos Richardson came into court and acknowledged his deeds of
lease & release for 150 acres of land to Thomas Dozer which
was ordered to be recorded

Ordered that this court be adjourned untill tomorrow morning
nine o'clock. Arthur Simkins, Hugh Middleton, Russell Wilson.

83 The court met according to adjournment 10th of April 1787.
Present the worshipful Arthur Simkins, Hugh Middleton, Russell
Wilson, Esquires.

Peter Hilliard, Charles Carter & George Carter being returned
defaulters 4 days each for not working on the road which Abram
Oadem is overseer ordered that they be summoned to shew why
did not work on the road at the next court

Present Leroy Hammond Esq.

Priscilla Jester (sic) came into court and acknowledged her
deed of gift to Thomas Jeter, William Jeter,Nancy Jeter,
Elizabeth Jeter her four children which was ordered to be
recorded

On application of John Hancock permission was granted him to
keep Tavern Securities James Vessels and Seth Howard

Lewis Nobles came into court and acknowledged his deeds of
lease & release for 50 acres of land to John Lucas which was

42

ordered to be recorded

Mrs. Zelpha Nobles was privately examined by Arthur Simkins Esq. one of the Justices relinquished her right of dower and thirds to the land conveyed by her husband to John Lucas which was ordered to be recorded

84 Deeds of lease and release from Benj. Harris for 260 acres of land to William Evans was proved by the oaths of Casper Neal and Meshak Wright which was ordered to be recorded

Ezekiel McClandol came into court and acknowledged his deeds of lease and release to Isaac Kirkland for 470 acres of land which was ordered to be recorded

On Petition of Sundry Inhabitants Ordered that Richard Johnston, Isaac Lewis, Lewis Clark, John Hill, John Gibson or any three of them to view the ground from Perkins ford to the Court House the nighest and best way for the purpose of opening a road and report to the next court

Ordered that road be opened from Harlins Ferry to Ninety Six agreeable to report of the commissioners first opening at Harlins Ferry James Hagwood appointed overseer, from thence to Hard Labour, from thence John Kenneday overseer, to Parkes old place on Long Cane Road thence Mathew Barret to Jesse Harris' Mill thence Jesse Harris to Ninety Six.

Ordered that the road be opened from the court to fall in the old Long Cane road near Roland Williams agreeable to the report of the viewers and Roland Williams is appointed overseer from his plantation to Jas. Barrentines from thence James Barrintine to the Court House

85 Bargain & Sale of one negro girl from Daniel Jones to Hugh Middleton was proved by the oaths of Frederick Tilman Sr., Arthur Kilcreas which was ordered to be recorded

A bond of conveyance of 100 acres of land from Richard Witherton to Wm. Stringer was proved by the oaths of Abram Oadum and John Herndon which was ordered to be recorded

Acknowledgment of a conveyance from William Arthur to Robert Stark was sworn to in open court by Mark Lott

Ordered that Jesse Scrugs be appointed overseer over the road beginning at Island Ford road near Harriss to Turkey Creek the Charles Williams old place in the rooms of Capt. Coursey excused who was appointed in the room of Anguish McDonald

Ordered that James Span be appointed overseer over the road from Amos Richardsons to Burtons place on the Ninety Six Road in Room of Dudley Pruet excused

The State vs James Tutt. Assault. The Jury being called... Toliver Cox, James Thomas, Robert Burton, William Watson, James Booth, Bryan Green, Jeffery Hill, William Murphey, Andrew Crozier, Jacob Brown, Solomon Lucas, Butler Williams, do say that the defendant is guilty. Butler Williams, foreman.

The State vs John Russell. Tavern keeping without license True Bill.   James Harrison, Foreman.

John Roebuck came into and acknowledged his deeds of lease and release to Benjamin Cook for 300 acres of land which was ordered to be recorded

Mrs. Mary Roebuck was privately examined by Arthur Simkins Esq. one of the Justices relinquishes her right of dower and third to lands conveyed by her husband which was ordered to be recorded

On Motion of the County Attys. Ordered that a Capias Issue to apprehend John Purssell and compell him to appear at this court to answer to the indictment found against him. Ordered that Clerk recieve the presentment.

Ordered that a sommonds Issue to compell the overseers of the roads from Burtons old place on Ninety Six Road to show cause next court why the road over which he is overseer is out of repair agreeable to the presentment of the Grand Jury.

87 Ordered that a Summon Issue against Joseph Burton to shew cause next court why he pond up the water of Ninety Six Creek to the damage of road crossings the said creek agreeable to the presentment of the Grand Jury

William Jeter Jr. vs James Lauder & Jos. C. Chandler. Major Fields Pardue and Edward Keating entered themselves special bail in this cause

Ordered the Court be adjourned untill tomorrow Morning nine O'Clock. LeRoy Hammond, Arthur Simkins, Hugh Middleton, Russell Wilson.

The Court met according to adjournment 11th of April 1787. Present the worshipful Arthur Simkins, Hugh Middleton, Russell Wilson, Esquires.

Ordered the appearance docket be called the first time

Deeds of lease and release from Telphinia Beal to John Furman for 200 acres of land was proved by the oaths of Philip Thurman and William Rodes which was ordered to be recorded

Administrator of Wilson vs Thomas Murphy. Attacht.

88 Timothy Cooper vs Thomas Murphy.
Edmond Martin Esquire came into Court and acknowledged that he had in his hands £ 41 s 2 d 10 the property of the aforesaid Thomas Murphy which came into his hands by the sales of lands as sheriff of the District.

Robert Stark Junr vs Benajah Rambo, Contd.

David Zubly vs John Tobler. Dist. at Pltf. cost

Francis Nichols vs Fields Pardue. Abates by Death of Pltf.

William Longmire vs Benj. McCarty. Dest. at Pltf. cost.

Samuel Evans vs Jones Rivers. Contd.

John Cargill vs John Spencer Contd.

Hamatil Foy vs John Berry. Contd.

John Williams vs Thomas Bezzel. Contd.

Elijah Hubbard vs Wm. Baker Harvey. Contd.

Robert Moseley vs John Rainsford. Contd. at Pltf cost.

Martin Cloud vs Neri Taylor & wife. Contd.

Will Farrel vs James Massey. Jesse Roundtree contd. himself
on special bail.

The Same vs John Canady. Contd.

Robert Deshaso vs Frederick Holmes Settled.

Garrett Buckelew vs Saml Ramsey. Dismt.

Solomon Edwards vs Wm. Toolwine. Contd.

John Mims vs George Miller. Contd.

John Randol vs Rolley Roebuck   Contd.

John Whitley vs John Gibson   Contd.

89 Jones Rivers vs Elizabeth King. Contd.

Thomas Franklin vs Frederick Williams Contd.

George Mee vs Stephen Bettis. Contd.

Robert Melton vs Laurence Rambo. Contd.

John Hoes vs Jesse Glover Contd.

Chas. Franklin & wife vs Frederick Williams. Contd.

The same vs Drury Glover. Contd.

Joshua Hammond vs James Christopher Contd.

David Burks vs James Christopher Contd.

Daniel Barker vs James Tutt. Contd.

Morris Calaham vs Drury Murphy. Settled at mutual cost.

John Clark vs John Hicks. Contd.

Elijah Warrin vs William B. Harvey. Contd.

Jesse Roundtree vs Joel Chandler. Contd.

Michael Odom vs Bryan Green. Contd.

Present John Moore Esquire.

Mary Wilson vs Thos Murphey. Attmt.
A Jury being called impannelled & sworn to try this attacht.
in the nature of a writ of inquiries to wit (same as before)
do say we find Ł 27.10 with interest from July 1760 till paid

Present Leroy Hammond Esquire.

Ordered that James Tutt be brought into court to receive the
sentence of the court which are that the said Jas. pay Ł 3
on or before the next court which sum Edward Martin Esq.
agreed to havepaid by this time

90 Elisha Stephens came into court and acknowledged his deeds of
lease and release to Moses Hubbard for 100 acres land which
was ordered to be recorded

John Anderson vs Henry Key.   Contd. at Pltf. Cost.

Nery Taylor proved his attendance for 10 days in the suit of
William Longmire agst. Benj. McCary.

On motion of Plfts. Attorney Ordered that the suit Meler vs
Roundtree be discontinued at Pltfs. cost for want of security
for costs

John Bullock was allowed s 7 d 6 for 3 days attendance admx.
of William Wilson vs Thomas Murphey

Lawrence Rambo came into court and acknowledged his deeds of
lease and release to Stephen Tilman for 100 acres of land
which was ordered to be recorded

Mrs. Mary Rambo being privately examined by Hugh Middleton
Esq. one of the Justices relinquished her right of dower and
thirds to the land conveyed by her husband to Stephen Tilman
which was ordered to be recorded

In suit Robert Stark Jr vs Benejah Rambo, Joel Pardue is
allowed s 17 d 6 for 7 days attendance in behalf of Plaintiff

Ordered that the Venire for the Grand Jury be not issue to appear till Oct. Court

Ordered that all the evidences attending in the suit of Robert
Mosley vs John Rainsford be allowed their attendance according
to their different charges

John Harris came into court and acknowledged his deeds of
lease and release for 60 acres of land to Mrs. Rachael Chaney
which was ordered to be recorded

91 Mrs. Mary Harris being privately examined by Hugh Middleton
Esq. one of the Justices relinquished her right of dower and
thirds to land conveyed by her husband to Rachael Chaney which
was ordered to be recorded

Ordered on the Prayer of Abraham Richardson that he be allowed
to administer on the estate of George Rogers Deceased the
widow privately relinquishes her right as first of kin securities Charles Banks and Jesse Roundtree

Harris Freeman vs Baswell Evans.   Dismissed at the desire of
Pltf.

Ordered that the court be adjourned to the second Monday in
July next.   Arthur Simkins, Hugh Middleton, John Moore.

The court met according to adjournment the 9th July 1787.
Present the Worshipful Arthur Simkins, John Purvis, Nicholas
Eveleigh.

Ordered that the Petit Jury be drawn to serve next court
The names of the Petit Jury

Sherwood Whatley	Edward Holmes
Wm. Rennolds	James Beal
Benj. Darby	Isaac Brunson
Absolom McDonald	John Hammond
John Roberts	Dudly Pruit
Isaac Foreman	Joseph Trotter
Richd. Bush	Lewis Etheridge
Wm. Clerk Senr.	Richd. Cowley
Sam Marsh	Isham Langley
Edward Vann	Thomas Sheriff
Edmond Boyd	David Lyles
Elisha Gentry	John Elum
Stephen Tilman	Thomas Youngblood
Sherwood Cowly	Drury Murphey
Thomas Pennington	Robert Newport

92   Ordered that the sheriff return the Writ of Venire for the
Petit Jury
The names of the Petit Jury that appeared

David Zigler	James Christopher
Lewis Clark	Shaderick Henderson
James Cox	Christian Gomelian
James Henderson	Peter Ramsy
John Clackler	Edmund Pursel
James Butler	Evan Morgan
Absolom Roberts	John Stuart
Henry Croft .	James Rustin
Samuel Ramsey Junr	Richard Henderson
James Harrison	Joel Chandler
	Samuel Deloach

Ordered that in future no application be made for the office
of Sheriff or any other office in the appointment of this
court but by letter addressed to the Justices of the court
from the persons who may be candidates for such office in
their own hand writing and presented by them at the setting
of the Court when such appointment is to be made and that
the appointment of such offices in future be made by ballot

Evan Morgan cane into court and acknowledged his deeds of
lease and release for 300 acres land to John Hardy ordered
to be recorded

David Segler came into court and acknowledged his deeds of
lease and release for 47 acres land to John Hardy which was
ordered to be recorded

Deeds of lease and release from John Davis to William Brooks
for 100 acres land was proved by the oaths of Amos Roberts
and James King which was ordered to be recorded

93   Deeds of lease and release from Thomas Hargins to John Hargins
for 200 acres of land was proved by the oaths of Ezeriah Lewis
and John Buckelew which was ordered to be recorded

Deeds of lease and release from William Moore Esq. to Mathew
McMillian for 250 acres land was proved by the oaths of
Fields Pardue and John Moore Esq. ordered to be recorded

Present John Moore Esq.

Reuben Beckham came into court and acknowledged his deeds of lease and release for 100 acres land to Auquil Miles ordered to be recorded

Mrs. Anna Beckham being privately examined by John Purves Esq. one of the Justices relinquished her right of Dower and thirds to lands conveyed by her husband Auquila Miles ordered to be recorded

Daniel Bird came into court and acknowledged his deeds of lease and release for 150 acres land to Solomon Bird ordered to be recorded

Mrs. Susannah Bird being privately examined by John Moore Esq. one of the Justices relinquished her right of dower and thirds to land conveyed by her husband to Solomon Bird which was ordered to be recorded

Deeds of conveyance from Samuel Ridgeway to Stephen Bostick for 413 acres land was proved by the oaths of Mathew Ramsey and James Gowdy to John Adams ordered to be recorded

94   Joseph Nun came into Court & acknowledged his Deeds of Lease and Release for 150 acres of land to John Adams ordered to be recorded

Deeds of lease and release from William Settle to Anna Bland for 225 acres land was proved by the oaths of Will Birds and Henry King which was ordered to be recorded

Deeds of lease and release from George Mason to Anna Bland for 200 acres land was proved by the oaths of Wm. Birds and Henry King which was ordered to be recorded

Deeds of lease and release from Thomas Berry to James Grigs- by for 100 acres land was proved by the oaths of Henry King and Thos Butler ordered to be recorded

Deeds of lease and release from Thomas Berry to James Grigs- by for 100 acres land was proved by the oaths of Henry King & Thomas Butler ordered to be recorded

Deeds of lease and release from Thomas Berry to James Grigs- by for 100 acres land was proved by the oaths of Henry King & Thomas Butler ordered to be recorded

John Cockburn came into court and acknowledged his deeds of lease and release for 26 acres land to Frederick Tilman or- dered to be recorded

Mrs. Hannah Cockburn being privately examined by John Purves Esq. one of the Justices relinquished her right of dower and thirds to land conveyed by her husband to Frederick Tilman ordered to be recorded

Deeds of lease and release from Lewis Boody to Drury Mims for 16 acres land was proved by the oaths of David Mims and James Boody ordered to be recorded

95   Present Leroy Hammond,Russell Wilson, Esquires.

John Hammond vs Benj. Joiner Case Petition for for Ŀ 1. 63 & cost

William Jeter vs Van & Josiah Swearingen. Case Petition Lay over

William Coursey vs Frederick Buckelew. Case dismissed no prosecution

Isaac Fresby vs Charles Ashley. Trover Dismd. no prosecution

Fields Pardue vs James West. Debt Ind for Ł 3.48 with int and cost

The same vs William Bailey. Indt. for Ł 5.0.0 & cost

The Same vs Sam Glover. Defrd. till tomorrow

Mary Dick vs David Zubly. Defd. till tomorrow

Robert Stark vs Jenkin Harris. Defd. till tomorrow

James Coursey vs John Allen. Defd. till tomorrow

Com. of Horns Creek Meeting House vs William Nichols. Debt Defd. til tomorrow

Elverton Squires vs Jacob Odum. Defd. till tomorrow

James Cox vs Peter McCowly Defd. till tomorrow

Richardson Bartlett vs Abram Odum. Defd. till tomorrow

Peter Holland vs Thos Bezle Defd. till tomorrow

Abram Tichardson vs Vann Swearingen Defd. till tomorrow

David Zubley vs John Tobler. Defd. till tomorrow

96   Ordered that this court be adjourned till tomorrow morning nine o'clock. Arthur Simkins, John Purves, Wm. Eveleigh.

The court met according to adjournment 10th of July 1787 Present the Worshipful Leroy Hammond, John Moore, Russell Wilson, Esquires.

Deeds of lease and release for 50 acres land from William Cox to Christopher Cox was proved by the oaths of William Cox and Toliver Cox ordered to be recorded

Deeds of lease and release from John Goode to Christopher Cox for 150 acres land was proved by the oaths of Toliver & William Cox ordered to be recorded

Deeds of lease and release from Andrew Pickens to Melines Conkling Leavensworth for 600 acres land was proved by the oaths of Fields Pardue & Chandler ordered to be recorded

Deeds of lease and release from Andrew Pickens to Melines Conkling Leavensworth for 10090 acres land was proved by the oaths of Fields Pardue and Joel Chandler ordered to be recorded

On application of Suckey Coody widow of Lewis Coody Dec'd adm of rights credits of said dec'd was granted to her she having entered into bond with Leonard Nobles & Adam Pardue

49

for the faithful discharge of the administration and was
qualified according to law

97   A receipt from William Hardin and Margaret Hardin to John
and Benjamin Ryan was acknowledged by the said William and
Margaret for the sum of Ł 200 and ordered to be recorded

A receipt from John and Benjamin Ryan was ackd. by the said
Ryans for the sum of Ł 200 to William Hardin and Margaret
Hardin

Ordered that warrant of appraisement issue to Lewis Nobles,
William Nobles, Lewis Tilman and Leleston Pardue authorizing
them or any three of them to appraise the goods and chattels
of Lewis Body decd' as may be shown by the administration

Mrs. Rachael Rambo being privately examined by John Purvis
Esq. one of the Justices relinquished her right of dower and
thirds to lands conveyed by her husband Benejah Rambo to
Fielding Rennolds ordered to be recorded

Deeds of lease and release from Henry Summerall to Thomas
Adams for 100 acres land was proved by the oaths of Frederick
Tilman and Edmond Whatley ordered to be recorded

Present Arthur Simkins, Wm. Eveleigh, Esquires.

Ordered that the administration of Jacob Foreman shall be
cited to shew cause the first day of next court why the admn.
granted to her should not be revoked

On application of Mrs. Mary Brooks widow of Jacob Brooks deceased the administration of the rights and credits of the
said deceased was granted to her she having intered into
bond with Benjamin Cook, John Garmon, James Carson, her securities for the faithful discharge of the administration
and was qualified according to law.

98   Ordered that a warrant of appraisement issue to Samuel Savage,
James McKay, William Abney, and Nathaniel Abney or any three
of them to authorize them to appraise the goods and chattels
of Jacob Brooks which will be shewn to them by Mary Brooks
administratrix

The State vs John Pursel. Tavern Keeping. a jury being
called and impanneled...to wit David Segler, Lewis Clerk,
James Cox, Shadrack Henderson, James Henderson, John Clask-
ler Junr., Absolom Roberts, Samuel Ramsey, Christian Gomelion,
Peter Ramsey, Edmons Pursel on their oaths do say and James
Harrison on his solum (sic) affirmation does say that the
defendant is guilty of selling the half pint rum but not as
a Tavern keeper, Samuel Ramsey foreman. on the verdict Mrs.
Carnes gave notice of motion in arrest of judgment

On petition of Sundry Inhabitants that a road be opened from
the Ferry on Saludy River called Lees Ferry to the court
house to fall into a road intended to be laid out to the
Court House from Perkins ford near Capt. Johnsons House &
James Allen, Frederick Williams, Thed. Harris & James Herrin
do view the ground and report to the next -- best and most
convenient way

99 Samuel Carter vs Drury Glover. Referred to James Harrison and Mathew McMillan with power umpirage and report to next court

Peter Hilliard vs Thomas Bezzel Case. Petition. Referred Benjamin Ryan and Edward Couch with power of umpirage and report to next court

The court proceeded to the appointment of Sheriff and Mr. William Covington was appointed to that office

Ordered that James Cobbs, William Jeter Junr., James Hargrove do view the ground from Thurmans to Adams Ferry to cross near the river Savannah as the ground will admit of and report to next court

Ordered that William Mathews overseer over the road leading from Burtons old place to Ninety Six do cut Burtons Mill dam of the road as damaged by the flowing of the water after the first day of September next

Joseph Morris vs Wm. Longmire. Debt. Judgmt. confessed according to note the tobacco in Ł 1 Ł 9 Pr. hundred and payment by instalments

William Jeter Senr vs Vann & Josiah Swearingen. Case. Pltf. non suited in this action

Fields Pardue vs Samuel Glover   Contd.

100 Ordered that the court be adjourned untill tomorrow morning nin o'clock. LeRoy Hammond, Arthur Simkins, John Purves, John Moore, Wm. Eveleigh, Russell Wilson.

The Court met according to adjournment the 11th July 1787 Present Leroy Hammond, Arthur Simkins, Wm. Eveleigh, Russell Wilson.

James Harrison came into court and acknowledged his deeds of lease and release for 200 acres land to William Reynolds which was ordered to be recorded

Mrs. Elizabeth Harris (sic) being privately examined by Russell Wilson Esq. one of the Justices relinquished her right of dower and thirds to land conveyed by her husband to William Reynolds and ordered to be recorded

Mary Dick vs David Zubly. Judgt. for the plaintiff 21/10 to be deducted out of a former verdict vs Plaintiff

Robert Stark vs Jenkin Harris. Case continued generally

James Coursey vs John Allen. Case. Judgment for Ł 1. 6. 6. for plaintiff

101 Thomas Beckham came into court and acknowledged his deeds of lease and release for 400 acres land to Edmond Martin ordered to be recorded

Com. of Hornes Creek vs William Nichols. Debt. Judt for Ł 7.10

Elberton Squires vs Jacob Odum & wife. Contd. by consent of

51

parties

James Cox vs Peter McCoverly Debt. contd.

Abraham Richardson vs Doct. Vann Swearingen. Debt contd.

Richardson Vartlett vs Abraham Odum. Case. settled

David Zubly vs John Tobler Case dismissed

Peter Hilliard vs Thos. Bezzell Case. referred

On application of Arthur Simkins Esq. it is ordered that he be allowed his account of L 19. 3. 3. for material toward the public buildings.

The court to a choice of a coroner & Robert Stark Junr was unamiously (sic) chosen to serve in that office

102 James Coursey vs John Allen. The following persons having proved their attendance as witness in this action viz James Lyon 6 days 15/ Wm. Dawson 4 days 10. Call Collins 4 day 10/ William Key 3 days 7.6 Sutha Duckworth 4 days 10/

William Anderson Esq. came into Court and acknowledged his Deeds to John Holloway for 300 acres land which was ordered to be recorded

The State vs John Pursell Indt. for Tavern keeping
The court after hearing the council on both sides on motion give Judgment for the defendant order him discharged on paying cost

Robert Stark Junr vs Benajah Rambo. Case. Indt. for the Pltf for L 50

John Garrett vs Jas. Morrow Case. contd.

Robert Stark vs Rolly Roebuck Contd.

John Cargill vs John Spencer Referred to Moses Harris and Nicholas Dillard with power of Umpirage and report to next court

John Williams vs Thomas Bezzell Contd.

Solomon Edwards vs Wm. Tolsion. Cont by consent

103 John Randal vs Rolley Roebuck Dismissed

John Williams vs John Crawford Contd. by consent of parties

Richard Johnson vs Frances Settle Dismissed

William Nichols vs Edward Couch & John Ryans Contd.

Isaac Davis vs Will Hightower. Contd.

John Goff vs John Kirkland. Continued till next court when to be fixed perm--

Samuel Evans vs Jones Rivers. Contd. till tomorrow

52

Ordered that this court be adjourned till tomorrow morning
9 o'clock, Prior to adjournment ordered that the Sheriff
take unto custody John Pursel untill he pays his fees
Leroy Hammond, Arthur Simkins, W. Anderson, Wm. Eveleigh,
Russell Wilson.

104 The Court met according to adjournment the 12th July 1787
Present the Worshipful Leroy Hammond, Arthur Simkins,
Wm. Eveleigh, Russell Wilson, Esquires.

Robert Moseley vs John Rainsford. Case, agreed before the
Court on to the plea of the Defendant & it is considered
by the court that the Defendant answer over and put in a substantial plea, whereupon the Defendant by Chalres Goodwin
his attorney pleads the general issue and puts himself upon
his Country and the Plaintiff doth the same whereupon came
a Jury (same as before)...the Defendant pay Ƚ 20. Samuel
Ramsey, foreman.
On motion of Mr. Goodwin attorney for the defendant a new
trial was granted

Dyer Frazier vs Jas. Robinson. Dismissed for want of securtiy for costs

Hannah Vann vs Martin Cloud. Mr. Henry Ware entered himself
security in this action for costs

105 Mossley vs Rainsford. The following persons having proved
their attendance as witnesses in this action to wit Ben
Moseley, 4 days 10/ Darrik Holsonback 4 days 10Ƚ Edmd
Coursey 23 miles 13/8 for the Plaintiff James Hargrove,
4 days 10/ Edward Vann 4 days 10/ Mary Vann 3 days 7/6
George Mossely 4 days 10/ Robert Moseley 4 days 10/
Philip Johnson 4 days 10/ Henry Summerall 4 days 10/
Those for Deft.

Jeter vs Lander & Chandler. Judg. according to bond for
Ƚ 27.10 and interest

Stark and Rambo On motion of the Defendants attorney for an
appeal in this action ordered that he be allowed till next
court to give his reasons why such appeal be allowed

Ordered that this court be adjourned till the second Monday
in October next. Leroy Hammond, Arthur Simkins, Wm. Eveleigh,
Russell Wilson.

The Court met according to adjournment 8th October 1787
Present the Worshipful Arthur Simkins, John Purves, Hugh
Middleton, Esquires.

Ordered that the Sheriffs commission be read which was read
accordingly and ordered to be recorded

Ordered that the Sheriff give bond and Security for the faithful discharge of his duty who give Abraham Richardson & John
Pursell in the sum of Ƚ 1500 agreable to law.

106 Ordered that the grand jury be drawn to serve in April next
The names of the Jurors drawn
Richard Johnson, Michael Buckhalter, Abraham Richardson, John
Clark, Philip Johnson, George Cowan, Thomas Lamar, Thomas Maw-
verry, William Jeter Junr, Nathan Howell, William Green,

Wm. Shinholster, John Thurman, John Bullock, William Spraggins, Solomon Pope, John Grey, Caleb Holloway, John Childs, Fields Pardue.

Ordered that the Sheriff draw the Petit Jury for next court
The names of the Jurors drawn

1. Thomas Adams	16. George Delater
2. John Morris	17. John Quddlebum (sic)
3. Edward Prince	18. Mathew Barrett
4. Thomas Putler	19. Janathis Stephens
5. Thomas Freeman	20. Peter Rootes
6. Thomas Palmer	21. James Martin
7. Stephen Butler	22. William Hollody
8. Jesse Jurnagin	23. Edward Bussey
9. Henry Youngblood	24. John Berry
10. Alex. Cowley	25. Henry Timberman
11. William Baker	26. John Adams
12. Lamar Mays	27. Mark Nobles
13. Drury Mathew	28. Abner Mays
14. Catlett Cowley	29. Peter McGrew
15. Robert Speers	30. Thomas Bezzel

Ordered that the Sheriff return the Writ of Venire for the Petit Jury. The names of the Petit Jury that appeared

1. Sherwood Whatley	9. Thomas Pennington
2. Benjamin Dary	10. Dudly Pruit
3. John Roberts	11. John Elam
4. Isaac Foreman	12. Thomas Youngblood
5. William Clark Junr	13. Drury Murphey
6. Edward Vann	14. Robert Newport
7. Edmond Boyd	15. Edward Holms
8. Stephen Tilman	

107 Sam Marsh was excused his attendance on this court as a Petit Jury on Acct. of his want of memory.

Present William Anderson Esquire.

Deeds of lease and release from Elizabeth Bell to John Childs for 100 acres land was proved by the oaths of Robert Huggins & James Harkins which was ordered to be recorded

Deeds of lease and release from William Robinson to Thomas Youngblood for 200 acres land was proved by the oaths of John Childs and Jesse Hopkins which was ordered to be recorded

Robert Cockran came into court & acknowledged his deeds of lease and release for 640 acres land to John Hammond which was ordered to be recorded

Christian Limkacker came into court and acknowledged his deeds of lease and release for 100 acres land to Mathew Devore Junr which was ordered to be recorded

Mathew Devore came into court & acknowledged his deeds of lease & release to Christian Limkecker for 110 acres land which was ordered to be recorded

Mrs. Rebecca Devore was privately examined by Hugh Middleton Esq. one of the Justices relinquished her right of Dower & thirds to land conveyed by her husband Chris. Lembecker which was ordered to be recorded

108 David Boswell came into court and acknowledged his Deeds of lease and release for 149 acres land to John Barns which was ordered to be recorded

David Boswell came into court and acknowledged his Deeds of lease and release for 120 acres land to Bryan Green which was ordered to be recorded

Mrs. Phebe Green was privately examined by one of the Justices relinquished her right of dower and thirds to land conveyed by her husband to John Barns which was ordered to be recorded

Bryan Green acknowledged his Bond of identification to David Boswell which was ordered to be recorded

Daniel Walker came into court & acknowledged his Deeds of lease and release to John Hofman for 66 acres land which was ordered to be recorded

John Gorman came into court and acknowledged his deeds of lease and release for 200 acres land to Michael McKey which was ordered to be recorded

Mrs. Hannah Gorman was privately examined by William Anderson Esq. one of the Justices relinquished her right of Dower and thirds to lands conveyed by her husband to Michael McKey which was ordered to be recorded

Drury Nipper came into court and acknowledged his deeds of lease and release to Jacob Fudge Senr for 100 acres land which was ordered to be recorded

109 Mrs. Eliza Nipper was privately examined by Wm. Anderson Esq. one of the Justices relinquished her right of dower and thirds to lands conveyed by her husband to Jacob Fudge Senr. which was ordered to be recorded

Deeds of lease and release from Peter Day to Joseph Cunningham for 95 acres land was proved by the oaths of John Hancock and Reubin Frazier which was ordered to be recorded

John Day came into court and acknowledged his deeds of lease and release for 167 acres land to John Handcock and Reuben Frazier which was ordered to be recorded

John Hancock came into court and acknowledged his deeds of lease and release for 240 acres land to John Day which was ordered to be recorded

The last will and testament of Richard Lowery was proved by the oaths of Joseph Collins and William Howie which was ordered to be recorded

Ordered that the Court be adjourned till tomorrow morning 9 o'clock. Arthur Simkins, Hugh Middleton, Wm. Anderson, Wm. Eveleigh.

The court according to adjnt. the 9th 1787. Present the Worshipful Leroy Hammond, Arthur Simkins, Hugh Middleton, W. Anderson, Wm. Eveleigh, Esquiers.

110 Roland Williams came into court and acknowledged his deeds

of lease and release for 100 acres land to Rachael Quenney
which was ordered to be recorded

Mrs. Martha Williams being privately examined by William
Anderson Esq. one of the Justices relinquished her right of
dower and thirds to land conveyed by her husband to Rachael
Quinsey and James Rowe which was ordered to be recorded

Roland Williams came into Court and acknowledged his deeds
of lease and release for 100 acres land to James Rowe which
was ordered to be recorded

On application of Benjamin Ryan Junr. he being of approved
age to choose came into court and made case of Benjamin Ryan
Senr as his guardina ordered that the said Benjamin Ryan
Senr give bond for the fiathful discharge of his duty as
Guardian & with George Cheney, John Cheney and John Gray in
the sum of Ł 1500

Ordered that the grand jury defaulters at this court shew
cause the first day of next court why the failed in attendance agreeable to their summons on this court

Ordered that the late Sheriff be fine in the sum of 20/ for
neglecting to summons Wm. Longmire Grand Jury

Deeds of lease and release from Richard Kirkland to Philip
Mays for 175 acres land was proved by the oaths of Alexander
Alexander and Charles Banks which was ordered to be recorded

111 Ordered that by consent of parties that Drury Pace, Richard
Johnson, and John Cheney be added to the grand jury on acct.
of several of the jury failing to appear at this court Capt.
Henry Key being appointed foreman

Ordered that the grand jury be sworn viz
1. Henry Key   8. Samuel Crafton
2. Thomas Anderson   9. Samuel Burgess
3. John Hancock   10. William Mathews
4. John Gorman   11. William Longmire
5. Benj. Cook   12. Drury Pace
6. Robert Belcher   13. Richard Johnson
7. James Coursey   14. John Cheney

Ordered that the coroner give bond and security for the
faithful discharge of his duty in the sum of Ł 1500 who give
John Gray & George Cowen according to law

The last will and testament of William Perrin was proved by
the oath of Thomas Littleton one of the subscribing witnesses
was ordered to be recorded

Ordered Abner Perrin one of the Executors mentioned in the
above will be sworn as Executor which was done accordingly

Wm. Murphey came into court and acknowledged his deeds of
lease and release for 50 acres land to James Butler which
was ordered to be recorded

On motion of Benjamin Darby one of the Petit Jury was excused
his attendance on this court on acct. of his indisposition

Leroy Hammond vs John Garret. On att. John Martin and Daniel Barksdale appeared in open court and acknowledged themselves special bail in this action

112 Abrah Richardson vs John Garrett. on attnt. John Martin and Daniel Barksdale appeared in open court and acknowledged themselves special bail in this action

Deeds of lease and release from Thomas Adams to Edmond Whatley for 100 acres land was proved by Butler Williams & Daniel Marew which was ordered to be recorded

Mrs. Rebecca Adams being privately examined by William Anderson one of the Justices relinquished her right of dower and thirds to land conveyed by her husband to Edmond Whatley which was ordered to be recorded

Peter Hilliard vs Thomas Bezzel. Petition referred Judgment for Ł 30.0 & costs

The State vs William Dawson & John Randal. a true bill Henry Key, foreman. Capt. Richard Johnson entered himself security for the Defendants tomorrow

The state vs Richardson Bartlett & William Dobey. True Bill Henry Key, foreman. Francis Settle intered himself security for the appearance of the Defendants tomorrow

The State vs Richard McCary. No bill Henry Key, foreman

David Burks came into court & acknowledged his deeds of lease & release for 44 acres land to Drury Mims which was ordered to be recorded

113 Mrs. Jean Burks was privately examined by William Anderson Esq. one of the justices relinquished her right of dower and thirds to land conveyed by her husband to Drury Mims ordered to be recorded

The last will and testament of James McGetta was proved by the oath of Peter Carnes Esq. which was ordered to be recorded

On application of Mrs. Elizabeth Roberts widow of Reubin Roberts deceased the administrator of the rights and credits of the said deceased was granted to her she having entered into bond with Rolan Williams, James Cox & John Carter for the faithful discharge of the administration in the sum of Ł 300 & was qualified according to law

Ordered that a warrant of appraisement issue to John Jones, Isaac Lewis, Richard Johnson Junr., and Richard Johnson Senr or any three of them to authorize them to appraise the goods and chattels or Reubin Roberst deceased that will be shewn them by Elizabeth Roberts Administratrix

Deeds of lease and release from Robert Bartlett to John Roberts for 150 acres land was proved by the oaths of Reubin Roberts and John Williams which was ordered to be recorded

Ordered that this court be adjourned till tomorrow morning 9 o'clock. Leroy Hammond, Hugh Middleton, Wm. Eveleigh.

114 The court met according to adjournment 10th October 1787
     Present the Worshipful Arthur Simkins, Hugh Middleton, Wil-
     liam Anderson, Esquires.

     The State vs Richardson Bartlett & William Dobey. Ordered
     that the defendant Richardson Bartlett give security to appear
     at the next court and not to depart without leave thereof who
     gave Ben Cook in the sum of Ł 25 himself in the sum of Ł 50

     The State vs Richardson Bartlett & William Dobey. Ordered
     that the deft. William Dobey give security for his appear-
     ance the next court who gave John Abney in the sum of Ł 20
     himself in the sum of Ł 50

     Ordered that Richard Weatherton give security to appear and
     prosecute next court Richardson Bartlett and Wm. Dobey who
     gave   -- Witherton in the sum of Ł 55 himself in the sum of
     Ł 50

     On application of Samuel Eskridge a youth he being of approved
     age the guardianship of the said Sam Eskridge was granted to
     Joseph Thomas on his giving bond with security who gave Isaac
     Lewis & Daniel Bullock in the sum of Ł 300

     On application of Charles Hammond a youth being of proper age
     the guardianship of the said Charles was granted to William
     Covington Esq. who on his giving bond and security who gave
     Hugh Middleton Esq. and George Cowan in the sum of Ł 300

115 Leroy Hammond being under age the court appointed the afore-
     said Wm. Covington as his guardian also who gave security as
     above

     Miss Elizabeth Warring Martin being under age the court ap-
     pointed Mrs. Betty Martin her guardian on her giving bond
     & security who gave Capt. George Cowan and John Martin in
     the sum of Ł 500

     The State vs Wm. Dawson & John Randal. Ordered that Wm Daw-
     son & John Randal give security for their appearance the
     next court & John Randal gave Abr. Richardson his security
     William Dawson gave Capt. John Ryan principal in the sum of
     Ł 50 securities in the sum of Ł 25 each

     John Parker prosecutor in this action gave William Doby his
     security to prosecute principal in the sum of Ł 50 security
     in the sum of Ł 25

     John Coursey came into court and ackd. his deeds of lease
     and release for 300 acres land to John Bridges which was
     ordered to be recorded

     Fields Pardue vs Sam Glover. Petition Dismissed at Pltfs
     cost

116 Robert Stark vs Jenkin Harris. Petition continued until
     tomorrow

     Elverton Squires vs Jacob Adams. Petition Judgment for
     33/ and cost

     The State vs Edward Vann True Bill Henry Key, foreman

58

Ordered that the defendant give security to appear next court
and not depart without leave who gave Lewis Nobles in the sum
of Ł 25 himself in the sum of Ł 50

The State vs Martin Cloud. Assault. Ordered that the defendant give security to appear next court and not depart without leave who give William Hardin in the sum of Ł 25 and
himself in the sum of Ł 50

Ordered that a road be opened agreeable to the report of the
viewers from Perkins ford to the court house viz to begin
at Perkins ford the nearest & best way to big creek at Mr.
John Gibsons then to red branch near Capt. Popes old mill
seat thence to Rocky creek near to Mr. Isaac Lewis plantation
thence to Turkey Creek at the ford of Augusta road below Mr.
Richd. Johnson Plantation thence to the line run by Mrs. Abney from the said ford to the said court house thence along
the said line to the court house and that the following persons be appointed to clear the same viz John Gibson from
Perkins ford to big creek keep in repair from thence to red
creek branch Lewis Clark thence to rocky creek Thomas Deloach Junr. thence to Turkey Creek, Isaac Lewis thence to
the court house Robert Burton

117 Ordered that the clerk receive the presentment of the grand
jury which are in the following words

We the grand jury of the county of Edgefield Present it as a
grievance that the road leading from Perkins Ferry -- creek
bearrins old bridge to the court house being out of repair
for want of working on

We present Mr. Swindle for retailing spiritous liquors ordered
that a capias issue to bring him to next court to shew cause

We present it as a grievance that the lands marks is not
renewed every give years the presentment be layed before the
legislature

We present it as a grievance that there is no notice taken
on profain swearing   Henry Key, foreman

Ordered that the following persons be allowed their attendance
in the action Squires vs Adams viz William Anderson 6 days
at 2/6 James Tomlin 6 days at 2/6

James Cox vs Peter McCoverly. Petition Continued by consent

118 John Goff vs John Kirkland Case nonsuited Joshua Warren
proved his attendance for 9 days @ 2/6 in this action

Samuel Evans vs Jones Rivers. Trover. dismissed

Elisha Hubbard vs Will Baker Harvey. Case dismissed

William Cook vs Jones Rivers Case Refd. Contd.

Robert Stark assinee vs Sarrah Harris. Contd. at Pltf cost

John Herndon vs John Randal Judt. by default. The same jury
as before who fined for the Plaintiff Ł 15. 9 with interest
and costs   Isaac Foreman, foreman

Martin Cloud vs Neri Taylor. Dismissed

The same vs. John Canady Dismissed

Samuel Hammond vs Allen Hinton. Judt. by Deft. on a writ
of Inquiry the same Jury as before who upon their oaths do
say that the debt Ⱡ 9 16.9 & costs. Isaac Foreman, foreman

119 James Vessels vs James Christopher. Case contd by consent

John Mims vs George Miller. Trover. Referred to Henry Ware
& Wm. Dawson who say that the defendant pay Ⱡ 10 and costs

William Evans vs Jesse Roundtree. Case Issue joined the
same jury as before upon their oaths do say we find for the
pltf. Ⱡ 34. 10 with lawful interest from 1 Jan 1786 and cost
Isaac Foreman, foreman

Benjamin Joiner vs John Herndon. Judgt. confessed according
to account

Rolly Roebuck vs Mark Lott. Dismist. at Pltfs cost

Abemelick Hawkins vs Thomas Lamar. Debt. Ordered that a
dedimus Issue to Mayor Forswith Dalziel Hunter to examine
Tabourn Jones and John Lamar in this action as witness for
the deft. and due notice be given to Capt. Wm. Key of the
time and place

Arthur Morrow vs William Dawson. Trover. contd.

120 John Hightower vs James Vessels Debt. Contd.

Jesse Roundtree vs David Barnett. Col. Hammond security for
costs

William English vs Thos & Raddy Smith. Asst. Contd. at
Pltf. cost

Jesse Roundtree vs Thomas Lamar. Case contd. Ordered that
a dedimus issue direct to Major Forsyth & Dalziel Hunter to
examine James Lamar in this action on behalf of the debt
giving due notice time & place

George Mee vs Stephen Bettis. Trespass Contd. till tomorrow

John Hoes vs Jesse Glover. Asst. The same Jury as before
...we find for the plaintiff Ⱡ 15 and costs. Isaac Foreman,
foreman

James Cockran 9 days attendance in this action on the part
& behalf of the plaintiff @ 2/6

John Hammond vs Robert Melton. Debt. Contd.

John Kilcrease vs George Cowan. Dismissed at Pltf. cost

Fields Pardue vs James C. Murphey. Dismisd.

121 Fields Pardue vs William Nichols. Debt Judgment by default

Samuel Ramsey vs Drury Glover Debt. contd.

David Van vs John Ballard Detinee contd. Edward Van entered himself as security

Martin Kinard vs Fields Pardue. Debt.   Contd

Lewis Coody vs Bennett Crafton Abates by death of parties

Peter Carnes vs James Anderson   Dismisd.

Arthur Watson & Robert Star Ex. vs Richard Johnson & Edward Couch. Debt. contd.

The same vs Richard Johnson & William Butler. Debt. contd.

Reubin Rambo vs Lewis Nobles. Debt. contd.

Hannah Van vs Martin Cloud Case contd.

122   John Davison vs Drury Murphey Debt. contd.

James Wilson vs Frances Settled. Debt referred Col. Hammond and Edward Kealing with power of umpirage

William Mead vs Thomas Hill. Case contd.

William Jeter Senr vs John Pounds Debt contd.

James Lyond vs John Allen. Case contd. at Pltfs cost

Edward Van vs John Spencer. Debt discontd. at Pltfs cost

John Fluker vs Charles Banks. Discontd at Pltf cost

John Herndon vs Robert Collins Debt contd.

Robert Alexander vs Frances Handcock. Debt contd

123   Alexander Alexander vs Philip May. Debt contd.

Ross & Currie vs Robert Moseley. Case judt. by deft.

George Miller vs Sam Burgiss Case contd.

Anna Minter vs John Garrett Attempment Contd. special bail Henry Ware

Thomas Franklin vs Alexander Wilson Slander discontd.

The same vs Presley Bland Asst. discontd.

The same & wife vs John Goff. Asst. non suited

Wm. Brooks vs James Vessells Asst. contd.

Ann Foreman vs Wm. Williams. Slander discontd.

John Randal vs William Nichols. Asst. Judt. by Deft.

Leroy Hammond vs Benjamin Breadlove Discontd. at the cost of Ulysses Rogers

124 William Covington vs Charles Bussey. Trover referred to

Edwd Keating and Edmond Martin with power of umpirage by order of court

John Randal vs William Nichols   Judt by Deft.

John Drunkard vs William Dean.   non suit

Richard Johnson vs John Watson   Asst. contd.

William Williams vs Isaac Foreman & Arthur Thomas.   Asst. discontinued.

Morris Calleham & wife vs James Lyon & wife.   Slander. Judgt. by deft.

William Anderson vs Thomas Chappel   Case   not to be red.

Benjamin Cook vs Edmond Martin   Case   contd.

Robert Moseley vs Robert Cockran   Trover   Contd.

Adams Pardue vs Edward Vann   Asst.   Contd.

William H. Moseley vs Thomas Lawson.   Trover.   Judgt by default

125   Thomas Morrison vs James Martin   Debt.   Contd.

James Martin vs Sampson Griffin.   Case   contd.

James Martin vs Fields Pardue.   Trover   contd.

James Gollihan vs West Cook.   Asst. discontd.

John Daimpert & wife vs David Bowers & Isaac Ardis.   Case contd.

Absolum Roberts vs George Cowan   Debt.   Contd.

Edmond Whatley vs Thos & Drury Adams   Case   discontd.

John Rainsford vs George Miller & James Booth.   Debt.   Judt. by Deft.

William Hardin vs Joshua Hammond   Debt   discontd.

Arthur Roades vs Ann Summeral   Case   contd.

126   Peter Hilliard vs William Robinson   Case contd.

John Hammond Senr vs James Vessels   Slander contd.

John Purves vs Francis Settle.   Debt   contd.

John Carter vs John Williams.   Debt   contd.

Adams Pardue vs Suckey Coody   Case contd.

Edith Coody vs Suckey Coody.   Discontd.

William Hammilton vs John Kennedy.   Case   Judt by deft.

Morning Williams & Father vs John Watson   Asst.   contd

The same vs The Same. Slander contd.

Robert Mosley vs John Rainsford Case Judgment confessed
for 1500 pounds of tobacco with stay of execution till 21
Dec next

Thomas Bezzel vs Christian Gomillian Trover contd.

127 Edward Mitchel vs Frederick Tilman. Judgment confessed according to note payable by instlnt.

Benjamin Blackley vs William Carson. Debt. Contd.

Thomas Dalton vs George Ragland. Attmt contd. Edward Couch
entered himself bail in this action

Leroy Hammond Esq. vs John Garrett. Attmt contd. John
Martin and Daniel Barksdale entered themselves as special
bail in this action.

William Carson vs Joseph Read Attmt Judt by Deft.

Drury Pace vs George Ragland Attmt Contd. Robert Melton
entd. himself special bail in this action.

William Anderson vs Thomas Wooten. Attmt Judt. by Deft.

Abraham Richardson vs John Garrett Attmt contd. bail given
as before

Samuel Mays vs George James Attmt contd. Judgmt by Deft.

Edward Bland vs Henery bolton Trespass Contd.

128 Charles Franklin vs Frederick Williams. Discontinued

Robert Melton vs Lawrence Rambo. Case. The same jury being
called impannelled & sworn as beofre do say we find for the
deft. with costs and the plaintiff to have the note given him

Charles Fraklin & wife vs Frederick Williams & others. Asst.
discontinued

John Garrett vs Robert Moseley. Case contd. by consent

Joshua Hammond vs James Christopher. Case discontinued

William Haregrove vs Benjamin Cook Debt. contd. by consent

Jesse Roundtree vs Joel Chandler Case continued by consent

Daniel Parker vs James Tutt Assault contd.

John Clark vs John Hix. Case judt by Deft.

John Anderson vs Henry Key. Trover Referred to Meyer Tutt
& George Cowan with power of umprage and report to next court

Timothy Russell vs Isaac Leafever & wife. Debt. continued

129 Samuel Carter vs Drury Glover. This action being referred to
Mathew McMillian and James Harrison do return their award

for Ł 28 s 10 d 6 and costs which is confirmed

Abraham Richardson vs Van Swearingen Dismst. at Deft. costs

John Hammond vs Frances Settle Judt. confessed according to note

The Same vs Joseph Toles. Judgmt. confessed for Ł 3 19.77

The same vs George Mayson Judg for Ł 1.8.10 and costs

The Same vs Abraham Little. Judgt. confessed Ł 3.16.7½

Hannah Van vs Moses Carter. Judgt. according to note

William Covington vs Warner Lewis Dismisd. by order of the pltf.

John Carter vs John Williams Judgt. confessed according to note with stay of execution for half the next court

Ephriam Sizemore vs Richard Pond. Judgt. confessed for Ł 5 and cost which is settled

Young Allen vs John Tole. Judgt. according to note

130 Ordered that the issue docket be called over

Jeremiah Web vs James Carson. Case non suit

Robert Stark vs Benejah Rambo. Judgt. confirmed for Ł 50 agreeable to the instalments upon the Def. giving security

John Garrett vs James Murry. Case.
a jury being called...Sherwood Watley, John Roberts, Isaac Foreman, William Clark Senr., Edward Vann, Edmond Boyd, Stephen Tilman, Thomas Pennington, Dudly Pruit, John Elam, Thomas Youngblood and Drury Murphey who say we find for the plaintiff Ł 18 s 1 d 3 with interest & costs
                              Isaac Foreman, foreman

Ordered that a road be opened from Lees Ferry on big Saludy the nearest and best way to the court house beginning at Lees Ferry thence to Clouds creek near Corley Mill thence to Richland Creek crossing at or near William Butlers Plantation thence crossing Dry Creek at or near the widow Rustins thence crossing mine creek at or near the plantation of William Herrins thence crossing rockey creek at Mr.Baruns thence to intersect with a road from Perkins pond to Mr. Richd Johnsons

131 Dalziel Hunter vs Rufus Inman. Debt Judgment according to specialty execution to issue agreeable to instalments the Pltf to pay the cost

The same vs The same. Debt. Judgment according to specialty The same order as above

Patrick Wullivan came into court & acknowledged his deeds of lease and release to Robert Belcher for 350 acres land which was ordered to be recorded

James Martin vs Fields Pardue. By consent of parties ordered that a dedimus Issue to Major Forsyth & William Freeman in the State of Georgia to take examination of Stephen Tucker on the part of the plaintiff giving the defendant due notice of time and place

Robert Stark vs Sarah Harris. Ordered that a dedimus issue to two magistrates in the state of Georgia to examine Thomas Robinson in this action on the part of the Plaintiff and they giving five days notice of time and place

Reubin Rambo vs Lewis Nobles. Ordered that a dedimus to John Shackleford to take the examination of Pitman at the house of Mr. S. D. Garmina the first of Nov. on behalf of the defendant

132 Ordered that the Petit Jury defaulters at this court shew cause next court why they failed attending this court

Samuel Mays vs George James Attmt. William Anderson Esq. who being summoned as garnishee sayeth on his oath that upwards of Ł 90 lawful money is due by him to George James

On application of Barshaba Blair widow of George Blair deceased ordered that the administration of all and singular the goods and chattels of the said deceased be granted to her she having entered into bond with Henry Key and John Martin in the sum of Ł 200 for the fiathful discharge of her duty & taken the oath accordingly

Ordered that the warrant of appraisement be issued directed to John Griffis, James Thomas, Christopher Blanton, William Key, or any three of them to authorise them to appraise the goods and chattels of George Blair dec'd which will be shewn them by Barshaba Blair the admx.

Samuel Carter vs Drury Glover. The following persons first having proved their attendance on this court as witnesses be allowed the same in this action John Blanton 6 days @ 2/6 David Rush 5 days @ 2/6 George Ragland 2 days @ 2/6 in behalf of the Plaintiff

133 Ordered that the court be adjourned till tomorrow morning 9 o'clock prior to adjmt the sheriff having signified to the court the appointment of Drury Mims to the office of Goaler the court approve the appointment. Arthur Simkins, Hugh Middleton, Wm. Eveleigh, Benj. Tutt.

The Court met according to adjournment the 11th of October 1787. Present the worshipful Leroy Hammond, Hugh Middleton, Wm. Eveleigh, Esq.

On application of Mrs. Frances Edwards late widow of William Martin deceased who proved the will of the dec'd in common form and produced the renunciation of the other executor Macness Goode Ordered that she be qualified as executrix

Mrs. Wesley Martin and Rieves Martin being of full age the guardianship of the aforesaid Wesly & Rieves was granted to Garland Goode on his giving bond and security who gave Wm. Mathews & Drury Mathews for the faithful discharge of the said trust in the sum of Ł 2000

Ordered that warrant of appraisement issue directed to John
Moore, William Robinson,Frederick Glover and Samuel Goode
or any three of them to authorise them to appraise the estate
of William Martin deceased which shall be shewn them by
Frances Edwards Exec. of the deceased est.

Robert Stark vs Rolly Roebuck Judgmt. according to instalments the first Inst. being paid Ŀ 6:1:10 with interest

John Cargill vs John Spencer case continued at Pltf cost

John Williams vs Thomas Bezzel Dismt. for want of jurisdiction of the court

Solomon Edwards vs William Goodwin contd. by consent

John Williams vs John Crawford Case non suit

William Nichols vs Edward Couch Settled at Deft. cost

Robert Stark vs Jenkin Harris Pltf. Judt. Ŀ 4.13.4 & cost

John Hoes vs Drury Glover. Assault dismd at Pltf. cost

David Burks vs James Christopher Dismd at Pltf cost.

Ordered that court be adjourned till tomorrow 9 o'clock.
Leroy Hammond, Arthur Simkins ,Wm. Eveleigh.

135 The court met according to adjournment 12th of October 1787.
Present the worshipful Leroy Hammond, Wm. Eveleigh, Russell
Wilson, Esquires.

Ordered Melines C. Leavensworth & Thomas Lamar of Horse Creek
be appointed overseer over the road leading from Perkings Fer-
ry on Savannah River to Horse Creek at Bevins bridge from
Horse Creek to the road leading to Fort Moore Bluff, Jacob
Zinn and Isaac Ardis in the room of Nathaniel Bacon & Benj.
Bowers

Ordered that the following persons be appointed to open and
keep in repair the road from Lees Ferry on Saludy to the Court
House to wit Andrew Lee, Clouds Creek thence where the road
is to cross the Ninety Six road Jacob Smith thence where the
road falls into the road leading from Perkins ford to the
Court House Robert Pow

Morris Calliham vs Drewry Murphey. Trover dismisd

Elisha Warren vs Will Baker Harvey. Assault non suit

Michael Odum vs Bryan Green Dismissed

Thomas Franklin vs Frederick Williams Assault Discontd.

Present Russell Wilson Esq.

George Mee vs Stephen Bettis case
The same Jury as before being called impannelled and sworn
to wit Sherwood Whatley, John Roberts, Isaac Foreman, William
clark, Edward Van, Edmond Boyd, Stephen Tilman, Thomas Pennington, Dudly Pruit, John Elam, Thomas Youngblood and Drury
Murphey who say that the Plaintiff recover Ŀ 15 cash.

66

The Deft by Peter Carnes his Atty. prays an appeal to which it is granted on his entering in to bond to prosecute the appeal with effect ordered that the appeal be dismist with stay of execution six months, Anderson Williams proved his attendance in this action 7 days @ 2/6 for Pltf.

Timothy Cooper vs Thomas Murphey Discont.
Ordered that the following persons be allowed their attendance as witnesses in this action Robert Melton vs Law Rambo viz to be paid by the Plaintiff

137 Thomas Adams 14 days @2/6 Mathew Durram 4 days @ 2/6 milage for 50 miles John Lucas 12 days @ 2/6

Ordered that this court be adjourned till the second Monday in January next. Leroy Hammond, Arthur Simkins, Russell Wilson.

The court met according to adjournment the 14day day of Jan 1788. Present the Worshipful Leroy Hammond, Benj. Tutt, Russell Wilson, John Moore, John Sturzennegger, Esquires.

Ordered that the Petit Jurors be drawn to serve next court. The names of the Petit Jury so drawn

1.	Nathaniel Bacon	16. Reubin Holloway
2.	James Heart	17. Robert Bland
3.	Kealan Smith	18. James Davis
4.	Alexander Oadum	19. Van Swearingen
5.	George Miller	20. Robert Deshaso
6.	Joel Cox	21. Samuel Stalnaker
7.	Gasper Miller	22. William Brown
8.	Isaac Leafever	23. Thomas Ross
9.	John Jackson	24. Ezekiah Odum
10.	Bartlett Bledsoe	25. William Arrington
11.	Joseph Cook	26. Amos Mitchel
12.	Jonathan Mire	27. Dudley Carter
13.	Robert Courtney	28. John Calliham
14.	Michael Deloach	29. Nicholas Minor
15.	Joseph Collier	30. Sampson Moore

138 Ordered that all the defaulters as Jury to be allowed 3 months in future to make excuse for their non attendance on this court

John Berry was excused his attendance on this court as a jury on acct. of his deafness

Ordered that James Harrison, James Stephens, George Perrin, Robert Belcher or any three of them do appraise the estate of William Perrin deceased

The last will and testament of Thomas Roberts deceased was proved by Sherwood Whatley and Edmond Whatley and Absolum Roberts was qualified as an executor according to law

The last will and testament of Edward Laremon was proved by James and William McCarter & Martha Laremon was qualified according to law an as executrix

Ordered that James Harrison, Arthur Warson, Edward Nelson and Thomas Warren or any three of them to appraise the estate of Edward Laremon deceased and make return according to law.

The last will and testament of Frances Posey was proved by Elijah Walker and Benj. Posey and Absolum Posey was qualified according to law as an executor.

Ordered that Lewis and Benjamin Clark, Ezekiah Walker and Richd. Bush or any three of them to appraise the estate of Frances Posey decd and make return according to law.

139 The administration of the estate of John Watsman deceased was granted to Elizabeth Manor she having given bond in the sum of Ł 300 with John Frederick and James Frederick as securities

Ordered that Thomas Warren, Sam Messer Obediah Johns, Nathaniel Howel or any three of them do appraise the estate of John Watsman and make return according to law

Permission was granted to Andrew Lee to keep tavern securities Arthur Watson and Howel Johnson

Permission was granted to John Gorman to keep tavern securities Andrew Lee & Drury Pace

Permission was granted to William Day to keep tavern securities John Gorman & James Beal

Permission was granted to James Coates and James Stuart to keep tavern securities Barkely Martin & Matt Martin

Permission was granted to Henry Ware to keep tavern securities Drury Mims and Edward Mitchel

Permission was granted to Thomas Swindin to keep tavern securities William Covington and James Vessels

Permission was granted to Anthony Butler to keep tavern securities Wm. Watson & Wm. Mosely

140 Permission was granted to Moses Harris to keep Tavern securities Daniel Bird and John Herndon

Permission was granted to Jinkin Harris to keep tavern securities Burgis White and Leonard Nobles

Permission was granted John Henrdon to keep tavern securities Daniel Bird and Moses Harris

Permission was granted to John Handcock to keep tavern securities Will Moseley and James Vessels

Permission was granted to Lileston Pardue to keep tavern securities James King and John Hendon

Permission was granted to Genry & Powers to keep tavern securities Will Covington and Fields Pardue.

Ordered that the court be adjd. till tomorrow morning 9 o'clock John Moore, John Sturzennegger, Leroy Hammond, Benj. Tutt.

The court met according to Adjt. the 15 of Jan 1788. Present the Worshipful Leroy Hammond, Benjamin Tutt, John Sturzenegger, Esquires

Henry Bolton came into court and acknowledged his deeds of lease and release to Will Humpris for 135 acres land which was ordered to be recorded

141 Deeds of lease and release from William Davis to Thomas Spraggins for 153 acres land was proved by the oaths of Enoch Grigsby & Ludwick Hill which was ordered to be recorded

John Arledged came into court and acknowledged his deeds of lease and release for 144 acres land to Samuel Jenkins which was ordered to be recorded

Deeds of lease and release from Peter Green to Isham Green for 344 acres land was proved by the oaths of John Moore Esq. and James Beal which was ordered to be recorded

Thomas Beckham came into court and acknowledged his deeds of lease & release for 150 acres land to Joseph Collier which was ordered to be recorded

William Brown came into court and acknowledged his deeds of lease and release to John Arledge for 100 acres land which was ordered to be recorded

William Doby came into court & acknowledged his deeds of lease & release for 100 acres land to John Oliphant which was ordered to be recorded

Mrs. Ann Doby being privately examined by John Moore Esq. relinquished her right of dower and thirds to lands conveyed by her husband to John Oliphant which was ordered to be recorded

Will Covington Esq. came into court and acknowledged his deeds of lease & release to John Hardy for 45 acres land which was ordered to be recorded

142 Richard Witherton came into court and acknowledged his deeds of lease and release for 55 acres land which was ordered to be recorded to Thomas Witherton

William Dovy came into court and acknowledged his deeds of lease and release for 250 acres land to Absolum Shearly which was ordered to be recorded

Mrs. Nancy Doby was privately examined by John Moore Esq. one of the Justices relinquished her right of dower and thirds to lands conveyed by her husband to Absolum Shearly which was ordered to be recorded

Richard Johnson came into court and acknowledged his deeds of lease and release for 464 acres land which was ordered to be recorded

Stephen Tilman came into court and acknowledged his deeds of lease and release for 100 acres land to Frederick Tilman Junr which was ordered to be recorded

Drury Mims acknowledged his deeds of lease and release to Jenkin Harris for ½ acre land which was ordered to be recorded

Mrs. Mims being privately examined by John Moore Esq. one of the Justices relinquished her right of dower and thirds to land conveyed by her husband to Jenkin Harris which was ordered to be recorded

Deeds of lease and release from Abner Mays to David Lyles for 90 acres land was proved by the oaths of Joseph Odham and William Ward which was ordered to be recorded

143 Deeds of lease from Ben Hughs, Anna Hughs, Esther Mayson & Ellen Mayson for 200 acres land was proved by Levi Jester & Charley Mock which was ordered to be recorded

Drury Mims came into court & acknowledged his deeds of lease and release for ½ acre land to Moses Harris which was ordered to be recorded

Mrs. Mims was prively examined by John Moore Esq. one of the Justices relinquished her right of dower and thirds to land conveyed by her husband to Moses Harris which was ordered to be recorded

Deeds of lease and release from Sullivan Stephens to James Youngblood for 200 acres land was proved by John Harkins and Davis Williams which was ordered to be recorded

Deeds of relinquishment from Daniel Bullock & wife to Jacob Smith & Enock Grigsby was proved by Russell Wilson Esq. & Ludwick Hill.

John Randal came into court and acknowledged his deeds of lease & release for 50 acres land to Daniel Day which was ordered to be recorded

Edmond Martin came into court and acknowledged his deeds of lease and release for 100 acres land to James Harrison which was ordered to be recorded

Robt Speer came into court & acknowledged his deeds of lease & release for 100 acres land to Ancel Roberts, Ord. to be recorded

144 Robert Stark assnee. vs John Williams Debt.Contd.

Frances Settle vs Daniel Wallicon. Debt. Contd. Bail taken

James Vessels vs Jesse Roundtree Case contd.

Ker & Brown vs William Hardy Debt contd.

Frances Settle vs Simon Cushman Debt contd.

John Wms & Cutts vs M. C. Leavensworth & Andrew Perkins. Case Contd.

John Williams vs Fields Pardue Contd.

John Randal vs William Nichols Asst. contd.

James Futch. Case contd.

Benj. Tutt vs George Ragland Debt contd. Bail

Ann Hammond vs Abraham Richardson case contd.

Edward Miles vs Drury Mims. Case contd.

Easter Mason vs James Coursey Case contd.

145 Benjamin Blackley vs William Carson   Slander Judt. by Deft.

The Same vs The Same. Assault Same order

Eliz. Reynolds vs Frances Moore & wife Slander contd.

Drury Mims vs John Cheney. Case contd.

William Brown vs John Purves Esq. Debt contd.

Sampson Griffin vs William Nichols Case contd.

Thomas Boon vs Charity Mock Case contd. Bail.

John Herndon vs John Randal Slander contd.

John & Benj. Ryan vs Exr of Lason Ryan vs Joshua Hammond.
Debt contd.

Jesse Roundtree vs James Butts & West Cook Case contd.

John Randall vs Robert Roebuck. Trover contd.

146 Allen Hinton vs Edward Flecker. Trespass contd.

Jesse Roundtree vs William Evans Case contd.

Joseph Burton vs Caleb Holloway Trover contd.

Nathan Johnson vs Jesse Scrugs. Slander contd.

John Perry vs James Massy. Attmt. Discontinued

John Handcock vs James Scoot. Attmt contd.

Mary Roberts vs David Hunter. Attmt. Contd. John Moore
Esq. sworn as Garnishee

Charles Goodwin came into court and acknowledged his deeds of
lease and release for ¼ acre of land ordered to be recorded

Deeds of conveyance from Richard Johnson to Leroy Hammond
Esq. for 100 acres land was proved by oaths of Joshua Hammond
& Robert Speer ordered to be recorded

Ordered that a dedimus Potestation Issue Major Forsyth &
Dalziel Hunter to take the Exn of Mrs. Ann Marbury to several
tracts of land conveyed by her husband to Peter Carnes & also
to John T. Lowe & also to take th ackn. of the said Marbury
to the said land.

147 Ordered that a dedimus issue to Major Forsyth and Dalziel
Hunter to take examination of Daniel M D Furges and James
Stuart subscribing witnesses to the land conveyed by McCarter
Campbel to Charles Goodwin Esq.

William H. Mosely vs Thomas Lawson. Ordered that a dedimus
issue to Henry Ware and Thomas Hughs to take the Exam. of

John Gorden and John Medium in this action for the defts.

The state vs John Randal. John Randal came into court and acknowledged to the County Ŀ 50, James Barrington acknowledged to owe the county Ŀ 25 in this action.

The State vs William Dawson. The defendant came into court and acknowledged to owe the County Ŀ 50 & George Cowan to owe Ŀ 25 as security

The state vs Edward Vann. The defendant came into court and acknowledged to owe Ŀ 50 to the County & Lewis Noble to owe Ŀ 25 as security in this action.

The State vs Martin Cloud. Recognizence renewed

148 The State vs William Doby. Recognizance renewed

The State vs Richd. Bartlett Recognizance renewed

Joshua Hammond came into court and acknowledged his deeds of lease & release to William Spencer for 164 acres land which was ordered to be recorded

Benjamin Cook came into court & acknowledged his deeds of lease & release to Charles Goodwin Esq. for 164 acres land which was ordered to be recorded

Deeds of lease and release from Jabith Hendricks to Edward Prince for 50 acres land was proved by the oaths of Hugh Middleton Esq. & Joseph Prince

Joshua Hammond came into court and acknowledged his conveyance to William Covington Esq. for 14½ acres of land

Isaac Kirkland came into court & acknowledged his deeds of lease and release for 343 acres land to William Odum

Jonathan Myers was appointed by the court of ordinary as Guardian to Gracy Sally and Leonard Myers children of Leonard Myers dec'd who gave John Sturzenegger as security in the sum of Ŀ 100

149 Isaac Mitchel was appointed by the court of ordinary as guardian to Lyda & Biddy Mitchel children of Daniel Mitchel Dec'd who gave William Covington in the sum of Ŀ 500

The last will and testament of William Harvey deceased was proved by the oaths of Hugh Middleton Esq. and Zepheniah Harvey was qualified as an executor

Ordered that a warrant of appraisement issue to William Brooks, Edward Prince, Stephen Smith & John Patterson or any three of them to appraise the estate of William Harvey deceased &make return according to law

Absolum Williams a youth son of Charles Williams being of full age chose Capt. Drury Pace as his guardian who gave William Reynolds & George Deluaghter in his security in the sum of Ŀ 200

Thomas Anderson was appointed guardian by the court ordinary to Abraham Yates son of Thomas Yates deceased who gave Capt. Richd. Johnson as security in the sum of L 200

Deeds of lease and release from Henry Summeral to John Rainsford for 100 acres land was proved by the oaths of Philip Johnson and Daniel Huff which was ordered to be recorded.

Isaac Kirkland came into court and acknowledged his deeds of lease and release to John Ryan for 300 acres land which was ordered to be recorded

150 Henry Foster came into court and acknowledged his deeds of lease and release to Daniel Rogers for 200 acres land which was ordered to be recorded

Joseph Hightower came into court and acknowledged his deeds of lease and release for 306 acres land to John Hammond which was ordered to be recorded

Benajah Rambo came into court and acknowledged his deeds of lease & release for 152½ acres land to Edward Mitchel which was ordered to be recorded

Mrs. Rachael Rambo came into court and was privately examined by John Moore Esq. one of the Justices relinquished her right of dower and thirds to land conveyed by her husband to Edward Mitchel which was ordered to be recorded

Fielding Reynolds came into court and acknowledged his deeds of lease and release for 100 acres land on John Herndon ordered to be recorded

Mrs. Elizabeth Reynolds being privately examined by John Moore Esq. one of the Justices relinquished her right of dower and thirds to land conveyed by her husband to John Herndon ordered to be recorded

Benjamin Tutt vs George Ragland Debt. Ordered that the defendant give special bail in this action and to continue in custody till done

Edmond Martin came into court and acknowledged his deeds of lease and release to William Hagwood for 300 acres land which was ordered to be recorded

151 Ordered that all the Jurors who were summoned to shew cause this court why they failed in their attendance last court as Jurors were excused except the following persons Thos L. Sheriff and Isaac Brunson.

Ordered that the late Sheriff shew cause why he neglected to summon Rights Nicholson and others as Jurors last court

The State vs Wm. Carson Ordered that his recognizance and that of his security be forfeited.

Permission was granted to Robert Stark to keep tavern securities Henry Ware and Arthur Watson.

Sion Fields bound himself to John Mallet by indentures in open court which was ordered to be recorded

Ordered that the clerk pay unto Mr. Henry Ware undertaker
of the court house 20 pounds out of the duty money to be
paid to Arthur Simkins Esq. if any residue to go in out of
building the jail

Ordered that the Sheriff furnish his collection and settle
by next court

152 Mary Roberts vs David Hunter. Attmt. Timothy McKinney
being summoned as garnishee maketh oath and sayeth that all
the property in the hands of his deponent consisted in acctn
to the amount of Ł 30 with notes of hand at the time of
serving the attachment and the said David Hunter was indebted
to the deponent in the sum of Ł 5 13 4.

Ordered that the overseers of the road leading from Lees
Ferry lay out the said road to intersect the road leading
from Perkins ford at or near Bells place.

Ordered that this court be adjourned till tomorrow 9 o'clock.
Leroy Hammond, Hugh Middleton, Benj. Tutt.

The Court met according to adjt. Jan 16, 1788. Present the
worshipful Leroy Hammond, Hugh Middleton, Benjamin Tutt,
Russell Wilson.

Benjamin Tutt vs Thomas Ragland. Debt. Shadrack Rozar came
into court and entered himself special bail in this action.

Francis Tilman vs Daniel Wallicon. Debt. Frederick Tilman
came into court and entered himself special bail in this
action.

153 Bargain and sale from George Raglin to Shadrack Rozar was
acknowledged in open court and ordered to be recorded.

Robert Farris vs Barkley Martin. Debt. Referred to Peter
Carnes & Thomas Carnes ordered to be renewed

Ordered William Williams who was approved of as a Deputy
Sheriff be qualified, was qualified according to law.

Henery Ker vs Joel Pardue Fifee Js. Judgmt. confessed for
Ł 4 5 6. with stay of execution till next court

Ordered that Edward Mitchel, John Gray and John Cheney be
appointed commissioners to let the laying the floors of the
Court House with seasoned good plank 1½ inch think 16 window
shutters 3 in each folding 3 pannels 2 folding pannels case
in side and out with the doors lined with ½ inch plank 3
pannels in a door the two end windows sashed, a neat stair
case & banister, the whole finished in a workman like manner
out of seasoned stuf.

Ordered that Russell Wilson and Robert Stark do view the
ground between James Spanns and the road leading from Ninety
Six to Charleston for the purpose of opening a road and
report to next court

Thomas Dalton vs George Raglin Attmt Discontinued at pltfs
cost

154 Ordered that Edward Mitchel, John Gray & John Cheney commissioners do pledge the faith of the county to the undertaking of laying the floorsand that they shall be paid out
of the first money after paying the ballance of the jail and
publick work already undertaken

Ordered that Barkley Martin be apptd. overseer over the road
leading from Ninety Six to Augusta from Gunnels Creek to the
Hornes in place of George Martin

From Hornes Creek to sweet water creek Thomas Key in the
room of John Handcock same road

Ordered that Butler Williams be appointed in the room of
Henry King as overseer over the road leading from the court
house to Lamars Ferry from Lewis Tilmans Old Fields to Mrs.
Martins old place from thence to Wares ford Stephens Creek
Capt. Cowan the same road

Ordered that Samuel Mercer be apptd. overseer over the
road leading from Cambridge to Charleston beginning at Dry
Creek to the County line in place of Arthur Watson.

Ordered that Edward Couch be appointed overseer over the
road leading from Frydays Ferry to Augusta beginning at the
Ridge to Edisto in place of George Mee

155 Ordered that George Perrin be appointed overseer over the
road leading from Hardlabour to Cuffeetown in place of
Samuel Stalnaker thence to the road of Cypress creek Robert
Belcher in place of William Carson

Ordered that John Coursey be appointed in room of Thomas Mc-
Ginnis over the road leading from the Island Ford to Augusta
from Log Creek to old Long Cane road thence to Ephriam branch
John Hargins in place of Benj. Lewis

Ordered that John Roberts & Adam Stalnaker be appointed overseer in place of James Barrintine and Roland Williams over
the road leading from the court house to Roland Williams

Ordered that a citation issue to summons the next of kin
of John Coates dec'd if any to appear next court otherwise
the administration will be granted to George Cowan of the
said deceased Est.

Ordered that a citation issue to summon the next of kin of
Richd. Stags dec'd if any to appear next court otherwise
the administration will be granted to George Cowan of the
said dec'd estate

Ordered that Isaac Kirkland be appointed county constable
who was qualified according to Law

Ordered that the court be adjourned till second Monday in
april next. Leroy Hammond, Hugh Middleton, Benj. Tutt,
Russell Wilson.

156 The court met according to adj. of the second Monday in
April 14th 1788. Present the Worshipful Arthur Simkins,
Hugh Middleton, Auquila Miles, Esquires.

Ordered that the grand Jury to be drawn to serve in October
next. the names of the grand jury so drawn
1. Thomas Key   11. Robert Lamar
2. Thomas Galphin   12. John Low
3. Philip Lamar   13. Arthur Watson
4. Abner Perrin   14. Thomas Dozer
5. Lud Williams   15. William Abney
6. James McMillian   16. Jacob Smith
7. George Forrest   17. Morris Guin
8. Sam Walker   18. Robert Lung
9. Sam Ramsey   19. William Glover
10. William Butler   20. John Myer

Ordered that the Petit Jury be drawn to serve next court
The names of the Petit Jury so drawn.
1. Joseph Nun   11. John Blocker   21. Lot Eskridge
2. Philemon (sic)   12. John Walker   22. Wm. Terry
3. William Deer   13. John Simkins   23. Russell Beckham
4. Thos Sellers   14. Josiah Stephens   24. William Brooks
5. Obdiah Kilcrease   15. Elias Gibson   25. Robert McCan
6. John Cunningham   16. Christopher Cox   26. Nicholas Dillard
7. James Buckelew   17. Gasper Nail Junr 27. John Chaney
8. John Pursel   18. Nathaniel Hender- 28. Thomas Deloach
9. Joseph Hightower   son   29. Frederick Tilman
10. Peter Zimmerman   19. Voluntine Zin   30. Michal Shaver
                       20. Saml Howard

156   On application of Joseph Hightower permission was granted
       to him to keep tavern securities Frances Settle and Nathaniel
       Bacon

       On application of John Boyd permission was granted to him to
       keep tavern securities John Calliham and Isaac Howard

       Elizabeth Harvey being appointed Executrix to the last will
       and testament of William Harvey dec'd was qualified in open
       court

       William Cook vs Jones Rivers. Case. This action being re-
       ferred to Hugh Middleton & Aquila Miles Esq. and not agree-
       ing opnion chose Barkley Martin as umpire do say that Jones
       Rivers do pay with 3 months to the said William Cook Ł 3

       Ordered that a citation issue to cite all the kindred &
       credits of William Martin dec'd to appear next court to shew
       cause why the administration of the dec'd Wm. Martin Est.
       should not be granted to Barkly Martin

       Ordered that Jacob Smith give security to keep the peace
       towards Daniel Bullock who gave Thos Anders & Saml Mays in
       the sum of Ł 50 each principal in 100 for 12 months

       Ordered that the sheriff return the writ of venire for the
       grand jury the names of the grand jury that appeared

       1. John Bullock   10. John Childs
       2. Richd. Johnson   11. John Clark
       3. Philip Johnson   12. George Cowen
       4. Thomas Lamar   13. Thomas Marbury
       5. William Jeter Junr   14. William Shinholster
       6. William Green   15. Solomon Pope
       7. John Thurman   16. Fields Pardue

                              76

8. William Spragins   17. Nathaniel Howel
9. John Gray   18. Caleb Holloway

The court appointed John Bullock foreman

Peter Carnes vs Edmond Boyd. Debt Judgment confessed for
the sum of Ł 6 10. 6. and cost. Execution stayed till the
first of October next

157 Martin Kinard vs Fields Pardue. Debt. Judgment according
to note payable by Instmt.

Ordered that the admn. of all and singular the goods & chattles rights and credits of Richd. Stages & John Cotes be
granted to George Cowan who gave Richd Johnson & William
Covington securities in the sum of Ł 300 who having first
cited the kindred and creditors of the said deceased

Ordered that the wheriff return the venire for the Petit Jury
The names of the Jury that appeared
1. Nathaniel Bacon   10. Thomas Ross
2. James Hart   11. Amos Mitchel
3. Gasper Galman   12. Dudly Carter
4. Joseph Cook   13. John Calliham
5. Joseph Collier   14. Nicholas Minor
6. Kiland Smith   15. Sampson Moore
7. James Davis   16. George Miller
8. Sam Stalnaker   17. Van Swearingen
9. William Brown   18. James Cox
                           19. Robert Deshaso

158 Adams Pardue vs Suckey Coody Admx. of Lewis Coody. Debt.
The defendant confessed Judgt for Ł 34. 14.4

William Rowen vs Lamulet Armstrong. Case. William Dawson
and William Bailey entered themselves as special bail in
this action

Ordered that Court be adjd. till tomorrow morning 9 o'clock
Arthur Simkins, Hugh Middleton, Russell Wilson, Aquila
Miles, John Sturzennegger.

The Court met according to adjt. 15th 1788. Present the
worshipful Arthur Simkins, Hugh Middleton, Russell Wilson,
Wm. Anderson.

William Anderson came into court and acknowledged his several
deeds of lease and release to the following persons' viz
Joseph Oldham for 100 acres to Thomas Ross for 100 acres
to Thomas Ross for 50 acres to James Anderson 2 tracts, one
containing 500 acres, the other 250 acres which was ordered
to be recorded Also to John Pool for 90 acres which was
ordered to be recorded

159 Nathaniel Howel and Calib Holloway two of the grand Jurors
appeared & was qualified as such their excuses for not appearing when first called was received by the court

Ordered that William Doby give security to keep the peace
towards Richd. Witherton who gave Will Murphey in the sum
of Ł 50 himself the sum of Ł 100 for 12 months

Ordered that Isaac Howard give security to keep the peace towards William Key who gave John Walker and Elisha Robinson in the sum of Ł 50 himself in the sum of Ł 100 for 12 months

Present Aquila Miles Esq.

Thomas Anderson vs Ansel Beardes. Case. discontd at Deft. cost

Ordered that the appearance docket be called over

William Nichols vs Philip May. Case contd.

160 Messrs Purves Tutt & Keating vs Samuel Burges. Debt. Discontinued

Dalziel Hunter vs Sam Hammond Debt Discontinued

James C. Murphey vs Isaac Hardiss Abated

Fields Pardue vs Nicholas Bugg Debt Judt by Deft.

The same vs the Same Debt Judgment by default

Thomas Gordon vs Frances Settle Slander non suit

Ann Summerall Admx. vs George Miller & James Thomas Trover. Contd.

Varner Lewis vs Thomas Lawson. Debt Judt by default

Henry Hampton, Henry Hunter & John Hamton vs Thomas Lamar & John Lamar. Debt Contd.

The Same vs The Same Debt the same order

161 The Same vs Edward Pretor & Richd Johnson Debt contd.

The Same vs The Same Debt contd.

John Purves vs Adam Pardue Debt contd.

Ann Summerall vs Edward Vann. Debt contd.

Edward Keating vs Thomas Lamar Debt contd.

The Same vs George Bryan Debt contd.

The Same vs John Purves Case Discontinued

Edward Boyd vs James Lyon Debt judgment by deft.

Robert Stark vs George Miller & John Herndon Debt contd.

Benjamin Tutt vs William Robinson & John Powel. Debt contd.

162 Frances Settle vs Thomas Gordon Case Judgment by default

Robert Stark vs John Randal Debt contd.

Samuel Wright vs Jesse Skinner. Debt. Contd. John Herndon and Clemon Cargil in open court entered themselves as special bail in this action

John Davison vs Benj. Burton   Debt.   Contd.

Robert Evan & Co. vs William Dawson   Debt contd.

Jesse Skinner vs Cornelius Cargil. Debt. Judt by deft.

Robert Stark vs Robert Melton.   Case   contd.

The Same vs Edward Couch Case contd.

Nathaniel Bacon vs Solomon Turner Attmt Judt by Deft.

Ann Summerall vs Henry Summerall Attmt John Martin being
summoned as garnishee & not appeared Ordered that he shew
cause next court why the money in his hands should not be
adjd. to the said amt.

163   Edward Keating vs George Cowan Contd. Thomas Lamar entered
himself special bail in this action

John Davison vs George Cowan Attmt. contd. The same order

Allen Hinton vs The Est. of Charles Williams. Attmt Contd.

Arthur Watson & Robert Stark Exrs. of M. Watson vs Richard
Johnson assignee of James Moore.

Present Arthur Simkins & Wm Eveleigh, Esquires.

John Williams vs Jesse Roundtree & Daniel Danely. Debt.
Judgment for Ł 10. 0. 0.

Deeds of lease and release from Oburn Buffington to Richard
Johnson for 200 acres land was proved by the oaths of Richard
Johnson Senr & Christian Gomillian was ordered to be recorded

Arthur Watson came into court & ack. his deeds of lease and
release for 35 acres land to John Watson which was ordered
to be recorded

164   Absent Aquila Miles Esq.

Thomas Lamar vs James Coobs. Judgt for Ł 5 confirmed.

Thomas Lamar vs James Coobs Judgt for Ł 4 11 6 confirmed

Peter Carnes vs Charles Wall Judt. confessed for Ł 1 1 9
and cost except Atty fee

Robert Stark vs Adams Pardue. Judgt confessed for Ł 3 1 3
with interest

Peter Carnes vs Edward Couch. Judgment confessed for Ł 1 1
9 and cost except Attys fee with stay of execution 2 months

The same vs The same The same order

Allen Hinton vs James Martin. Judgt. confessed for Ł 5 0 0

The State vs James Maxwell. Petit True Bill Jno Bullock
foreman. Ordered that the Deft. be continued over to the

next court on this first recognizance

Abemeleck Hawkins vs Thomas Lamar   Debt.   contd.

165   Jesse Roundtree vs Thomas Lamar.   Case.   Ordered that this
cause be referred to Thos Lamar Senr and John Carter with
power of umprage and report next court

John Hammond vs Robert Melton.   Judgt. according to note
payable by instalments

David Van vs John Ballard   Trover   discontinued at deft. cost

Arthur Watson & Robert Stark Exrs. vs Richard Johnson &
Edward Couch.   Debt.   Judgment.   According to note payable
Oct. and payable by instalments

The same vs Richard Johnson & Will Butler.   Debt.   The same
order

John Davison vs Drury Murphey.   Debt.   Judgment confessed
for Ł 9 3 payable by instalment

John Herndon vs Robert Collins   Discontd. at Plfts. cost

Ross & Curry vs Robert Mosely.   Judgment confessed for Ł 5
& cost stay of execution until 1st Oct. next

William Covington vs Charles Bussey   Trover   discontinued

166   Adams Pardue vs Edward Van   Assault   discontd.

Samuel Mays vs George James   Attmt   continued

Edward Bland vs Henry Bolton   Trespass   Discontinued at
Deft. cost

Robert Stark vs John Williams.   Judgment confd. according
to note with stay of execution to Oct. court

Daniel Parker vs James Tutt   Asst.   discontinued at Deft
cost

Esther Mason vs James Coursey.   Case   Abates by death of
Plaintiff

Elizabeth Reynolds vs Frances Moore.   Discontd. equal cost

Jesse Roundtree vs William Evans.   Contd. to next court

Nathan Johnson vs Jesse Scrugs   Ordered that this cause be
referred to John Blocker, Henry Key, Will Dawson, Joseph
Dawson & report next court

Ordered that this court be adjourned to tomorrow Morn 9
o'clock.   Arthur Simkins, Hugh Middleton, Wm. Eveleigh,
Wm. Anderson.

167   The court met according to adjt. the 16 1788.   Present the
worshipful Arthur Simkins, Hugh Middleton, Wm. Eveleigh, Esq.

Daniel Parker vs James Tutt   Asst.   John Lucas proved his
attendance 10 days @ 2/6   Levi Jester proved his attendance

8 @ 2/6 and David Shackley 15 days @ 2/6 evidences in this action for the Plaintiff

John Watson Admr. having returned an acct. of the sales and expenditures of John Anderson Estate ordered that the clerk examine and report to next court the justness of them

Present Benjamin Tutt Esq.

Ordered that David Lasly be committed to the custody of the Sheriff for a contempt of court

Absent Arthur Simkins Esq.

Edward Couch Asst. vs George Cowen Asst. The court after debating this matter giving their opinion untill tomorrow

Present Arthur Simkins Esq.

John Oliver vs Thomas Lamar. Debt. Judgment for ₺ 5. 34 with interest from 1st Nov last.

Present Leroy Hammond Esq.

James Vessels vs Amon Roberts. Dismissed

168   Dr. James Lander vs Joel Chandler. Debt. Dismissed

The Same vs Thomas Lamar. Dismissed

Peter Carnes Esq. vs William Shaw. Esq. Judgment for ₺ 5

David Burk vs Thomas Beckham Case Dismissed

Drury Pace vs Simon Gentry Judgment for ₺ 5

Peter Hillard vs Robert Melton. Dismissed at mutual cost

Phill May vs William Nichols Judt. for ₺ 4 10 5 Int. from 1st Jan 1785

Thomas B Scoot vs Isham Mitchell Dismissed

William Jeter vs Dr. Van Swearingen Judt for Deft.

William Wilson vs Richd. Jones. Judgment for ₺ 1 17 3 with int. from 1 Oct 1786

An Summerall vs Henry Summerall. Att. John Martin summoned as garnishee on this attmt ack. in open court to owe Henry Summerall ₺ 43 5 . payable in tobacco or horse flesh agreeable to acct given in

169   James Cox vs Peter McCoverly Judgment for ₺ 2 10. & cont.

Peter Carnes vs Granger Parkman. Contd.

Robert Stark Jr. vs John Hammond. Judgment for ₺ 1728 Int. from 9 Jan 1787 Joseph Hightower proved his attendance in the above action for the Plaintiff for 3 days.

Robert Stark Jun. vs Thomas Beckham. Judgment confessed for ₺ 10 agreeable to the instalments.

James Gunnels proved his attendance as evidence in this action for Plaintiff 3 days @ 2/6 and 66 miles @ 4 mile

John Hammond vs Robert Melton. Joseph Hightower proved his attendance four days.

Robert Stark vs Mary Hunter. Judgt for Ŀ 3 interest from 1st day of Jan 1787. James Gunnels proved his attendance in this action for his attendance as evidence in this action for his attendance as evidence @ 2/6 & his coming 66 miles at 4 ¢ a mile

Robert Stark vs Christian Gomillian. Judt according to note Jas. Gunnels

Philip May vs Will Nichols. Eliza. Runnels, Philip Mayson, James May proved their attendance two days each for the Plaintiff as evidences in this action

170 James King vs Nicholas Ware. Judgment for Ŀ 7 10 interest from 3 Sept 1787

Thomas Gordon vs Isaac Davis Dismissed

Peter Carnes vs Michael Cass Contd.

James Lanthren vs James Melton Continued

Allen Hinton vs Charles Blackwell. Judgment agreeable to note interest according to the date not agreeable to the instalment act

Edward Mitchell vs John Thos. Spencer. Judt. for Ŀ 8 1 7 with int. from 16 Nov 1787

James Cox vs Peter McCoverly. David Lasley proved his attendance for 6 days @ 2/6 in this action as evidence for plaintiff

Isaac Davis vs William Hightower. On attmt. A Jury being impannelled & sworn to try this writ of Inquiry. Viz: James Hart, Gasper Galman, Joseph Cook, Joseph Collier, Keland Smith, Jas Davis, Sam Stalnaker, Wm. Brown, Amos Michel, Dudly Carter, Jno Calliham & Nicholas Minor   upon their oaths...the Deft pay $10 with interest from 6 Jan 1785
Kealand Smith, foreman

171 The State vs Wm. Dawson & John Randal. Tavern Indct. The same jury as above do say we find for the Defts guilty.

Leroy Hammond, Hugh Middleton,Wm. Eveleigh.

The Court met according to Adjt. the 17th 1788 Present the Worshipful Leroy Hammond, Arthur Simkins, Hugh Middleton.

Frances Little vs Richard Johnson. Defd. till tomorrow

The State vs Martin Cloud. Asst. Indict. On motion of the county atty ordered that this action be discontinued on acct. of Ann Cannady the prosecutor not attending on this court

The state vs William Dawson. Issue traversed. Who having been found guilty by the jury it is considered by the court that William Dawson pay 40/ and John Randal Ł 5 to be recovered of the goods & chattles etc. excn. to stay until 1st day of next court

172 The State vs Richardson Bartlett & William Doby. Issue traversed. A jury being called...(same as before)the deft. Richardson Bartlett guilty of assaulting an Officer in executing of his office they also say that William Doby is guilty of an assault taking a prisoner out of the possession of an officer

John Hammond vs James Vessels. Slander contd.

James Hargrove vs Benjamin Cook. Debt discontinued

The State vs Edward Van. Ind. assault On motion of the County atty ordered that this action be discontinued on acct of Adams Pardue being called as prosecutor not appearing

The state vs William Pardue. The defendant being bound to keep for peace for 12 months towards Sanders Nobles security gave Henry Ware in the sum of Ł 20 himself in the sum of 50 in case of failure to be recovered of their goods and chattles.

173 The State vs James Brada The defendant being bound to keep the peace for 12 months towards Sanders Nobles gave Edward Vann his security in the sum of Ł 25 himself in the sum of Ł 50...

The State vs Sanders Nobles. The defendant being bound to keep the peace for 12 months towards William Pardue and James Brada who gave John Ryan his security in the sum of Ł 25....

The State vs Richardson Bartlett & William Doby. Asst. traverse indictment. The defendant being guilty it is considered by the court that they pay each Ł 3 to be recovered of thier goods and chattles & execution to stay until 1st day of next court

Robert Stark Asnee vs Sarah Harris Exr. Case The same jury as before who say that the deft. pay to the plaintiff Ł 8 15 with interest from 11th Dec 1778 agreeable to the instalments provided the deft. give security

Solomon Edwards vs William Forturine. Discontinued.

174 James Vessels vs James Christopher Contd.

Abemeleck Hawkins vs Thomas Lamar. continued

Arthur Morrow vs William Dawson Discontinued Keland Smith proved his attendance as witness in this cause for deft. 7 days

John Hightower vs James Vessels Contd.

William English vs Thos & Roddy Smith. Discontinued

Fields Pardue vs William Nichols. Judg by default cont.

83

Samuel Ramsey vs Drury Glover. Contd.

David Van vs John Ballard Discontinued at pltfs cost.

Reuben Rambo vs Lewis Nobles. Debt. The same jury as before
do say on their oaths, we find for the defendant.

Hannah Van vs Martin Cloud. Discontinued.

175 Reuben Rambo vs Lewis Nobles. Debt. The following persons
proved their attendance in this action viz John Ryan 4 days
@ 2/6 John Pitman 12 days @ 2/6

John Rainsford vs Miller & Both. Continued by consent

Nathaniel Powel vs Solomon Turner. Ordered that the sheriffs
sell the property attached being perishable according to the
return delivered in by the sheriff

The Court met according to adjournment 16th 1788. Present
Leroy Hammond, Arthur Simkins, Hugh Middleton Esquires.

Ordered that the strays subject to sale shall be sold on the
first day of next court by Burges White and that he return
the money arising from the sale unto court

176 Robert Farris vs Bartlett Martin. Debt. Thomas Peter Carnes
& Peter Carnes Esqrs. and Robert Harper Esqr umpire do say
that the deft. pay the sum of ₺ 9.10 Exn. to be staid untill
1 Dec next and cost

James Wilson vs Frances Settle Debt continued

John Davison vs John Carter Discontinued

William Mead vs Thomas Hill Discontinued

William Jeter vs John Pounds. Debt. A jury being called
(same as before)...we find for the Plaintiff ₺ 14 with int.
from 20 Dec 1785 and cost

Robert Alexander vs Philip May. Contd.

177 Anna Maria Minter vs John Garrett. Continued.

George Miller vs Samuel Burgess Case. The same jury as
before who say we find for the Pltf. ₺ 18 payable by instalments with cost of suit

William Brooks vs James Vessels Discontinued.

John Garrett vs Robert Moseley Case The same jury as before
who...the plaintiff suffered a non suit

John Randal vs William Nichols. Asst. Discontinued at the
Deft cost

William Covington vs Charles Bussey. Trover Discontinued

John Randall vs WilliamNichols Asst. Discontinued.

178 William Jeter vs John Pound. Philip Johnson proved his
attendance in this action for 4 days @ 2/6 for pltf.

John Herndon vs John Randol. Mrs. Ann Hammond proved her attendance in this action for 4 days @ 2/6 for plaintiff

Morris Calliham & wife vs James Lyon & wife. Slander. Ordered that this cause be referred to Henry Key & Richd. McCary with power of umprage and report to next court and to be made a rule of court

Frances Settle vs Richd Johnson. Judgment confirmed for Ł 2. 3. 5.

John Randal vs William Nichols Asst. discontinued at Deft. cost

Richard Johnson vs John Watson Asst. contd.

Benjamin Cook vs Edmond Martin case contd.

Robert Mosely vs Robert Cockran Trover continued

William Hatteway Moseley vs Thomas Lawson. The same Jury as before do say we find for the plaintiff Ł 5 and cost

179 On motion of the Plaintiff attorney ordered that a dedimus issue to Major Forsyth and William Freeman Esqrs. Justices in the State of Georgia to take the examination of James Cox in two actions brought by Henry Hunter, Henry Hampton & John Hampton against Richard John and Edward Preton also a dedimus directed to Henry Allison Hampthon to take the examination of John Appling a witness to actions brought by the parties above Thomas & John Lamar

Thomas Morris vs James Martin Debt continued

James Martin vs Fields Pardue continued

John Deyampert & wife vs David Bowers & Isaac Ardis Case contd.

Absolom Roberts vs George Cowan Judgment confessed for Ł 30 in principal indents the interest to be paid in special indents with stay of execution for 3 months if the deft pays the indents in to Clerks hands if he does not an execution to issue for Ł 12 in special

Thomas Morrison vs James Martin Debt contd.

180 Arthur Rodes vs Ann Summerall Case Discontinued at Pltfs cost

Peter Hillard vs William Robinson case contd.

John Purves Esq. vs Frances Little Debt Discontinued at the deft. cost

John Carter vs John Williams. Judgments confessed for Ł 19 3. 2. with interest from 1 Jan 1787 staying execution 1 October court

William Hamilton vs Alexander Canada Contd.

Morning Williams vs John Watson. Asst. Ordered that the plea of the defendant be overruled as frivelous and inconclusive

and that the parties be ruled to plead on the merits of the
cause with a good and substantial plea

Morning Williams vs John Watson. Assault. The same jury as
before on their oaths do say that we find for the plaintiff
Ł 10 and cost of suit

181   Jesse Roundtree vs Joel Chandler. Case. On motion of the
parties ordered that this cause be referred to John Carter
and Ephriam Ferrol with power of umprage and report to next
court to be made a rule of court

Ordered that the clerk record the presentment of the grand
jury which are as follows viz, we present the overseer of
the road from mill creek to Pritty run by information of
Bartlett Martin

We do present the overseer of the road from Campbels ware
house to Adams Ferry road

We present the overseer of the road on each side of horse
creek bridge ordered that the clerk issue a summons that the
overseers shew cause next court why they failed in keeping
the said road in repair

Morning Williams vs John Watson The following persons proved
their attendance as evidence in this action 5 days each @
2/6 to wit Henry Webb, Ann Watson and Celia Anderson

Leroy Hammond vs John Garret. Att. Ordered that this
cause by consent of Parties be referred to Edwd Keating
and his award to be returned to this court & be a judgment
thereof

182   The court met according to adjournment the 14th July 1788.
Present Arthur Simkins, Hugh Middleton,Benjamin Tutt,
Nicholas Eveleigh, Russell Wilson, Esquires.

Ordered that the Petit Jury be drawn to serve October Court

1. John Cockburn	16. Philip May
2. Ezekiel Smith	17. John Whitloe
3. John Hill	18. Will Huggins
4. Thomas Banks	19. Frances Whitney
5. Drury Pace	20. John Morrow
6. James Hollingsworth	21. Ogdon Cockeroff
7. Robert Laws	22. Paul Abney
8. John Jas Steffel	23. Daniel Clark
9. Richard Dean	24. Henely Webb
10. John Canada	25. John Wallace
11. Littleberry Adams	26. William Green
12. John Hoes	27. Robert Anderson
13. Will Robertson	28. William Howle Jr.
14. David Burks	29. John Coursey
15. Frances McRath	30. Nathan Cawley

Ordered that the sheriff return the writ of venire for the
Petit Jury The names of the Petit Jury that appeared viz

1. John Purcel	13. Gasper Nail Jr.
2. John Walker	14. Russell Beckham
3. Joseph Nun	15. William Brooks
4. William Dean	16. Josiah Stephens
5. John Blocker	17. Thomas Sellers
6. Christopher Cox	18. Nathaniel Henderson

7.	Thomas Deloach	19.	Samuel Howard
8.	Obediah Kilcrease	20.	Peter Zimmerman
9.	Nicholas Dillard	21.	Valuntine Zin
10.	Michael Shaver	22.	William Terry
11.	Philemon Boxman	23.	Frederick Tilman
12.	Joseph Hightower		

William Jeter vs John Pounds. Debt On motion of Mrs. Carnes
Ordered that an execution issue for the whole debt entered
last term and not be instalments

James Buckelew, Elias Gibson & John Cunningham returned to
serve as Petit Jurors made default. ordered that they shew
cause next court why they failed to attend at this court

Jesse Harris overseer of the read leading from Harlins Ferry
to Ninety Six returned on oath the following persons as
defaulters viz James Rustin, 1 day Frances Lightfoot 2 days
Timothy McKinney 1 day Robert Combs 1 day Shadrack Henderson 2 days Thomas Johnson 2 days William Huggins 4 days
Nelson Fields 2 days

Charles Goodwin Esq in open court ackd. his deeds of lease
and release to John Cook for ¼ acre of land which was
ordered to be recorded

184 Ordered that all defaulters in future where no excuse for
their non attendance is allowed to pay the fees due to the
officers of the court but where excused are allowed it shall
be deemed publick service and no fees taken

Mrs. Rebecca Cook being prively examined by Hugh Middleton
one of the Justices relinquished her right of dower to the
lands conveyed by her husband to Charles Goodwin Esq. 18.40
acres land which was ordered to be recorded

George Walker having produced his admission and certificate
as Sollicitor and attorney was publickly read in open court
and approved of and ordered to be recorded

The State vs Thomas Lawson. Ordered that the recognizances
of the said Lawson stands over together with Richard Walker
& Samuell Garner to the next court principal in the sum of
Ł 50 securities in Ł 20 each

185 The State vs Richard Walker & Jeremiah Walker. Ordered that
the recognizances of the said Richd. & Jeremiah Walker together with Morris Calliham and John Kelly their securities
stands over to the next court principal in the sum of Ł 25
each

Russell Wilson Esq. and Robert Stark being appointed on petition of James Span to lay out a road from his house leading
to the publick road from Cambridge to Charleston report that
a road be opened from the house of the said Spans South 20
degrees West across redbank to the end of the lake thence
south seven degrees west to the said road along a blazed way
made by the said Wilson and Stark

Ordered that the admn. of all and singular the goods and
chattles of William Martin deceased be granted to Barkley
Martin on his giving bond and security who gave James Martin
and James Cobbs in the sum of Ł500 lawful money

Ordered that the petitions & summons be called over

Peter Carnes vs Granger Parkman. Debt. Continued untill tomorrow.

186 The Same vs Michael Caps. Debt Judgment for Ł 3 5 3

James Lauder vs James Watson Case dismissed

Absent Arthur Simkins Esq.

Edward Couch vs George Cowan Judgment confessed for Ł 5

Present Arthur Simkins Esq.

John Garrett vs Reubin Rambo Case Judgment for Ł 10

Winfrey vs Robert Melton Debt Continued untill tomorrow

William Brown vs Robert Melton. Debt Judgment for Ł.1.2.0

Ordered that the court be adjourned untill tomorrow morning 9 o'clock. Arthur Simkins, Hugh Middleton, Wm. Eveleigh, Russell Wilson.

The Court met according to adjournment the 15th 1788 present the worshipful Arthur Simkins, Hugh Middleton, Wm. Eveleigh, Russel Wilson, Esquires.

187 George Mosely vs Edmond Whatley Debt dismissed

Presley Bland vs Robert Melton. Case dismissed

Daniel Wallicon vs Thomas Lamar Debt dismissed at pltfs cost

Ezekiel Harris vs David Zubly. Case dismissed

The same vs James Coleman. Debt the same order

John Dean vs James Martin Debt dismissed

Fields Pardue vs Sterling Hightower Debt dismissed

The Same vs Adams Pardue Debt dismissed

Julius Smith vs James Wash. Debt Judgment confessed for Ł 9 1 6 staying execution untill Christmas

Samuel Wilson vs Edward Prince Debt dismissed

Alexander McIver vs Timothy Cooper Debt dismissed

188 Samuel Wilson vs Charles Warley Debt dismissed

The Same vs William Watson Debt dismissed

James Martin vs Allen Hinton Dismissed

Robert Stark vs Welles Odum Dismissed

Robert Stark vs Benjamin Cook Case Judgment for Ł 3 12 3 with staying execution 3 months

88

The Same vs John Pounds. Judgment for Ł 7 8 8 not subject
to instalments

William Glasscock vs Frances Little   Debt   contd

Richard Win vs Benjamin Cook   Dismissed

Conrade Galman vs Adams Pardue   Dismissed

Thomas Dixon vs John Williams   Dismissed each party paying
his own cost

189 William Longmire vs David Burks.   Judgment for Ł 6 3 0 for
rent

Martha Oadum vs Thomas Lamar   Judgment for Ł 5 5 7 with stay
of execution for 3 months.

Present John Moore Esq.

Peter Carnes vs Granger Parkman.   Judgment for Ł 3 5 3 with
stay of execution 3 months

Winfrey Whitlock vs Robert Melton.   Judgment for Ł 3/6 for
defendant

Present Hugh Middleton Esq.

A mortgage for negroes from Isaac Crowther to William Roberson was proved by the oath of Charles Goodwin Esq. which was
ordered to be recorded

The last will and testament of Sophia Miles was proved by the
oaths of Isaac Ardis and William Shinholster was qualified
and Isaac Ardis, Jacob Zin, Valentine Zin and Gasper Nail
or any three do appraise the goods and chattles of the said
deceased estate

Present Benjamin Tutt, Wm. Anderson & Aquila Miles, Esq.

190 Ordered that Robert Stark Esq. be authorised to collect and
receive all money due to the County on any account whatsoever
that such money shall be liable on to the orders of this court
That he do render in exact & fair account of receipt and disbursements of all money due the county every court for the
inspection of the bench and that he be allowed 2½% all the
receipts the same on disbursements and that he the said
Robert Stark do give bond and approved security for the due
and faithful discharge of the said trust

Ordered that the first monies that do come into the treasurers hands after the payment of the publick buildings already
engaged shall be appropriates to the purpose of building a
shed room adjoining to the Court House for the Clerks Office

Permission was granted to Enock Grigsby to Keep Tavern securities Russell Wilson Esq. and Jacob Smith.

The State vs William Maxwell   Traversed Indt.   Pet Larceny
a jury be called impannelled...John Purcel, John Walker,
Joseph Nun, John Blocker, Christopher Cox, Thomas Deloach,
Obediah Kilcrease, Nicholas Dillard, Michael Shaver, Joseph

Hightower, Gasper Nail, Russell Beckham...the defendant guilty.

Absent Russell Wilson Esq.

On motion of Mary Mintor the adm. of all and singular the goods & chattles of John Mintor decd was granted to Mary Mintor widow of the said dec'd who give bond and security agreeable to law give William Terry and James Coursey in the sum of Ł 500. John Thurman, Jesse Scrugs, John McFatrick and Nathan Tally or any three of them to view and appraise the goods & chattels rights and credits of the said deceased

Received in open court by virtue of a judgment obtained last court of George Cowen full satisfaction

The State vs William Maxwell. On motion of the County Attorney ordered that William Maxwell receive 15 lashes on the bare back instantly & stand convicted untill he pay his fees

192   Ordered that the appearance docket be called over

Frances Jones Adm. vs Edward Couch & John Duglish.   Debt Contd.

Alexander McGrigger vs David Zubly.   case contd.

John Tobler vs The Same.   Case contd.

Robert Stark vs Edward Couch & Will Williams.   Debt   contd

The Same vs Edward Couch   Debt   contd.

The Same vs George Dean Debt   contd.

William Hinton vs William Patterson   Debt   contd.

Alexander McIver vs Joseph Cook   Debt   contd.

Samuel Willison vs William Dawson   Debt judgment confd. with stay of execution 3 months according to note

John Carter vs William Nichols   Debt   continued

193   John Davison vs William Mathews.   Debt   discontinued

Jeremiah Walker vs John McCary   Asst.   contd.

Richard Walker vs John Walker.   Asst.   contd.

LeRoy Hammond vs Frederick Tillman   Dbbt   Burnell Johnson bail   judgment by default

The Same vs John Pounds & Frederick Tillman.   Debt   Burnell Johnson & Charles Warley bail   contd.

Purves Tutt & Keating vs Samuel Burgess.   Case   continued

Ann Cunningham Admx. vs Robert Melton   Case   contd.

James C. Murphey vs Ezekiel Harris   Case   contd.

90

Elizabeth Williams vs Isaac Ardis & Bowers   Case contd.

Felix Gilbert vs Moses Lucas   Debt   contd.

Susannah Stidham vs Keating Smith   Asst contd.

194 Richardson Bartlett & William Doby vs Richard Witherton
case continued

James Harrison & wife vs John Watson   Case continued

Nathan Johnson vs Jesse Scrugs   Assault continued

Winfrey Whitlock vs John Cardin   Trespass contd.

Elisha Roberson vs William Reynolds & James Thomas   Debt
contd.

William Glascock Exr. of Benefield vs William Evans & Nathan
Howel.   Debt contd.

William Freeman & Hodges vs Frederick Glover.   Case contd

John Kenedy vs Wm Ross & Robert Bonner.   Debt   Leroy Hammond Esq. Bail

195 John Garrett vs Crooks Shands & Sheers.   Debt   Ordered to be
referred to Edward Keating and William Wallace with power
of umprage and report next court & to be made a rule of court
by consent of parties

Charles Goodwin Esq. vs John Sharpton & John Randal.   Debt
Judgmetn by default vs Sharpton

Jesse Roundtree vs James Vessels   Case contd.

Fields Pardue vs Isaac Norrel.   Case continued

Freeman & Murray vs Frederick Glover.   Case   contd.

Robert Stark vs Samuel Ramsey.   Case   contd.

Frances Davis vs Mordica Madocks   Case   Nonsuited

Samuel Willison vs Anthony Powel.   Attmt   William Shinholster
entered himself special bail   contd.

Peter Hillard vs Michael Oadum & Jane Oadum   Attmt   Contd.

196 Richard Johnson vs Oburn Buffington   Attmt   Joel Chandler
garnishee came into court and says he give a bond to Richard
Johnson for Ł 100 which bond he is informed is in the hands
of the deft. and on its being produeed he is willing to discharge when due on getting a receipt for the same.

Mathew Gayle vs Wm. Gilbert   Attmt. Judgment by default.

Kemp T. Stroather vs John Wonack. Attmt   Judgment by default

George Cheney vs John Hampton. attmt   Judgment by default

Alexander Oden vs George Dooly   Attmt   Judgment by default

On motion of Thos Peter Carnes ordered that a Siri Facias
issue against John Sharpton garnishee in this cause to shew
cause next court why judt should not be entered up against
him

In the court of ordinarys ordered that the executors to make
up their accounts

197 John Gorman in open court acknowledged his deeds of lease
and release to Thomas Berry for 177 acres land which was
ordered to be recorded

Robert Stark vs Sarah Harris. James Roberson proved his attendance 9 days in this action @ 2/6 pr day and mileage 20
miles

Richard Johnson vs John Watson Asst. The deft paying his
own cost and 9/4 towards the Plaintiff cost

Ordered that the moneys arising from the sale of the estrays
this court be equally divided between the publick undertakers
of the Court House

Ordered that Drury Pace be appointed guardian to Charles
Williams son of Charles a minor untill he arises to proper
age to choose for himself who gave Benj. Tutt Esq. as securtiy in the sum of Ł 300

Ordered that this court be adjourned untill tomorrow morning
9 o'clock. LeRoy Hammond, Arthur Simkins, W. Anderson,
Wm. Eveleigh.

198 The court met according to adjournment the 16 of July 1788
Present the Worshipful LeRoy Hammond, Hugh Middleton, Russell Wilson, Esq.

Nathan Johnson vs Jesse Scrugs Slander The referees having
reported that this action be dismissed at the Deft cost which
report was confirmed and ordered to be recorded.

Absent LeRoy Hammond Esq.

In the court of ordinary
On motion of Mary Watson and Patience Watson they being of
full age to choose their guardians do choose Leroy Hammond
Esq. and Jacob Oadum their guardians who give bond and
security Richard Johnson Senr and Richard Johnson Junr in
the sum of Ł 1000

Leroy Hammond Esq. vs Frederick Tilman. Debt Judgment
confessed according to note with stay of execution 3 months

Leroy Hammond Esq. vs John Pounds & Frederick Tilman. Judgment confessed according to note with stay of execution 3
months

199 Present Leroy Hammond Esq.

John Deyampter & wife vs Isaac Ardis & David Bowers. discontinued

Samuel Wilson vs Frances Little. Debt Judgment confessed
according to specialty subject to instalments.

William Anderson vs Thomas Wooten. Judgmt for Ł 4 7 0 with
interest for 18 months. Ordered that the sheriff sell the
attachment effects of Thomas Wooten

Ordered that William Brooks be appointed Petit Juror in the
room of Joseph Nun excused

Benjamin Blackly vs William Carson Debt Ordered that this
suit be referred to Richard Tutt and John McDaniel with
power of umprage and report next court

James Vessels vs James Christopher Debt Judgment confessed
for Ł 21 3 and cost when assets that Christopher retains own
debt as admr.

200 Abemeleck Hawkins vs Thomas Lamar Debt a jury being impannelled and sworn viz (same as before)...we find for the
plaintiff 15 guineas.

Richard Johnson asnee vs Arthur Watson & Robert Stark Exrs.
Debt continued by consent

Robert Alexander vs Frances Handcock Debt Nonsuited for
want of security for costs

John Hightower vs James Vessels & others. Debt Judgment
confessed according to specialty subject to deduction for
4 7 4 dollars paid in part of the note also the judgments
cost on attmt of Isaac Davis subject to instalments

Jesse Roundtree vs Thomas Lamar discontd. at mutual cost

Fields Pardue vs Will Nichols Debt Judgment confessed for
Ł 25 19 7 and interest according to note

Samuel Ramsey vs Drury Glover. Debt to issue by instalments
The same jury as before who say we find for the Pltf Ł 9 18
9 with interest and cost

201 Ker & Brown vs William Hardy Debt Judgment confessed for
Ł 3 5 with interest from the 1st of Jan 1788 with stay of
execution untill 1st of Dec next

Anna Minter vs John Garrett on attmt the same jury as
before who says we find for the pltf Ł 32.19 with interest
and cost

Morris Calliham & wife vs James Lyon wife wife. Slander
discontd.

Benjamin Cook vs Edmond Martin Case The same jury as before
who say we find for the Plaintiff Ł 10 2. 2. with interest
from 10 Oct 1786 till 16 July 1786

John Herndon vs John Randal Slander discontd. the deft.
pays cost

Jesse Roundtree vs William Evans Case On motion of Mr.
Harper council for the Pltf ordered that the plea filed by
the Deft. be qualified for insufficiency and the said deft.
do plead the general issue non assumsit

George Cheney vs John Hampton   Attmt.   Ordered that the
attached property be release on the Deft. giving special
bail who give Edward Van and Martin Cloud

202   Benjamin Cook vs Edmond Martin.   The following persons having
proved their attendance viz Joseph Cook 11 days @ 2/6
Moses Carter 6 days @ 2/6   Frances Moore 5 days @ 2/6 and
coming 30 miles for Plaintiff

James Martin vs Fields Pardue   Trover   A jury being with
drawn by consent the Plaintiff non suited

Jesse Roundtree vs Joel Chandler.   Case   The same jury as
before who say we find for the defendant and cost of suit

James Martin vs Fields Pardue.   Ephriam Ferro proved his
attendance in this action for 6 days @ 2/6 for plaintiff

James Vessels vs James Christopher   James Martin proved his
attendance in this action as evidence for 9 days @ 2/6 for
deft

Ordered that this court be adjourned until tomorrow Morning
8 o'clock.   Arthur Simkins, John Moore, Russell Wilson.

The court met according to adjournment the 17th of July 1788
Present the Worshipful Arthur Simkins, John Moore, Russell
Wilson.

203   Thomas Morrison vs James Martin   Debt.   To be continued over
to next court and then to be dismissed at the Plaintiff costs
provided the deft makes titles to the land when required

Ordered that the County Treasurer pay unto Henry Ware out
of any Publick money he may received before next court Ł 20

John Rainsford vs George Miller & James Booth.   Debt.   Jury
being called (same as before)...we find for the Plaintiff
Ł 15 4 6 with interest and cost

Benjamin Cook proved his attendance in this action of Rainsford vs George Miller and James Booth 6 days @ 2/6   also
Thomas Marbury 10 days @ 2/6

John Hammond vs James Vessels   Slander   The deft. pleads
guilty and pays cost
The following persons proved their attendance viz Elenor
Beck 6 days @ 2/6   Joseph Hightower 9 days @ 2/6 in this
action

204   William Hammelton vs Alexander Kenady.   Case   Judgment by
default   contd.

James Harrison & wife vs John Watson Junr.   non suited

Ordered that John Randal be summoned as witness in the
action Harrison & wife agt Watson Junr for plaintiff

Thomas Bezzel vs Christian Gomillian   Trover   discontinued

Leroy Hammond Esq. vs John Garrett   Attmt   contd. by consent

William Carson vs Joseph Read Attmt   non suited

The following having proved their attendance in the action
Harrison & wife vs Watson in behalf of the defendant viz
Edward Couch & Christian Gomillian 3 days each

On motion of the admn. of Samuel Gibson ordered that William
Dawson be appointed guardian for John Gibson a minor who
give securities Joseph Dawson and Richard Johnson in the sum
of Ł 500

The following persons having proved their attendance in this
action of Morrison vs Martin viz Simon Martin 6 days @ 2/6
Ann Hammond 11 days @ 2/6 in behalf of the deft

206 Drury Pace vs George Ragland Attmt.   The same jury as before
...we find for Plaintiff Ł 14

Mathew Gayle vs Felix Gilbert Writ inquiry. The same jury
as before upon their oaths do say we find for the plaintiff
Ł 298 13 8 and cost

The Same vs The Same Writ inquiry The same jury as before
upon their oaths do say we find for Plaintiff Ł 160 and cost

Ordered that the attached effects be sold and to go in discharge of the above Judgments

Abraham Richardson vs John Garrett Attmt. Dismissed for
want of Jurisdiction of the court

Robert Ewing & Co. vs William Dawson.   Debt Judgment confessed according to note styain execution six months and
issue agreeable to instalments

John Clerk vs John Hicks trespass Continued

John Anderson vs Henry Key Discontinued

Timothy Russel vs Isaac Lefeaver Discontinued

206 Frances Settle vs Daniel Wallicon Abates by death of the
defendant

Thomas Pennington proved his attendance as witness in the
cause of Russell vs Lefeaver & wife 15 days at 2/6

Frances Little vs Simeon Cushman Debt case The same jury
as before upon their oaths do say we find for Pltf. Ł 12 12
2 & cost

Richard Pond proved his attendance as evidence in the suit
Settles vs Cushman 11 days @ 2/6 and 11 days in the suit
Vessels vs Christophes

Thomas Boon vs Charity Mock. Ordered that the defendant
give special bail in this action who gave Abraham Richardson
and Ansell Lee

Charles Goodwin vs John Sharpton Writ inquiry case on appearance The same jury as before who say we find for the
plaintiff Ł 21. 15 with interest and cost

95

Alexander Oden vs George Dooly. Debt Judgt by Deft on
app writ of inquiry. The same jury as before..we find for
Pltf Ŀ 10 with int from 10 5672 till 17th July 1788 444
and cost of former suit expended & cost of present suit

207 Jesse Skinner vs Cornelius Cargil. Debt writ of inquiry
The same jury as before...we find for Pltf. Ŀ 16 6 3 with
interest and cost

John Williams & Malica Butts vs Andrew Pickins & John Owen
& John Lewis Gervias. On motion of Wm. Goodwin ordered that
the name of M. C. Leavensworth be struck out as one of
the defendants. The same jury as before say we find for
the Deft. Ŀ 3 2 6 3/4 and cost

John Carter proved his attendance 7 days for plaintiff @
2/6 in this action

John Hammond vs Jesse Roundtree. Judgment of the magistrate
Leroy Hammond confirmed for Ŀ5 & cost

The same vs The same Judgment of the Magistrate confirmed
for Ŀ4

The same vs The same Judgment of the magistrate Leroy Hammond confirmed for Ŀ 3 and cost

Henry Hunter & others vs Thomas Lamar & John Lamar. Judgment confessed according to bond intitled to the instalments
law on giving security

208 The same vs The Same Judgment confessed according to bond
The same order

Fields Pardue overseer of the publick road leading from the
Cherokee Pond to Campbels ware house having returned the
following persons as defaulters on the said road viz Leroy
Hammond Esq. 5 days, Samuel Willison 1 day, Thomas Lamar 3
days, General Pickens 3 days, Robert Cockran 1 day

Ordered that the above defaulters shew cause next court why
they should not be fined according to law

Benjamin Tutt Esq. vs George Ragland. On attmt writ of
inquiry The same jury as before upon their oaths do say we
find for the Plaintiff Ŀ 25 and interest according to note
and cost

Robert Stark vs Robert Melton. Judgment reversed

Ordered that a Seri Facias Issue agt John Sharpton summoned
as garnishee on attmt Alexander Oden vs George Dooly to
shew cause next court why judgment should not go against
him

The County Treasurer gave bond approved security agreeable
to a former order

209 Ordered that the court be adjourned till the second Monday
in October next. Arthur Simkins, John Moore, Russell Wilson.

The court met according to adjournment the 13th day of Oct.
1788. Present the worshipful Leroy Hammond, Russell Wilson,

96

Aquila Miles, Esq.

Ordered that the Grand Jury be drawn to serve in April next
The names of the Grand Jury drawn

1.	John Herndon	11.	John Lucas
2.	Jones Rivers	12.	George Martin
3.	Benj. Cook	13.	James Lyon
4.	Mathew McMillian	14.	Isaac Lewis
5.	William Childs	15.	William Green
6.	Charles Martin	16.	Robert Belcher
7.	John Cheney	17.	David Zubly
8.	Robert Samuel	18.	William Mathews
9.	Thomas Wilson	19.	William Shinholster
10.	James Anderson	20.	John Gray

Ordered that the Petit Jury be drawn to serve next court
The names of the Jurors drawn

1.	Seth Howard	16.	John Tillery
2.	David Richardson	17.	Michael McCarter
3.	Christopher Ward	18.	William Moseley
4.	Thomas Spraggins	19.	Frederick Williams
5.	Rolley Roebuck	20.	Phil May Junr
6.	John Anderson	21.	William Cockran
7.	Samuel Gardner	22.	Lewis Clark Red B.
8.	Joshua Hammond	23.	Richard Moore
9.	Robert Anderson	24.	Shadrack Rozar
10.	James Farquar	25.	James Vessels
11.	William Key	26.	John Wheler
12.	George Buckelew	27.	John Rivers
13.	Dennet Abney	28.	Joseph Culbreath
14.	Jacob Harveland	29.	David Thompson
15.	Mathew Turpin	30.	John Sprat

Ordered that the sheriff return the writ of venire for the
grand jury. The names of the Grand Jury that appeared

1.	John Lowe, foreman	8.	Thomas Dozer
2.	James McMillian	9.	William Abney
3.	Samuel Walker	10.	Jacob Smith
4.	Samuel Ramsey	11.	Robert Long
5.	Robert Lamar	12.	John Myer
6.	Arthur Watson	13.	Philip Lamar
7.	John Clark		

Ordered that Mr. Duncan Campbel have permission to retail
spiritous liquors as law as a quart untill January next he
having paid the duty

Ordered that the sheriff return the writ of venire for the
Petit Jury The names of the Petit Jury that appeared

John Cockburn	Little Berry Adams
Ezekiel Smith	William Robinson
John Hill	Frances Whitney
Thomas Banks	Ogdon Cockeroff
Drury Pace	John Wallace
James Hollingsworth	Robert Anderson Jr.
John James Stiffel	William Howle Junr
John Cannady	John Coursey

Ordered that Grand Jurors defaulters at this court shew cause
next court why they failed attending the court

Mrs. Zelphy Clark relinquished her right of dower to the
land conveyed by her husband to Samuel Walker before Auquila

Miles, Esq.

The last will and testament of Ellis Marcus was proved by
the oaths Barkley Martin and Peter Chastain ordered to be
recorded

Ordered that the bond taken by the Commissioners from Isaac
Foreman one of the builders of the court house be filed in
the Clerks office

Ordered that Mr. Smith sell the Estray Filley taken up by
him and return the money to the Clerk in thirty days

212 Samuel Wright vs Jesse Skinner. John Herndon special bail
in this action delivered the body of the defendant in open
court

Ordered that the sheriff take body of Jesse Skinner in custody until he renews his bail. Leroy Hammond, Russell
Wilson, Auquila Miles.

The court met according to adjournment the 14th of October
1788. Present the worshipful Leroy Hammond, Russell Wilson,
Auquila Miles.

Ordered that Thomas Key be appointed overseer of the road
from Horns Creek to Sweet Water in room of John Handcock
discharged

Ordered that John Clark be added to the grand jury by consent
of parties

Joseph Deck one of the executors of the last will and testament of John Deck deceased was qualified as such

Absent John Purves Esq. Present Hugh Middleton Esq. Absent
Leroy Hammond Esq.

213 Ordered that a citation issue that the kindred and creditors
of Ann Goode deceased should not shew cause next court why
the administration of the goods & chattels, rights and credits of the deceased should not be granted to William Longmire

Present John Sturzenegger Esq.

Ordered that all persons living within five miles of the
road thats to be opened leading from white hall near Samuel
Andersons from thence to Charles Williams on Turkey Creek
thence to John Thurmonds on Beaver Dams tence near Charles
Martins on Honres Creek thence to Seth Howards on Chavers
Creek thence the most convenient way to the ware house opposite the town of Augusta and that John Thurman, Seth
Howard, James Haregrove and Pulds (sic) Pardue and Robert
Anderson call upon the inhabitants aforesaid to clear out
and open the same and that they have power to fine the de-
faulters according to law

Ordered that Peter Chastian, Joseph Collier, John Martin and
Marshal Martin or three of them be appointed appraisers of
the Estate of William Martin decd.

214 Ordered that a citation issue that the kindred and creditors
     of William Minter-deceased should shew cause next court why
     the admn. of the goods and chattels of the said deceased
     should not be granted to William Brooks

     Robert Stark acknowledged his deeds of lease and release to
     John Day for 200 acres land which was ordered to be recorded

     Present Hugh Middleton Esq.

     William Anderson Esq. appointed collector of the Publick
     taxes for this county gave bond and security agreeable to
     the order of law

     Ordered that Robert Anderson be discharged from attending at
     this term as a petit juror on account of his indisposition

     Present Leroy Hammond Esq.

     Ann Summerall vs Henry Summerall On attmt A jury being
     called...Ezekiel Smith, John Cockburn, Thomas Banks, Drury
     Pace, James Hollingsworth, John James Stiffel, John Cannady,
     Littleberry Adams, William Roberson, Frances Whitney, William
     Howle Junr, John Coursey upon their oaths do say we find
     for the plaintiff Ł 33 13 4. Ezekiel Smith, foreman

215 Ordered that Abraham Richardson be appointed overseer over
     the road leading from sweet water into Pickens Ferry Road

     Varner Lewis vs Thomas Lawson Discontinued at the Deft cost

     The State vs Jack Johnson & Morris Pardue. Assault. True
     Bill. John Lowe, foreman Ordered that a capias agt. the
     Defendants

     The State vs Richd. Walker & Jeremiah Walker. Asst. true
     bill. Ordered that the Deft. give security who give William
     Carson & Thomas Broughton in the sum of Ł 50

     The State vs Ben Parker. Asst. true bill Ordered that a
     capias issue

     The State vs Samuel Carter & Abraham Odu. Asst. true bill
     Traversed. Ordered that the defendants give security who
     give Roland Williams in the sum of Ł 25 himself in the sum
     of Ł 50

216 The State vs Banjah Rambo. Asst. true bill Ordered that
     the deft. give security who give securities Edward Van,
     John Pursel in the sum of Ł 25 each principal in the sum of
     Ł 50

     The State vs Samuel Carter. Ordered that the deft. give
     security who give John Randal in the sum of Ł 25 principal
     Ł 50

     Nathan Johnson vs Jesse Scrugs. discontinued pltfs cost

     John Williams vs Charles Williams John Myer ordered himself
     special bail in this action.

     Ordered that the court be adjourned till tomorrow morning
     9 o'clock. Leroy Hammond, Russell Wilson, Aquila Miles.

The court met according to adjournment 15th day of Oct 1788
Present the worshipful Leroy Hammond, Russell Wilson &
Aquila Miles, Esq.

217   Ordered that a warrant of appraisement issue to John Myer,
David Bowers, John Clerk, Samuel Burges or any three of them
to view and appraise the goods and chattels rights and credits of John Dick not heretofore appraised

Ordered that a citation issue to summon the kindred and
creditors of John Tobler dec'd Savannah to shew cause why
letters of administration should not be granted to John Bar-
ber next court this citation to be published in Beach Island

David Zubly acknowledged his lease and release to Leroy Hammond Esq. for 239 acres land which was ordered to be recorded
also a mortgage for 10 negroes which was ordered to be recorded

Daniel Bullock and Roland Williams was qualified in open
court as constables for the county

Robert Stark vs John Pounds. James Gunnels proved his attendance in this action 1 day @ 2/6 and coming 66 miles a 4 d.

218   Robert Stark vs Benj. Cook. James Gunnels proved his attendance in the action 1 day @ 2/6 and coming 66 comes @ 4 d.

Robert Stark vs Edward Couch. James Gunnels proved his attendance 1 day in this action & coming 66 miles @ 4d.

William Brown vs Robert Melton. James Gunnels proved his
attendance 1 day & coming 66 miles @ 4d.

Present John Sturzennegger Esqr

Ezekiel Harris entered himself security in the action for
cost John Cannady vs Robert Bonner.

Henry Ware reported to the Court that he had finished the
work he had under taken to do to the Court House was approved
of by them.

Ordered that a dedimus issue directed to Henry Allison and
Chalres Crawford Esq. in the State of Georgia to examine
Mathias Bevers as a witness for Ezekiel Harris at the suit
James C. Murphey giving 10 days notice of the time and place

Nathan Johnson vs Jesse Scrugs. The following persons proved
their attendance in this action viz. John Thurman 2 days @
2/6 and John Terry 2 days @ 2/6 for the Defts in an action
of an asst.

219   Ordered that a dedimus issue directed to Henry Ware & Capt
Hughs to take examination of Katy Bradley a witness for John
Williams at the suit of Charles Williams giving 10 days no-
tice of time and place

Col Collins vs David Burks. Plaintiff Judgment for cow &
calf and cost

James Harris vs John Harris Plaintiff Judgment confessed
for the sum of ₤ 6 0 6 with interest for 7 months stay of

execution 2 months

The following persons proved their attendance in the action
of Collins vs Burks   viz   William Brooks 3 days   Elizabeth
Holmes 2 days   William Holmes 2 days @ 2/6 each

Solomon Edwards vs Hugh Carson.   Pltf   Contd. at Deft cost

William Prescot vs James Clerk Spraggins.   Judgment for Ł
6.10 with interest from 1 Nov 1784 and cost

John Garrett vs Crook Shanks & Speers.   Case   Refns report
that the Deft pay the sum of Ł 22 14 6 and the sum of Ł
5 5 9 interest payable by instalments Sam Willison and Richd
Johnson securities for the residue

On motion of Roland Williams ordered that Mrs. Mary Roberts
be cited to appear next court to shew cause why she wastes
the Estate of her husband

Thomas Morrison vs James Martin   Discontd. at Pltfs cost

Winfrey Whitlock vs John Carden. discontinued.

Betsey Williams of full age chose Frederick Swearingen her
guradian who give his securities Van Swearingen in the sum
of Ł 50

Deeds of lease and release Leod. Marbury to John Lowe for
200 acres land was proved by Peter Carnes ordered to be recorded

Ordered that the appearance docket be called.

Crook Shanks & Co vs David Zubly.   Debt   contd.

Robert Stark vs Thomas Cotton   Trover   contd.

Mary Lott Admx. vs Elisha Brooks & John Bullock.   Debt
abates

221 John Leach vs James Vessels   Debt   Judgment confessed for
Ł 24 11 with interest from 16th Jan 1786 stay execution 11th
Jan subject to instalments

Absolom Tillery vs Frances Settle   malicious prosecution
contd

John Randal vs Lewis Clark.   Assault contd.

Frances Davis vs Mordica Maddock.   Trover   contd.

John Herndon vs Fields Pardue.   Asst.   discontd.

Robert Bonner vs James Martin   Case   continued

The Same vs Frances Settle   Case   contd.

John Purcel vs John Handcock   Debt   contd.

Arthur Watson & Robert Stark vs George Mee & Edward Couch.
Debt   contd.

David Zubly vs Wm. Evans Debt continued

222 The Same vs The Same Debt contd.

Edward Van vs Thomas Ray Trover contd.

John McCoy vs Richd. Walker case contd.

Martha Hightower vs John Hightower Attmt discontinued

John Williams vs Charles Williams Attmt contd.

Drury Pace vs Lewis Watson Attmt contd.

Samuel Wright vs Henry Crags Attmt discontd.

Ebenezer Hill vs John Sharpton & Benj. Reynolds. Attmt
contd.

John Thurmon vs John Sharpton & Benj. Reynolds. Attmt
discontd.

The State vs Richard Walker & Jeremiah Walker. Ordered
that the defendants continue in custody untill he give bail

Drury Pace & John Coursey entered themselves security for
their appearance next court Ł 25 each principal Ł 50

223 On motion of Mr. Harper on the part of William Doby complains
of extraordinary fees charged by the clerk agt him and Richard
Bartlett in an indictment for an assault ordered that the
bill of cost & execution be referred to the county attorney
and that he do report on the validity of the same at the
next court and should they on examination appear illegal
that then the sentence of the law be in force

Jesse Roundtree vs James Vessels James Vessels vs Jesse
Roundtree The above causes referred to Leroy Hammond,
Edward Keating and John Carter and report to next court and
to be a judgment

Ordered that this court be adjourned untill tomorrow morning
9 o'clock. Leroy Hammond, Russell Wilson, Aquila Miles

The court met according to adjournment Present the worshipful John Purves, Russell Wilson, Aquila Miles, Esq.

224 On motion of William Covington formerly chose and appointed
guardian to Charles and Leroy Hammond that Hugh Middleton
and George Cowan his securities not attending to enter into
bond that other securities be appointed their room Ordered
that Fields Pardue and Barkley Martin be appointed in their
room

On motion of the Clerk that a deputy be appointed to offi-
ciate in the said office who offered Alexd Boling Stark which
said Alexander was appointed by the court

The grand Jury returned their presentment are as follows
viz 1st We present it as a very great grievance that the
District or Circuit Courts are not made courts of record
to be laid before the Legislature

2nd. We present it as very great grievance that there is
not some move adopted for the preservation of Orphans so
that they might be brought up in a Christian like manner,
the same order

3rd Location office is kept in the remotest part of the
District where the law says it shall be kept in the center
to the disadvantage of the lower part of the District, the
same order

225 4th We present it as grievance that the bridge and cassway
over Horns Creek is not kept in better order ordered that
the overseers shew cause next court why they are not kept
in repair

5th We present William Evans of Beach Island for frequently
abusing his wife by information of David Zubly ordered that
William Evans give security to keep the peace towards his
wife

6 We present Leonard Nobles for living in adultry with Ann
Jones by information Patty Ryan this presentment appears
out of the jurisdiction of the court

John Lowe	Samuel Walker
John Myer	Arthur Watson
Robert Lang	Samuel Collins
William Abney	James McMilliah
Robert Lamar	Philip Lamar
Thos Dozer	John Clerk
Jacob Smith	

Ordered that Jesse Skinner be returned from the custody of
the sheriff

Absent John Purves Esquire

On motion of the county attorney ordered that William Evans
be in custody of the sheriff untill he give security

Present LeRoy Hammond Esq.

William Hammelton vs Alexander Canady Debt discontinued

Absent Leroy Hammond Esq.

226 LeRoy Hammond Esq. vs John Garrett Case referd. Ordered
that the former order in this cause be renewed and the
referees report next court

Alexander Alexander vs Philip May Debt contd.

Benjamin Blackly vs William Carson Debt non suited

John Williams vs Fields Pardue Case for the debt A jury
being called impannelled...we find for the defendant the
sum of Ł 11.04.9 3/4

John Handcock vs James Scott Attmt discontinued

Brown & Gallman Adm vs John Purves Esq. Lewis Nobles entered
his attendance as a witness in behalf of John Randol vs
Rolly Roebuck 13 days @ 2/6

227 Robert Stark vs Robert Melton Case Referred to John Lowe
and Benj. Cook with power of umprage the awards to be entered next court and to be a judgment of the court

Robert Stark vs Edward Couch Debt Judgment according to
note

The same vs William Williams & Edward Couch. Debt Judgment
according to note

The Same vs Edward Couch. Case Judgment for Ŀ 8.10 with
interest ordered that the execution stay untill the 7th
Dec next

Dalzell Hunter vs Samuel Hammond Debt discontinued at
Pltf. cost

Joseph Burton vs Caleb Holloway Trover discontinued at
mutual cost

Samuel Mays vs George James Attmt discontinued

Ann Hammond vs Abraham Richardson. Trespass as mutual cost

Benjamin Blackley vs William Carson Asst discontd. at Pltf
cost

228 The same vs The Same Slander discontd. at Pltf cost

James Futch vs John Futch. Case the same Jury...the plaintiff was non suited. The following persons was allowed
this attendance as witness in this action viz. John Pursley
11 days @ 2/6, Richard Jones 7 days @ 2/6 George Mock 3
days @ 2/6

Edward Miles vs Drury Mims case non suited

Daniel Rogers proved his attendance for 4 days in this action
on behalf of the deft @ 2/6

Drury Mims vs John Cheney Debt Judgment confd. for 2000 of
tobacco or 4 pr hundred with interest staying execution one
month

229 John Ryan and Capt. Richard Johnson proved their attendance
as witnesses in this action Miles vs Mims Ryan 7 days and
Richard Johnson 4 days

On application of George Miller he was appointed Guardian to
Daniel and Elizabeth Nail the children of John Nail deceased
who give Frederick Tilman and William Dawson his securities
in the sum of Ŀ 100 for the faithful dischraging of his trust

James Martin vs Sampson Griffin Case Isaac Foreman entered
himself bail in this action

Sampson Griffin vs William Nichols. Case One of the jurors
not appearing ordered that the pltf be nonsuited, Richard
Johnson proved his attendance as a witness in this action
in the behalf of the plaintiff 6 days

John Williams proved his attendance in the action of Warner
Lewis vs Thomas Lawson 6 days

104

Ordered that Joseph Cimbol lunatick be continued in jail
untill he appears to be sufficiently recovered to be set at
liberty

William Evans gave his security for his future tender treat-
ment towards his wife Frances Little in the sum of Ł 25
principal in Ł 50

230 Ordered that this be adjourned untill the second Monday in
January next   John Purves, Russell Wilson, Aquila Miles.

The court met according to adjournment the 12th day of Jan
1789. Present the worshipful LeRoy Hammond, William Anderson, Benj. Tutt, Russell Wilson, Esquires.

Ordered that the Petit Jury be drawn to serve next court
The names of the Jurors so drawn

1.	Henry Zimmerman	16.	Timothy Rawdon
2.	William Cox	17.	Jesse Roundtree
3.	William Simkins	18.	Isaac Norrel
4.	Mathew Devore	19.	Robert Kilcrease
5.	Joseph Summerall	20.	David Shadwick
6.	Robert Wilson	21.	Thos Swearingen
7.	John Allen	22.	William Bryant
8.	Julius Dean	23.	John Henderson
9.	Chrisn. Glanton	24.	Abner Thornton
10.	William Holms	25.	John Norwood
11.	William Murphy	26.	John Bell
12.	Elisha Roberson	27.	Nathan Melton
13.	John Davis	28.	William Roten
14.	Thomas Edwards	29.	John Mims
15.	Barret Travis	30.	Charles Simons

Ordered that the sheriff return the writs of venire for the
Petit Jury   The names of Petit Jury that appeared

1.	Seth Howard	9.	Mathew Turpin
2.	Phill May Junr.	10.	John Tillery
3.	Thomas Spraggins	11.	Lewis Clerk
4.	John Anderson	12.	Shadrack Razar
5.	Samuel Gardner	13.	John Wheler
6.	James Vessels	14.	Joseph Culbreath
7.	George Buckelew	15.	Frederick Williams
8.	Denet Abney		

The last will and testament of Robert Belcher was proved
by the oath of James Harrison which was ordered to be recorded.

The last will and testament of Richard Allison was proved by
the oaths of William Anderson Esq. and Abney Mays, Mrs. Sarah
allison Ex. to the decd Richd. Allison was qualified according to law
The following persons were appointed to appraise the said
dec'd Estate viz Thomas Anderson, Wm. Anderson, William
Abney and William Hill

The administration of the goods and chattles of Samuel Ramsey was granted to Elenor Ramsey widow of the deceased who
give Thomas Anderson, John Harkins in the sum of Ł 500

232 and the following persons was appointed to appraise the said
Estate viz John Williams, John Moore Esq., William Roberson,
Wm. Mathews

The last will and testament of Thomas Roberts was proved by
the oaths of John Martin, Jeremiah Roberts and Mary Roberts
was qualified as executor to the said estate
And the following persons was appointed appraisers to the
said Estate viz John Martin, Shirley Whatley, John Pursel,
Thomas Key.

The administration of the goods and chattels of the estate
of William Minter was granted William Brooks   securities
Henry Key and William Holms in the sum of ℔ 1500

Ordered that a citation issue to cite the kindred and creditors of William Hargrove to shew cause why the administration
should not be granted to James Hargrove

Ordered that a citation issue to cite the kindred and creditors of David Murray to shew cause why the administration
should not be granted to Robert Stark Junr.

Ordered on motion of Henry Bolton who had his ear bit off in
affray which was proved by John Perryman be admitted to the
records of this court

233 Ordered that a citation issue to cite the kindred and creditors of John Davison deceased to shew cause why the administration of the said estate should not be granted to Edward
Keating

Ordered on motino of James Harrison that John Watson adm of
Charity Anderson produce his vouchers on the first day of
next term and make a final settlement of the said estate

Ordered that a citation issue to summon the kindred and creditors of Daniel Wallicon to shew cause why the administration
of the said deceased estate should not be granted to Frances
Little

On application of Joseph Hightower permission was granted
him to keep tavern Abraham Richardson

On application of Jenkin Harris permission was granted him
to keep tavern securitys James Lyon

On application of Abraham Richardson permission was granted
him to keep tavern security Joseph Hightower

On application of Drury Mims permission was granted him to
keep tavern   security   Edward Mitchel

234 On application of Coalter and Gibson permission was granted
them to keep tavern securitys   Barkley Martin

On application of Lewis Clerk permission was grnated him to
keep tavern securities Samuel Stalnaker and Bartlet Bledsoe

On application of John Herndon permission was granted him to
keep tavern   security Richard Johnson

On application of John Purcel permission was granted him to
keep tavern security Absolum Roberts

On application of Thomas Anderson permission was granted him
to keep tavern security Russell Wilson Esq.

On application of Andrew Lee permission was granted him to keep tavern security Russell Wilson Esq.

On application of Moses Harris permission was granted him to keep tavern security Isaac Foreman

On application of Robert Stark permission was granted him to keep tavern security Abraham Richardson

On application of William Dnerson permission was granted him to keep tavern security Thomas Anderson

235 On application Enoch Grigsby permission was granted him to keep tavern security Russell Wilson

Charles Banks acknowledged his deeds of lease and release to 2 tracts of land to Abraham Richardson one for 275 acres land the other for 200

Mrs. Susannah Banks relinquished her right of dower to the said land

Charles Banks acknowledged his lease and release to Robert Speers for 200 acres land

Mrs. Susannah Banks relinquished her dower to said land

Ordered that the court be adjourned to 9 o'clock tomorrow morning LeRoy Hammond, Benjamin Tutt, Russell Wilson, William Anderson.

The court met according to adjournment the 13th day of Jany 1789. Present the worshipful Leroy Hammond, Benjamin Tutt, Russell Wilson, W. Anderson, Esq.

236 Peter Carnes Esq. vs William Mathews Debt the Deft confesses judt for the sum of £ 85 3 4

Fields Pardue Cunnington and Moore vs John Spencer Judgment revived

The Same vs Van Swearingen Judgment revived

The same vs Simon Gentry Judgt revd.

Alexander Oden vs John Sharpton Judgment revd.

The same vs George Miller Judgment revd.

Permission was granted to Shadrack Razar to keep tavern security James Vessels

On application of James Frazier ordered that a citation issue to summon the kindred and creditors of William Frazier to shew cause why the admn. should not be granted to the sd. James next court

Lyon Henry vs Vincent Rowel Ordered that a dedimus issue to take the examination of Edward Rowel & others for the Pltf. giving due notice of time and place

237 Permission was granted to Thomas Clerk to keep tavern, securities Leonard Nobles and John Mallet

Ordered that the clerk have power to issue citations which
are to be published at some place of publick worship at
least three weeks before the setting of the court that the
administration is to be granted

John Rainsford vs Philip Johnson Dismd.

On application of Joseph Dick he was appointed guardian to
John and William Dick minors children of Thos. Dick gave
security John Clerk and Jonathan Myer in the sum of Ł 200

The State vs Moses Carter. The debt came into court and
acknowledged to owe Ł 50 and James Harris Ł 25 his security
in case the said Moses Carter fails to appear at the next
court and abide by the judgment of the court

John Cotten and Daniel Gunnels ackd. to owe the county Ł 25
each in case they fail to appear to prosecute the said Carter

The State vs Celia Watson The Deft. ackd. to owe the County
Ł 50 James Barrentine & John Coursey Ł 25 each in case the
deft failed to appear and abide the judgment of court

238 On motion of the clerk ordered that he have judgment against
the sheriff for the fees of the clerk thats now due

Ordered that Henry Ware be appointed in room of Lewis Tilman
overseer of a road from the court house to Lewis Tilmans old
field on the road to Lamars Ferry Ordered that Daniel Huff
be appointed in the room of Butler Williams

Ordered that James Walker be appointed in the room of Isaac
Lewis overseer of the road leading from John Jones to Amos
Richardsons

Ordered that Isaac Lewis be appointed overseer over the road
from Rockey Creek to the Island ford road

Ordered that John Bostick be appointed overseer of the road
in the room of Thos Anderson

Ordered Jacob Odum be appointed overseer in the room of
Samuel Messer

Ordered that William Terry be appointed in the room of James
Coursey overseer of the road leading from Cambridge to Augusta beginning at Turkey Creek to Gunnels Creek

Ordered that William Howle be appointed in the room of Barkley Martin overseer of the road leading from Cambridge to
Augusta beginning at Horns Creek to Gunnels Creek

239 Ordered that John Ryan be appointed in the room of Benj.
Cook overseer of the road from Chavous Creek to Horns Creek

Ordered that John Abney be appointed in the room oj James
Spann overseer of a road

Ordered that Edward Holmes be appointed overseer of the road
in the room of Joseph Nun

Ordered that Samuel Deloach be appointed overseer of the road
in the room of Thomas Deloach

Ordered that Thomas Lamar be appointed overseer of the road leading from Pickens Ferry on Savannah River to Bivens bridge on Horse Creek including the bridge

Ordered that Jacob Zin be appointed overseer of the road from Bivens bridge to the red house and fort more bluff

Ordered that William Key, Thomas Freeman, Isaac Lefever view the ground from Harlins Ferry to cross Turkey creek at John Allens thence to the Charleston road near the beaverdam creek and report to next court

Leroy Hammond Esq. vs John Garrett   Debt discontd.

240 Felie Gilbert vs Moses Lucas.   Judgment confessed by Wm. Covington for Ⱡ 23 & cost staying execution 6 months

Ordered that Treasurer pay the sum of Ⱡ 11 to Arthur Simkins Esq. and the residue of the publick money to be paid to the undertakers of the publick buildings Coroner & Constables, Clerks and Sheriffs

Ulysses Rogers vs John Cheney. Debt   Judgment confessed for Ⱡ 9.2 and cost stay of execution 2 months

Ordered that the county Attorney prefer a bill of inditement against the clerk on the complaint of William Doby and Richardson Bartlett and John Hammond and that they be bound over to give evidence to next court

Allen Hinton vs Edward Flecker.   Referred to Abraham Richardson and James Vessels with power of umprage and report next court.

Permission was granted John Hammond to retain spiritous liquors

On motion of Nancy Reynolds to choose her guardian she chose John Herndon who give Phill May as security in the sum of Ⱡ 200

Permission was granted to John Handcock to keep tavern security Shadrack Razier

On motion of the clerk ordered that Robert Stark be appointed deputy clerk who was qualified according to law

241 Ordered that Jacob Odum be allowed Ⱡ 90 out of the Estate of Michael Watson dec'd for the board of the children of the said Watson

Ordered that all the jurors defaulters be excused for their non attendance last term

Ordered that a dedimus directed to William Anderson Esq. to take the examination of Mary Edwards touching the relinquishment of her dower to lands conveyed by her husband to William Hill

John Williams vs Charles Williams.   Ordered that a dedimus issue directed to Capt. Hughs and Henry Ware to take the examination of Caty Bradly in this action

Henry Hunter & others vs Richard Johnson & Edward Preator
Discontinued

The Same vs The Same   Discontinued

Ann Sumerall vs Edward Vann   Discontinued deft. to pay clerks
fees

Ordered that Leroy Hammond settle with the Treasurer and
report to next court

242   Richardson Bartlett and William Doby acknd. to owe the county
Ь 25 each in case they fail to prosecute the clerk for extortion

Ordered that this court be adjourned to the second Monday in
April next   LeRoy Hammond,Benjamin Tutt, Russell Wilson,
Aquila Miles.

The court met according to adjournment the 13th of April
1789.   Present the Worshipful Leroy Hammond, Arthur Simkins,
John Purves, Benj. Tutt, Russell Wilson, Hugh Middleton,
Aquila Miles, John Sturzenegger, Esq.

Ordered that the Sheriff return the venire for the grand
Jury.   Ordered that the grand jury be drawnt to serve in
October   The names of the grand jury drawn.

1. Henry Key	10. Samuel Crafton
2. Thos Galphin	11. Philip Johnson
3. John Thurmon	12. Fields Pardue
4. Robert Lamar	13. William Jeter Sr.
5. Abner Perrin	14. Abraham Richardson
6. John Clerk	15. Thomas Anderson
7. James Harrison	16. Morrice Guin
8. James Coursey	17. Thomas Dozer
9. Thomas Lamar	18. John Bullock

Ordered that the Petit Jury be drawn to serve next court
The names of the Petit Jury drawn

1.Patrick Sullivant	16. Abraham Fanning
2. Henry Bolton	17. William Wilson
3. Isaac Evans	18. George King
4. Nicholas Glazier	19. John Smith
5. Moses Roberson	20. William McCartney
6. Samuel Middleton	21. Nicholas Minor
7. Joseph Dick	22. John Sweringham
8. William Humphreys	23. Amos Richardson
9. Isaac Mathews	24. Arthur Kilcreast
10. William Nobles	25. Frederick Weaver
11. John Tobler Sr.	26. John Covington
12. Thomas Boon	27. Thomas Harris
13. Allen Hinton	28. John Ackridge
14. John Pound	29. Thomas Pully
15. Joseph Covington	30. Peter Day

244   Ordered that the sheriff return the write of venire for
the grand Jury   The names of the grand Jury that appeared

1. John Herndon	10. James Lyon
2. Mathew McMillian	11. David Zubly
3. William Childs	12. William Mathews
4. Charles Martin	13. William Shinholster
5. Robert Samuel	14. John Grey

6. Thomas Wilson	15. Isaac Lewis
7. James Anderson	16. John Cheney
8. John Lucas	17. Jones Rivers
9. George Martin	

Ordered that the Sheriff return the writ of venire for the Petit Jury

1. William Cox	11. Robert Kilcrease
2. William Simkins	12. David Shadewick
3. Joseph Summerlin	13. John Henderson
4. Christohper Glanton	14. John Norwood
5. William Holms	15. Nathan Melton
6. William Murphy Junr	16. William Rotten
7. Elisha Roberson	17. John Mims
8. Timothy Rawden	18. Barrot Travis
9. Jesse Roundtree	19. Thomas Swearingen
10. Isaac Norrel	20. Mathew Devore

James Frazier came into court and acknd. to owe the county Ⱡ 10 in case he failed to appear in court tomorrow to give testimoney on behalf of the state against Moses Carter

245 Ordered that a road be opened from John McCoys ferry on Savannah river to the Rogus shoals on Stephens Creek from thence to Turkey Creek through John Allens land from thence a direct course unto the Charleston road near the Beaver Dam

Ordered that Thomas Freeman be the overseer of that part of the said road to the Rogue Shoals to the Ferry

And William Key from the rogue shoals to turkey Creek and James Coursey from thence into the Charleston road near the Beaver Dam

On complaint of James Harrison Ordered that John Watson Admx. of Charity Anderson give counter for the relief of James Harrison and that he be served with a copy of the order

Ordered that the admn. of all and singular the goods and chattles rights & credits of George Tillman decd. be granted to Lewis Tilman and Frances Tilman and that they give bond in Ⱡ 1000 security Butler Williams, Edward Mitchel, James Hargrove for the faithful discharge of the said trust and that George Martin, Daniel Huff and Willoby Tilloty & Edmund Boyd or any three of them appraise the said Estate.

Ordered that the court be adjourned till tomorrow morning 9 o'clock. Hugh Middleton, Russell Wilson, Aquila Miles.

The Court met according to adjournment on the 14th of April 1789. Present Leroy Hammond, Arthur Simkins, Benj. Tutt, Aquila Miles, John Sturzenegger, Esq.

Samuel Evans came into court and acknowledged to owe the county Ⱡ 50 and William Brooks and Thomas Howle Ⱡ 25 each in case the said Samuel Evans does not keep the peace towards Benejah Rambo and towards the citizens in general of this state this recognizance to continue in force for 12 months

The State vs Benajah Rambo. Asst The bail having surrendered the body of the defendant

247 a jury being called William Cox, William Simkins, Joseph
    Summerall, Christopher Glanton, William Murphey Junr, Isaac
    Norrell, Robert Kilcrease, David Shadewick, John Herndon,
    John Norwood, Nathan Melton, John Mims...we find the defen-
    dant guilty

    Ordered that the admn. of all and singular the goods and
    chattels & credits of William Haregrove dec'd be granted to
    James Hargrove and that he enter into bond of Ⱡ 500 for
    the faithful discharge of the said trust securities Seth
    Howard, Philip Johnson, William Terry and that Thomas
    Marbury, Littleberry Adams, William Jeter, John Lucas or
    any three of them appraise the said estate

    The State vs Benjamin Barker. Assault. A bill found
    Ordered that a bench warrant issue to take the body of the
    said defendant

    Samuel Willison vs Anthoney Powel Attmt referred to Fields
    Pardue and James McQueen with power of umprage

248 The State vs Benajah Rambo Asst. It is considered by the
    court that the deft. be fined Ⱡ 5

    The State vs Moses Carter. Petit Larceny No bill David
    Zubly, foreman

    The State vs Robert Stark Clk of Edgefield County Extortion
    True Bill

    The State vs James Stroop Assault True Bill

    Ordered that a capias Issue to take the body of the defendant

    Ordered that William Key, James Coursey, Christopher Glanton,
    John McFatrick appraise the estate of William Minter deceased
    or any three of them

    The State vs James Stroop. Asst. Thomas Pulley came into
    court and acknowledged to owe this county Ⱡ 25 in case he
    failed to appear here next court to prosecute the deft.

    James West came into court and acknowledged his lease and
    release for 17 acres of land to William Jeter which was
    ordered to be recorded

    Mrs. Celia West being privately examined by Hugh Middleton
    Esq. ackd. her right of dower to the land conveyed by her
    husband to William Jeter

249 On motion of Charles Goodwin Esq. Attorney of this county
    that in consequence of an inditement preferred against Robert
    Stark Esq. clerk of this court and found by the grand jury
    for extortion in his office that the court proceeded to the
    removal of said Robert Stark from the office of clerk the
    court thereupon proceeded and were unanimously of opinion
    that said Robert Stark not appearing and the court having
    reason to believe that he has absented from the County and
    State ordered that he be immediately removed from his said
    office

    The admn. of all and singular the goods and chattels rights
    and credits of James Clerk deceased was granted to Margaret

Clerk and that the interest into a bond of Ł 100 for the
faithful discharge of said trust her security Thomas Adams
and that Benjamin Teary, Thomas Adams, Littleberry Adams,
Frederick Tilman or any three of them appraise the estate of
the said deceased

250   Ordered that this court be adjourned untill tomorrow morning
9 o'clock. Arthur Simkins, Benjamin Tutt, Aquila Miles,
John Sturzenegger.

The Court met on Monday 13th July 1789 agreeable to law
Present Arthur Simkins, John Purves, Benjamin Tutt, William
Anderson, John Mooore, Russell Wilson, Aquila Miles, John
Sturzenegger, Esq.

The court proceeded to the election of a clerk by ballot
when in casting up the votes it appeared that Richard Tutt
Esq. was duly elected by a majority of the justices of the
County

251   Ordered that the Petit Jury be drawn to serve next court
The names of the Petit Jurors

1. Elkinah Sawyers	16. Solomon Bird
2. James Rowan	17. Joel Lipscomb
3. John Green	18. William Walker
4. James Campbel	19. Robert Allen
5. Messer Smith	20. Samuel Satcher
6. John Hill	21. Shadrack Rozar
7. Jacob Fudge Junr	22. Thomas Youngblood
8. Thomas Berry	23. Robert Anderson
9. Isaac Ardis	24. John Anderson
10. James Stroop	25. John Tillery
11. Garrett Buckelew	26. Jesse Scrugs
12. Drury Nipper	27. John Curry
13. John Body	28. Richd. Quals
14. George Abney	29. Phill May Junr
15. Richard Bush	20. Thomas Spraggins

Benjamin Blackley vs William Carson Damage. On motion of
Mr. Carnes attorney for the Plaintiff and by consent of
the Deft. It is ordered that the matters in dispute be referred to Samuel Anderson and Richard Tutt arbitrators indif-
ferently chosen between the parties to settle....

252   Ordered that the court be adjourned till tomorrow nine
o'clock. Arthur Simkins, John Purves, Benj. Tutt, Aquila
Miles

The Court met according to adjournment the 14th July 1789
Present Arthur Simkins, Aquila Miles, John Sturzeneger,
John Moore, Esq

Daniel Gunnels vs James Vessels Junr. Appeal from the magistrate judgment. Ordered that the judgment be confirmed

William Brown vs John Pound. Appeal from the magistrates
judgment. Ordered that the judgment be confirmed

Tolfero Bostick vs Frederick Ward Appeal from the magistrates
judgment Ordered that the judgment be confirmed

The court resolved itself into a court of Ordinary

On motion of William Shinholster it is ordered that the said
Shinholster be appointed guardian to William Shinholster Jr.
son of John Shinholster he giving bond and approved security
in the sum of Ł 100 Isaac Ardis and John Clerk offered themselves as securities who were approved of by the court

253 On motion of Elizabeth Addison widow of Joseph Addison for
letters of admn. on her deceased husband Estate ordered that
the said letters be allowed on her giving bond with William
Brown, Seth Howard, Bartlett Brown, and James Brown securities in the sum of Ł 500

Ordered that Arthur Simkins Esq. deliver the records of this
court to the clerk

Present LeRoy Hammond, Esq

Samuel Willison vs Anthoney Powel Arbitration. The award
of the arbitrators being produced and the awards overruled
by the court ordered that the rule of reference be reversed
and the cause reinstated

On motion of John Gorman and James Casson securities for the
admn. of Jacob Brooks Estate stating that they believe the
Estate wasting ordered that the clerk issue a citation against
Vachel Clary and Mary his wife to appear at the next court
to answer the above complaint

Ordered that Toliver Bostick be allowed tavern license untill
January next he giving bond and security as the law directs
William Beal & Robert McCombs are approved of by the court
as sufficient security

254 William Covington Esq. Sheriff of Edgefield County came into
court and acknowledged his deeds of conveyance for 100 acres
land to Joseph Rambo and was ordered to be recorded

Present Russell Wilson, Esq.

John Olliver vs Robert Anderson. Appeal from the magistrates
Judgment contd. for want of evidence

Ordered that John Miles be sworn as constable was sworn accordingly also that a dedimus be directed to William Anderson to swear Daniel Rodgers as constable

Toliver Bostick vs Thomas Farquchar. Appearl from Magistrates
judgment ordered that the judgment be confirmed

The last will and testament of John Tobler was proved by the
oath of John Myers and ordered to be recorded

William Longmire came into court and proved a citation which
appeared to the satisfaction of the court have been duly
published

On motion of William Longmire for letters of admn. on the
estate of Thos Goode deceased Ordered that the said letters
be allowed him on his giving bond with Henry Key and Jesse
Scrugs security in the sum of Ł 500

255 Alexander McIver vs Joseph Cook. Judgment confessed for
Ł19 5 7 3/4 with interest from 1 Jan 1787 to 1 Dec 1789

Arthur Watson and Robert Stark Exrs Michael Watson decd. vs
George Mee & Edward Couch. Judgment confessed for Ł 34 s 17
d8 with interest according to note

On motion of John Gorman ordered that a citation issue for
the next of kin or others to shew cause why letters of admn.
should not be granted to the said John on the Estate of
Samuel Carson

Solomon Edwards vs Hugh Carson Petition Trover. Judgment
for Plaintiff for Ł 8

Howel Johnson proved his attendance as a witness in this
cause 11 days for the plaintiff coming and going 27 miles
5 courts George Mee proved his attendance as a witness in
this action 10 days

Samuel Willison vs Anthony Powel Attmt. reinstated On
motion of Thos. P. Carnes atty for Pltf. Ordered that a
Dedimus potestatem iddue directed to Robert Forsyth and
William Freeman Esqs to take the disposition of William
Stratham a witness for pltff. giving the deft. 10 days notice
of the time and place of such examination to be read in evidence on the trial

256 Lyon Henry vs Vincent Rowel On motion of Peter Carnes Atty.
for Plaintiff Ordered that a dedimus potestatem issue directed Thomas Lewis, David Emanuel & Hugh Lawson Esq. or any
two of them to take deposition of Christopher Kelby a witness for pltf. The pltff. giving the deft. 10 days notice
of time and place of such examination to be read as evidence
on the trial

The court proceeded to the election of a sheriff by ballot
when on casting up the votes appeared that Bartley Martin
Esq. was duly elected

Ordered that the court be adjourned till tomorrow 9 o'clock
LeRoy Hammond, Arthur Simkins, Benj. Tutt.

Wednesday July 15, 1789. The court met according to adjournment. Present the worshipful Arthur Simkins, Benjamin Tutt,
Aquila Miles, John Purves, Leroy Hammond.

257 Samuel Willison vs Anthony Powel Attmt. On motion of P.
Carnes Attorney for Deft. ordered that dedimus potestatem
issue directed to Robert Forsyth and William Freeman Esqrs.
to take the deposition of Edmond Bugg Hicks the Deft. giving
the pltf. 10 days notice of the time and place of such examination to read as evidence on the trial

A deed of lease and release from Colon. Leroy Hammond and
wife to John Hammond for 15½ acre of land was produced and
acknowledged by Col. Leroy Hammond as his act and deed whereupon it was ordered to be recorded

A deed of Feoffment from John Hammond and Elizabeth Hammond
his wife to Leroy Hammond for upwards of 6 acres of land was
produced in open court and acknowledged by John Hammond as
his act and deed with leving and lessin thereon indorsed
which was ordered to be recorded

A deed of lease and release from John Hammond and Elizabeth

his wife to Leroy Hammond for 114 feet square of land was produced in open court & ackd. by Jno Hammond as his act & deed which was ordered to be recorded.

258 James C. Murphey vs Ezekiel Harris Case On motion of Peter Carnes Esq. Deft. atty. Ordered that a dedimus potestatem issue directed to William Freeman and Robert Forsyth Esqs. in Augusta to take the deposition of Mathias Beavers a witness for Deft. The deft. giving the pltf. 10 days notice of time and place of such examination to be read as evidence on the trial

James Vessels was appointed constable by Leroy Hammond Esq. and qualified accordingly.

The citation for the kindred & creditors of John Davison to shew cause why administration should not be granted to Edward Kating was returned and Samuel Willison as creditor to the decd. Davison appeared and claimed a right to the admn; after argument the court ordered that letters of admn. be granted to Edward Keating on his giving bond with John Hammond and William Covington securities in the sum of Ł 700 and the said Keating qualified accordingly

On motion of John Hammond & Ephriam Hendon for letters of admn. on the Estate of Silverster Elden decd. ordered that the said letters be granted to the said John Hammond and Ephraim Hendren on their giving bond with Edward Keating & William Covington in the sum of Ł 100 and the sd. Hammond qualified accordingly.

259 On motion of Charles Goodwin Esq.,Ephraim Ramsey Esq. was introduced to this bar and inroled as an attorney he having promised to produce his credentials to the next court

Leonard Nobles vs Robert Stark Attmt. Edward Vann came into court and acknowledged himself special bail in the above action

Robert Stark former clerk of Edgefield County vs William Covington. On motion of Thos P. Carnes Esq. for pltff. exhibiting an account for fees due in the hands of the said Covington as Sheriff of this county Ordered that judgment be entered agreeable to the County Court law for Ł 231 s 10 d 6½

On motion of Mr. Carnes ordered that a citation issue requiring William Brooks to shew cause why he does not produce to this court the will of William Minter deceased

Ordered that Richard Tutt late sheriff of this county produce to the next court a full account together with the original books of all monies received and yet due for the county tax

260 The last will and testament of George Troop was proved by the oath of George Miller and ordered to be recorded

Ordered that this court be adjourned till court in course. Leroy Hammond, J. P., Arthur Simkins, John Pruves, Aquila Miles, Benj. Tutt.

At a court held for the county of Edgefield on 12 Oct 1789

Present the worshipful Arthur Simkins, Aquila Miles, John
Sturzenegger, Esq.

Ordered that the grand jurors be drawn to serve at next
April court and the following persons were drawn to wit

1. John Lowe	11. Robert Long
2. Nathaniel Howle	12. James McMillian
3. Thomas Key	13. John Childs
4. Nathl. Abney	14. Thos Marbury
5. Sam burges	15. Jones Rivers
6. Isham Green	16. William Longmire
7. William Spraggins	17. Jacob Smith
8. Caleb Holloway	18. Ludwell Williams
9. William Butler	19. William Childs
10. John Myers	20. William Glover

Ordered that the Petit Jury be drawn for the next court &
the following persons were drawn to wit

1. Joseph Nun	16. Benjamin Darby
2. James Butler	17. Joseph Trotter
3. Jonathan Myer	18. William Reynolds
4. Hinly Web	19. Stephen Tilman
5. David Boswill	20. Peter McGrew
6. Nathan Cawley	21. Thos Pinnington
7. Thos Deloach	22. John Roberts
8. Michael Shaver	23. John Cunningham
9. David Burks	24. William Holliday
10. Robert Spears	25. Casper Nail Junr
11. William Brooks	26. Sherwood Corley
12. John Rivers	27. George DeLaughter
13. Will McCarter	28. Frances Mucklerath
14. Samuel Garner	29. Ebenates Stephens
15. Ogdon Cockeroff	30. Stephen Bettis

Richd. Dickerson Esq. produced his credentials as an attorney which were read in open court and the said Dickerson is
hereby enroled as an attorney of this court

262 Ordered that the sheriff return the writ of venire for the
grand jurors   The names of the grand jurors that appeared

1. Henry Key	10. Samuel Crafton
2. John Thurmon	11. Fields Pardue
3. Thomas Galphin	12. William Jeter
4. Robert Lamar	13. Abraham Richardson
5. Abner Perrin	14. Thomas Anderson
6. John Clark	15. Morrice Guin
7. James Harrison	16. Thos Dozer
8. James Coursey	17. John Bullock
9. Thomas Lamar	18. Philip Johnson

Ordered that the sheriff return the writs of venire for the
Petit Jurors   Returned and read accordingly when the following persons appeared

1. James Rowan	16. Joel Lipscomb
2. John Green	17. Solomon Bird
3. James Campbel	18. Robert Allen
4. Jacob Messer Smith	19. Samuel Satcher
5. John Hill	20. Jesse Scrugs
6. Jacob Fudge	21. John Curry
7. Thomas Berry	22. Richard Quals
8. Isaac Ardis	23. Philip May
9. James Stroop	24. Thomas Spraggins
10. Garrett Buckelew	25. Shadrack Rozier

11. Drury Nipper
12. John Body
13. George Abney
14. Richard Bush
15. William Walker

26. Thomas Youngblood
27. Robert Anderson
28. John Anderson
29. John Tillery

263 Scoot & Wood Exrs. of D. Willicon Decd vs Thomas Lamar & Thomas Lamar Debt. Judgment confessed agreeable to note subject to instalments with stay of execution 3 months

On application of Benjamin Mock he the said Benjamin was appointed guardian for Caleb Niblet an orphan under age to choose for himself a son of John Niblet

The last will and testament of Robert Belcher was proved by the oath of Alexander McKey, Susannah Belcher executrix John Win and James Harrison executors of the last will and testament of Robert Belcher was qualified according to law and the following persons were appointed to appraise the said estate to wit Thomas Bacon, John Adams, Robert Anderson and Robert Anderson Jr.

The last will and testament of William Talbert was proved by the oaths of William Key in open court Mrs. Martha Talbert Executrix was qualified accordingly and the following persons appointed to appraise the estate of the said Talbert to wit Marshel Martin, James Talbert, William Longmire & John McFatrick

The last will and testament of Samuel Marsh was proved by the oath of John Oliphant and Mrs. Sarah Marsh executor was wualified accordingly and the following persons were appointed to appraise the estate viz John Frazier, Nicholas Dillard, John Oliphant, and Benjamin Rhodes

Lewis Tilman and Frances Tilman Exr and Extx. of the goods and chattles of George Tilman deceased was qualified according to law

Barkley Martin Esq. was qualified as sheriff for this county according to law by taking the oath of office and the oath of the United States having produced his commission which was read securities Jonathan Wright and Jones Rivers

Peter Carnes vs Thomas Forquhar.   Petition dismd at Deft cost

The Same vs Nathan Johnson Pltf. Dismd at Deft. cost

The Same vs Martin Cloud. Pltf. Dismd at Deft. cost

Moody Burt vs Littleberry & Joel Harvey. Dismt. ordered that a judicial attachment issue

265 Ezekiel Harris vs David Zubly. Non est renew

Teasdale & Co. vs Richd. Johnson non est renew

Pickens & Co. vs Jno Herndon non est renew

The Same vs Wm. Brooks Same order

Howel Johnson & son vs John Powel non est dismissed

118

Jesse Johnson vs Jno. Powel non est dismissed

Thomas Ray vs James Mayson non est renew

Kershaw Chesnut & Co vs William English. Dismissed at the Deft. cost

Nicholas Bezel vs John Timmerman. non est dismissed

266 Wm. Wafford Admrs. of Wm. Wafford Jr. vs Samuel Hammond & Abner Hammond. non est renew

Coatler & Stuart vs George Tankersley. non est dismisd.

Daniel Danoly vs Richd. Johnson non est renew

Pickens & co vs Same. Same order

The Same vs Philip Lamar same order

Same vs Thomas Lamar B M Same order

Same vs M. C. Leavensworth Same order

Same vs Richd. Johnson same order

Same vs Richd Johnson Same order

Same vs Johnathan Myers Same order

The Samve vs Thomas Lamar H. C. Same order

267 Benjamin Barker vs William Williams Asst non est renew

Melbine C. Leavensworth vs Patrick Hays Attmt contd.

Sam Edwards vs Benajah Rambo Contd.

Henry McMurdy vs Lewis Watson contd.

Robt Stark & Arthur Watson vs Edward Couch & Geo Mee. Dismissed at Pltf cost

Edward Couch vs Hester & Hester Dismissed at Pltf cost

Thomas Smiths vs Joseph Lewis Non est renew

Charles Banks vs James Thomas Walch. non est renew

Ordered that the court be adjourned till tomorrow morning 9 o'clock. Arthur Simkins, Aquila Miles, John Sturzenegger.

268 Tuesday the 13th Oct 1789 the court met according to adjournment. Present the worshipful Leroy Hammond, John Purves, Aquila Miles, John Sturzenneger, Esq.

The State vs James Troop. Assault The deft came into court and confessed the fact laid in the indtctment whereupon the court find him s 20

Barkley Martin Esq. high Sheriff presents Jeremiah Hatcher to the court for their approbation as Deputy who was approved of & qualified accordingly by taking the oath of office and the oath for supporting the constitution of the United States

Ordered that the clerk of this court do in future write to
the grand & petit jurors defaulters at this court to make
good and lawful excuses upon oath for their non attendance
or at next sitting of the court they will be fined agreeable
to law

269 Edward Couch appt. vs Robert Stark respondt. The judgment
of John Moore Esq. appeal from a single Magistrate. The
appellant came into court and confessed that the judgment
be confirmed to the respondent for Ł 5 and cost of suit

Samuel Anderson vs James Davalun. Appeal from John Moore,
Esq. Single magistrate the parties was heard by their coun-
cel whereupon the court ordered that the judgment be reversed
and that the appellant recover the cost of suit of James
Davalen the respondent ordered that the clerk in the above
case execution for cost

Judith Moseley vs William Dooley. Appeal from a Magistrate
judgment confirmed for Ł 1 s17 d 8 and cost of suit

The Grand Jury (to wit) John Clerk, foreman; Henry Key, John
Thurmon, Abner Perrin, James Harrison, James Coursey, Thomas
Lamar, Samuel Crafton, William Jeter Senr., Morrice Guin,
Thos Dozer, John Bullock & Philip Johnson were sworn and
charged

270 William Carson ads Benjamin Blackley. These suits having
been referred to Samuel Anderson and Richd. Tutt

William Carson ads Benjamin Blackley. They return their
award and do say that both actions be deft. at mutual cost

Mr. James Frazier produced a citation in court citing the
creditors and next of kin of William Frazier dec'd to shew
cause why letters of admn. should not be granted to him ordered that the said letters be granted to the said James
he giving bond with John Ollephant and Levi Jester in the
sum of Ł 200 as securities and that the following persons
were appointed to appraise the said estate(viz) John Holmes,
Benj. Rhodes, William Marsh, and Childs Marsh.

The administrator of Silvester Elder having produced an
inventory of the said Estate which was ordered to be recorded

Ordered that the following persons be appraised of this estate of Joseph Addison decd to wit, George Miller, Fredrick
Tilman, Stephen Tilman & James Cobbs

271 John Gorman produced a citation in court citing the creditors
or next of kin of Samuel Carson to shew cause why letters of
administration should not be granted him, which appeared to
have been duly published ordered that the said letters be
granted to the said Gorman on his giving bond with Amos
Richardson & William Abney in the sum of Ł 100 and that the
following persons be appraisers of the said Estate (to wit)
Thomas Spraggins, Thomas Berry, Nathaniel Abney, Joseph Trotter. John Gorman qualified according to law as admn.

The State vs Saml. Carter. Indt. assault. A jury being

impannelled and sworn (viz) James Rowan, foreman; James Troop, Drury Nipper, John Body, William Walker, Solomon Bird, Jesse Scruggs, John Curry, Phil May Junr., Thomas Spraggins, Thomas Youngblood do say we find the deft. Samuel Carter & Abraham Oadum guilty. James Rowan, foreman.

The State ads Benj. Parker   Indt. assault   The deft. came into court and pled guilty and put himself on the mercy of the court

The State ads Robert Stark Esq. Clk.   Judt   True Bill, John Clerk foreman.   Extortion.

The grand jury returned their genl presentment received the thanks of the court and were discharged.

John Hammond ads. Robert Stark.   Information for exacting illegal fees.   Peter Carnes Atty.
The parties appeared by their attorneys and after a full investigation of the facts, the court are of the opinion that the defendant Robt. Stark has exhorted Ł 5 s 4 d 11 whereupon it is considered that the said Stark pay four fold (viz) Ł 20 s 19 d 8 and cost of information

Ordered that this court be adjourned till tomorrow morning 9 o'clock.   Leroy Hammond, Aquila Miles, John Sturzenegger.

The court met according to law on Wednesday the 14th day of Oct 1789.   Present the worshipful Aquila Miles, Russell Wilson, John Sturzenngeer, Esq.

273   On motion of Mr. Carnes atty. for Richard Tutt Esquire for permission of the court to prove the subscription of Nuby Mann to a deed of lease and release for 100 acres land sit- uate on the waters of Cuffee Town Creek dated 17 Jan 1778 It was ordered the evidence of Benjamin Tutt and John Purves Esq. be admitted as evidence to prove the hand writing of said Nuby Mann and that upon such proof the deeds be admit- ted to be recorded in the Books of this Court as it is re- presented to the Court as the party making such deed and all the subscribing witnesses are deceased.

John Kennady ads Robert Bonner.   Debt.   Judgment confessed agreeable to bond with stay of execution six months subject to all legal sets off which the deft. can produce within the time of 6 months & subject to the instalments law if the defendant produces satisfactor proof to the court that the debt is payable by instalments.

274   Alexander Alexander ads Philip May.   Discontinued at Peter Carnes Esq. cost

Lyon Henry vs Vincnet Powel   Attmt.   The parties consent to take the deposition of Frances Malory to be read in evidence at the trial

John Rainsford vs Robert Stark.   Judgment confessed by R. Stark Junr. for the sum of Ł 6 s 10 & cost

John Tobler vs David Zubly.   Abated by death of Plaintiff

Richardson Bartlett & William Doby ads Richard Weatherton. Discontinued at mutual cost

Glascock Ex. of Bennefield vs Wm. Evans & Nat. Howle.
Dismissed Deft. Cost

Elisha Robertson vs Reynolds & Robertson. Discontinued

Jesse Roundtree vs James Vessels. Award returned and judgment accordingly.

Robert Stark vs Sam Ramsey. Abated by death of Deft.

275 Kemp T. Strother vs John Wommack. discontinued

George Cheney vs John Hampton. discontinued

Absolum Tillery vs Frances Little. discontinued at Plaintiff cost except one guinea

John Randal vs Lewis Clark. Contd.

In the matter of the last will and testament of William Minter deceased. In the court of ordinary.
The above will having been brought into court and proved in
common form it is hereby ordered that all former orders respecting the admm. of the said Minter to William Brooks re-
scinded and it is also further ordered that one of the executors named in the said will being dead and the reason of the
appointment of the other Lewis Tilman having ceased that
administration with the will annexed be granted to James
Coursey and William Key by and with the consent of the parties entered in the said estate on their giving bond in the
sum of Ł 1500 with Drury Pace and Jesse Scruggs securities
the following persons were appointed to appraise the sd. Estate (viz) Henry Key, John Griffis, William Terry and William Longmire, the admrs. qualified according to law.

276 Ordered that Wm. Brooks pay all cost accrued in this matter
above

Samuel Stalnaker ads Ezekiel Smith. Appeal from the judgment of John Moore Esquire a magistrate of this county. Judgment received with costs

Robert Anderson vs John Olliver. Appeal from the judgment
of John Moore Esq. a magistrate of this County dismissed
each party to pay their own cost

The State vs Saml. Carter & Abraham Odum. The jury being
sworn as in this case yesterday found the defts. guilty wherefore the court fined Samuel Carter Ł 5 and Abraham Oadum
Ł 3 with costs

The State vs Morriss Pardue & Jack Johnson. Judt assault
the defts. came into court and plead guilty wherefore the
court fined them s 1 each and costs

277 Frances Jones ads John Duglas & Edward Couch. Judgment
confessed according to bond subject to instalment

William Longmire admr. of all and singular the goods and
chattles of Thomas Goode dec'd came into court and was qualified according to law whereupon the court appointed James
Coursey, John McFatrick, William Terry & Jesse Scrugs appraisers of the said estate

122

Charles Goodwin Esq. ads John Randal. Judgment confessed according to note for 20 guineas & interest from date with stay of execution 6 months

Jesse Roundtree vs West Cook. Continued by consent

George Walker Esq. produced to the court a writ of certeorari Issued by the John J. F. Grimke Esq. one of the associate Judges commanding the court to cause the proceedings in the case The State vs Robert Stark on an Judgt. for taking illegal fees as clerk of this court to be sent up to the District Court to be held at Cambridge 26 Nov next ordered that the clerk certify the proceedings accordingly.

278 Thomas B. Scott ads Isham Mitchel. Pltf. debt Judgment for Ł 5 with cost

Benjamin Jonakin vs William Melton. Pltf Dismissed at Pltf cost

Thomas Braughton vs Absolom Tilley. Pltf Dismissed at Pltf cost

James Harris vs Absolom Tilley. Pltf Dismissed at Pltf cost for want of papers

Mathew Duncan vs John Frederick Pltf. dismissed at Pltf. cost for want of papers

Sarah Holson & Willis Frederick proved 10 days attendance each in the above case and Sarah Holston is allowed mileage for 100 miles

John Watson vs McKey & Butler Pltf. dismisses at want of service

Charles Jenkins vs James Stuart. Pltf. case contd. by consent

Benjamin Jarnagan vs William Melton. Pltf dismissed at Deft cost

279 John Wallace vs John Allen Pltf. Dismissed for want of papers

John Garrett vs Burges White Pltf. dismissed for want of papers

Peter Carnes vs James Coody. Pltf. dismissed for want of papers

Thomas Adams vs John Walls. Pltf continued by consent

Thomas Collins vs Benjamin Parker. Continued on application of the defts. attorney

John E. Calhoun vs John Sharpton & Thomas Beckum. Judgment for Plaintiff for Ł 6.10 & interest from 12 Dec 1786 & cost

Arthur Simkins vs Edward Couch. discontinued

James Monday vs James Teagwood continued

Peter Carnes vs Moses Carter. Judgment for Plaintiff for
Ł 2 s 3 d 6 & costs

Joseph Prince vs Benj. Mock. Pltf. contd. by consent

280 Matt Martin vs Stephen Glover Dismissed at the Defendants
cost

Isaac Teasdale vs Richd. Johnson Pltf. continued

Samuel Wright vs John Herndon Pltf continued

Ezekiel Harris vs David Zubly. Pltf. continued

Samuel Wilson vs Frances Little. Whereas a judgment has
been detained in this court on a note of hand which was a
negroe payable according to the instalments and the parties
having agreed to value the negroe at Ł 40 with interest from
1 Jan 1785 credit to be given for Ł 20 12 7 on 17 June 1786
and Ł 12 on Jan 1789 Ordered that execution be issued according to the instalments

John Purcel vs John Handcock Debt referred to Aquila
Miles and Hugh Middleton Esq. with power of umprage and their
award to be made a rule of this court

281 Ordered that the court be adjourned till tomorrow 9 o'clock
Leroy Hammond, Arthur Simkins, Aquila Miles

The court met according to adjournment on Tuesday the 15th
Oct 1789. Present the worshipful Leroy Hammond, Arthur
Simkins, Aquila Miles, John Sturzenegger.

Peter Hillard vs William Roberson case discontinued

Thomas Boon vs Charity Mock Case discontinued at Pltf cost

Jesse Roundtree vs James Butts & West Cook discontinued

John Randal vs Robert Roebuck. discontinued

Allen Hinton vs Edward Fletcher. discontinued

282 Jesse Roundtree vs William Evans. Case on assumset. The
jury being called...William Walker, James Rowan, Robert Anderson, James Troop, Drury Nipper, John Body, Solomon Bird,
Saml. Satcher, Jesse Scruggs, John Curry, Thomas Spraggins,
Thomas Youngblood...we find for the pltf Ł 20 with lawful
interest from 7 Nov 1785. The Deft. prayed an appeal which
is granted upon the defendant giving security as the law
directs

James Tutt vs Thos. Carson & Wm. Johnso Debt contd. James
Carson Junr. Bail
James Carson the defendants bail came into court and delivered them up they being ruled by the court to give bail The
defendants are considered to be in custody of the sheriff
untill such special bail be given

Edmond Boyd vs James Lyon Debt continued by consent

283 John Purves Esq. vs Adams Pardue Debt The same jury as

before...we find for the plaintiff the principal & interest
Ł 20 sterling with int. from 17 Oct 1784 with cost suit
                              William Walker, foreman

Edward Keating vs Thomas Lamar Debt Judgment by default

Edward Keating vs George Bryant Judgment by default

Ann Summerall vs George Miller & James Thomas. Trover
non suit

Robert Stark ads George Miller & John Herndon. Debt judgment confessed subject to all legal lets. discounts the
deft. may produce to the clerk within one month

Frances Suttles vs Thomas Gordon Case non suit

284 Robert Stark vs John Randol. Debt The same jury as before
returned a verdict...we find for the Plaintiff debt and interest from date of the note according to instalments....

Robert Bonner vs Frances Settles Case referred to Col.
Leroy Hammond and Edward Keating with power of an umpire &
their award to be judgment of this court

Robert Stark vs Robert Melton Case The same jury as before
being impannelled and sworn...we find for the Plaintiff Ł 4
12 2 with interest from 1 Dec 1786.

285 Samuel Willison ads Anthony Powel Attmt On motion of Thos.
P. Carnes attorney for Pltf. Ordered that a commission
issue directed to John G. Noel and Robert Forsyth Esq. in
the State of Georgia to take the examination of Dalziel
Hunter as a witness on the part of the pltf, he giving the
defendant 10 days notice....

Robert Stark vs Robert Melton Case James Gunnels proved
12 days and traveling 66 miles 5 times

John Kennady vs Robert Bonner. Debt ordered that a commission issue to John Young Noel and Robert Forsyth in the
State of Georgia to take the deposition of George Hunter and
Dalziel Hunter giving the Defendant 15 days notice of time
and place

Lyon Henry vs Vincent Rowel. Attmt. Ordered that a commission issue to Robt. Forsyth and John Noel in the State
of Georgia to take the deposition of any witnesses the Deft.
thinks proper he giving 15 days notice of time and place

Nathaniel Powel vs Solomon Turner. Attmt non suit

286 Edward Keating vs George Cowin Attmt. Contd. at Pltfs cost

The Jury were sworn to execute all writs of enquity that
should be presented to them this court

Mary Roberts vs David Hunter. Attmt. Judgment by default
a writ of enquity The same jury...we find for the plaintiff
according to specialty with cost of suit

John Sullivant proved one days attendance in this cause

Allen Hinton vs The Estate of Chas. Williams. Judgment by default

The appearance docket was called overthe second time

Sampson Griffin vs Thos. Broon. Case contd.

James Nipper vs Leonard Nobles & John Herndon Debt continued

287 John Randal vs John Cheney Assault continued

Mathew Duncan vs Robt. Hart & Arthur Watson Esq. Case contd.

Thomas Galphin & William Dunbar Exrs. of George Galphin vs Isaac Foreman. Case continued

James Lauder vs Joel Chandler Case contd.

John Powel vs Sherwood Cauley. case non suit

Joshua Thorn & wife vs Allen Hinton case continued

Adam Stalnaker vs James Murrey Trover continued

Will. Hardy assnee vs Thomas Lamar. Settled at Deft cost

Lyon Henry vs Vincent Rowel. Attmt contd.

288 Ordered that all causes on the appearance dockett when attornies are employed on both sides shall be continued as at issue untill the next court

Barney Caffery vs Thomas Lawson Case judgment by default

John Satterwhite vs William Hardy. Debt Judgment by default

Henry McMurdy vs Lewis Watson. Attmt Judgment by default
Ezekiel Hudnel garnishee
Ordered that a si fa issue agst the said garnishee to shew cause why judgment should not go against him

Isaac Mitchel vs John Fure. Abated by death of Plaintiff

Thomas Connell & Gordon vs Joseph Cook. Debt Judgment by Deft for Ł 5 s 4 d 8 with interest from 25 March 1786

289 Thomas Pulley vs James Stroop Assault dismissed at Defts costs

John Cook vs Geo. Tankersley & Benj. Harris Debt Judgt by default

Jacob Messer Smith vs Isaac Hill Trover Judgment by default

John Moore vs James Shepherd Debt Judgment by default for Ł 35 agreeablt to note with interest from 1 Sept 1787

Edmond Martin vs Reubin Beckum Judgment by default

Richard Dozer vs Daniel Dinkle Trespass Dismissed at Matt Gayles cost

Mordica Maddock vs John Randal   Debt   non suit

Thomas Palmer vs Demsey Beckum & Thos Beckum   Judt by default

Leonard Marbury vs Richard Call   Debt on Judt. for 16 10

290   Leroy Hammond Esq. vs Randal Griffin & George Dooley.   Judgment by default

Edward Couch vs Solomon Edwards   Attmt   Judgment by default

Mark Lott vs Robt. Cooper   Judgment by default

Leroy Hammond vs George Dooly   Attmt   Judgment by default

Charles Goodwin vs George Dooley   Attmt. Judgment by default

Thomas Booth vs Charity Mock   Stephen Hutchenson proved his attendance in this cause 10 days

Ordered that this court be adjourned until tomorrow 9 o'clock Arthur Simkins, Aquila Miles, John Sturzenegger.

The court met according to ajmt. on Friday 16 Oct 1789. Present the worshipful Leroy Hammond, Arthur Simkins, John Sturzenegger, Esq.

291   Conrade Golman ads Robert Stark   Case entered by consent of Parties without process Judt for the Pltf Ł 1 s 17 d 4 with interest from 26 March 1784

Robert Stark vs John Pounds.   Debt   Judgment for Plaintiff Ł 8 s 2 d 8 with stay of execution till adj. court

Richard Johnson vs Watson & Stark Exrs.   Debt.   The same jury...we find for the Plaintiff Ł 107 s 8 d 11 payable by instalments   William Walker, foreman.

John Selman vs Thomas Jones   Debt.   Ordered that a dedimus issued directed to Hugh Lawson & William Little in Berk Co. in the State of Georgia to take the deposition of Blassengham Harvey Junr and James Stubbs on the part of the defendant he giving 10 days notice of time and place

Richard Johnson vs Oburn Buffington   Attmt.   Judgment by default

292   Freeman & Hodges vs Frederick Glover   Case contd. at Pltf. cost Ezekiel Harris entered himself security for cost in this court

John Cook vs George Tankersley   Debt   Judgment by default On a writ of inquiry the same jury...we find for the Plaintiff s 14 per hundred wieght for tobacco with interest from date of note with cost of suit

Edmond Martin vs Reubin Beckham.   Debt   Judgment by default. ...we find for the Plaintiff s 14 per Hundred weight of tobacco with interest from date of note with cost of suit....

Alexander McGregger vs David Zubley.   Debt   the same jury ...we find for the plaintiff Ł 11 s 4 d 9 with cost of suit.

127

Richard Johnson vs Watson & Stark Exrs of Michael Watson.
Debt. Roland Williams proved his attendance in this court
10 days and Edward Couch fifteen days each

Robert Stark vs George Dean Case continued Pltfs cost

William Stinson vs William Patterson Non suit

Purves Tutt & Keating vs Samuel Burgess Case contd.

Richard Johnson vs Oburn Buffington Attmt. judgment by
default writ of enquity The same Jury...we find for Richard
Johnson Ł 50 with cost of suit Joel Chandler garnishee having
come into court and confessed that he give a bond to Richd
Johnson for Ł 100 which bond he is informed is in the hands
of Oburn Buffington & that he is willing to pay it. Ordered
that Judgment be entered up agt Joel Chandler as garnishee....

294 James Harrison & wife vs John Watson. Slander Dismissed
Pltf. cost

Ann Cunningham vs Robert Melton. Case Judgment confessed
according to note Ł7 and cost of suit

James C. Murphey vs Ezekiel Harris Dismissed

Susannah Stidham vs Keating Smith Judgment by default

Fields Pardue vs Isaac Norril Case contd. at Plaintiff
cost

William Freeman & Murrey vs Frederick Glover Contd. at Pltf
cost

Elizabeth Williams vs Bowers & Ardis Case contd. at Deft.
cost

Thomas Gordon & Connel vs Philip Johnson. Debt Ordered that
a commission issue to Robert Forsyth and John Y. Noel Esqrs.
in Augusta to take the deposition of James Mearewether on
the part of the plaintif he giving 10 days previous notice
of time & place

295 Present John Purves Esq.

Peter Hillard vs Michael & Jane Oadum. Attmt The same jury
as before...we find for the Plaintiff Ł 20 with interest &
cost of suit.

Crookshands & Co. vs David Zubly. Debt continued

Robert Stark vs Thomas Cotten Trover non suit

Robert Boner vs James Martin Case Dismissed at Deft. cost

John Randal vs Lewis Clerk Assault continued

John McCoy vs Richd. Walker Discontinued at Pltfs cost

John Williams vs Charles Williams Debt Judgment by default
final judgt for Ł 40 with interest & cost

296 Peter Hillard vs Michl. Oadum & Jean Odaum Debt Frederick
Swearingen proved his attendance in this cause 18 days
Rolley Roebuck 10 days

James C. Murphey vs Ezekiel Harris. Nicholas Shaffer proved
his attendance 13 days in this cause

Thomas Boon vs Charity Mock. Benjamin Mock proved his attendance in this cause 10 days George Mock proved his attendance
15 days in the above action

Robert Stark vs Thomas Cotten Edward Couch proved his attendance in this cause 12 days

Ordered that this court be adjourned till tomorrow morning
9 O'clock. Leroy Hammond, Arthur Simkins, John Sturzeneger.

297 The court according to adjt. on Saturday 17 Oct 1789.
Present Leroy Hammond, Aquila Miles, John Sturzenegger. Esq.

David Zubly ads William Evans. Debt continued by consent

Present Arthur Simkins Esq.

Drury Pace vs Lewis Watson Attmt Richard McCary being
summoned as garnishee appeared being swron acknowledged to
owe the estate of Charles Williams dec'd 1200 weight of
tobacco

Edwd. Vann vs Thomas Ray. Case the same jury as before...we
find for the defendant.
Isaac Ray proved his attendance in this cause 16 days 26
miles & coming 5 times Joel Pardue 8 days attendance in the
same

298 Peter Chastian appeared in court as a deputy sheriff to
Barkley Martin Esq. for this county and being approved of by
the court The oath required by law were administered to him
accordingly

Thomas Boon vs Charity Mock. Dinah Sellers appeared her
attendance 12 days in this case

Drury Pace vs Lewis Watson Attmt contd.

The court proceeded to take under their consideration the
presentments of the grand jury when the following orders
were made

Ordered that the Clerk issue citations to the overseers of
the road from Charles Williams old place oposite Edgefield
Court House Also Capt. Key & Abraham Richardson surveyors
of the road from Horns Creek to Campbelton to appear at the
next court and shew cause why the roads are not in good
repair Agreeable to the presentment of the grand jury

Ordered that the tax collector furnish the sheriff with an
exact list of the taxable inhabitants in this county

299 The grand jury present as a great grievance the Duty laid on
the importation of salt by the legislation of the United
States, ordered that a copy thereof be gransmitted to the
Governor to be sent forward to the delegates of South Carolina

129

now in Congress

The grand jury present as a grievance the want of a joal in the District of Ninety Six Ordered that a copy thereof be transmitted to the Clk of the Senate & the Clk of the House of Representatives

James Carson came into court & made oath that he was unable to discharge the prison fees being committed to Joal at the instance of John Waggoner & proved also that he had given notice to the Plaintiff of this his application whereupon the court ordered he should be discharged

The State vs Moses Carter. The securities John Carter and Presley Bland came into court & renewed their recognizances for the appearance of Moses Carter at next court

Ordered that Arthur Simkins Esq. employ a person to put up temporary seats & a bar in the court house of this county

300   Ordered that this court be adjourned till second Monday in January 1790. Arthur Simkins, Aquila Miles, John Sturzenegger.

The court met according to adjournment on Monday 11th Jan 1790. Present the worshipful Hugh Middleton, Benj. Tutt, Russell Wilson, Esq.

Ordered that the Petit Jurors be drawn then the following persons were drawn

1. Nathaniel Bacon
2. Hez Gentry
3. Robert Russell
4. Robert Courtney
5. Edward Couch
6. John Stuart
7. Absolom McDaniel
8. Matt Martin
9. Peter Rambey
10. William Murphey
11. Absolum Roberts
12. Fredk. Williams
13. Ed. Pursel
14. Christian Gomillian
15. Edward Van
16. Evan Morgan
17. William Clark Senr
18. Henry Parkman
19. William Hill
20. Seth Howard
21. Jesse Jarnagin
22. David Lyles
23. Bryant Green
24. Isaac Foreman
25. Philip Shipes
26. Lileston Pardue
27. Henry Zimmerman
28. Richd. Henderson
29. John Corley Junr
30. Shadrack Henderson

301   Ordered that the sheriff return the writs of venire for the petit Jurors. The names of the Petit Jurors that appeared

1. Joseph Nunn
2. James Butler
3. Jonathan Myers
4. Henley Webb
5. David Boswell
6. Thomas Deloach
7. Michael Shaver
8. David Burks
9. William Brooks
10. Robert Speer
11. John Rivers
12. William McCartney
13. Samuel Garner
14. Ogden Cockerof
16. Joseph Trotter
17. William Reynolds
18. Stephen Tilman
19. Peter Megrew
20. Thomas Pennington
21. John Roberts
22. John Cunningham
23. William Holliday
24. Gasper Nail
25. Sherwood Corley
26. George Delaughter
27. Frances McIllrath
28. Ebnates Stephens
29. Stephen Bettis

130

15. Benjamin Darby

Edward Prince was excused as overseer of the road from the old meeting house to the Rockey Pond

The relinquishment of the right of Dower by Mrs. Elenor Cowen to a tract of land conveyed by her husband George Cowen to Jones Rivers was produced in court and ordered to be recorded

Ordered that John Myers, Jasper Nail, Isaac Ardis and Jonathan Myers or any three be appointed appraisers of the Estate of John Tobler deceased

302 Christian Tobler qualified as an executor to the last will and testament of John Tobler dec'd

The State ads Moses Carter. Daniel Rogers came into court and acknowledged himself to owe to the county Ł 25 in case he fails to attend next court as a witness in this case

Edward Holmes was excused as an overseer of that part of the road between Amos Richardson and Dry Creek and Mumford Perriman appointed in his room

George Bussey was sworn as constable for this County

On application permission was granted to William Day to keep tavern money paid securities Emery Day & John Day

On application permission was granted to Joseph Hightower securities Abraham Richardson & Charles Banks paid 30/5

On application permission was granted to Andrew Lee to keep tavern securities Henry Ware and Elijah Martin 30/ in full

On application permission was granted to Thomas Clark to keep tavern securities Samuel Garner & George Bussey 3/clk fees paid

On application permission was granted to Elijah Martin to keep tavern securities Matt Gayle James Roberson 11/14 paid in full

303 On application permission was granted to Moses Harris to keep tavern securities Henry Ware and David Boxwell 30/5 paid

On application permission was granted to John Herndon to keep tavern securities Thomas Adams and Robert Speer

On application permission was granted to Jenkin Harris to keep tavern securities Jonw. White and John Mims 30/

On application permission was granted to John Hall to keep tavern securities Jno. Herndon & Joseph Tucker

Ordered that Henry Ware be allowed his account provided it be produced which is Ł 29 d 4 for building the Court House

John Newson produced a citation citing the kindred and creditors of Luke Devoare to appear at the next court which

131

was published Ordered that the said Letters of admn. be
granted to the said John Newson and the following persons
were appointed to appraise the said Estate to wit, Abraham
Richardson, Charles Banks, Joseph Day & John Hammond; Charles
Banks & John Randal in the sum of Ŀ 250

304 Lease & release from John Arlridge to Drury Hern for 100 acres
land was acknowledged & ordered to be recorded

On application permission was granted to Joseph Burton to
keep tavern securities Joel Lipscomb and Peter McGrew

Philip Shipes was excused as an overseer of the road leading
from Augusta to the Ridge and Bibb Bush appointed in his room

The last will and testament of Samuel Howard was proved by
the oath of James Howard & Joseph Wallace

Robert Melton vs Laurence Rambo Richard Jones proved his
attendance in this action 2 days @ 2/6

Ordered that this court be adjourned till tomorrow morning 9
o'clock. Hugh Middleton, Benj. Tutt, Russell Wilson.

The Court met according to adjournment on Tuesday the 12 Jan
1790. Present the Worshipful Hugh Middleton, Benjamin Tutt,
Russell Wilson, Esq.

305 Blassengham vs Joseph Tucker. Attmt. This suit with all
matters in dispute between the parties referred to Benj. Tutt
& John Purves Esq. with power of umprage returnable to July
Court

John Wallace one of the executors of the last will and testament of Samuel Howard was qualified according to law

Joseph Duke vs McCartin Campbell & Thomas Galphin. Debt.
Judgment confessed for Ŀ 32 subject to instalments

Mrs. Elizabeth Kennady produced a citation citing the kindred
and creditors of John Kennady which was duly published
Ordered that the said letters of admn. be granted to the said
Elizabeth on her giving bond with Michael Blocker and John
Blocker in the sum of Ŀ 200 and the following persons was
appointed to appraise the Estate, to wit, Thomas Hagins, John
Oliphant, Nicholas Dillard and Lewis Youngblood. Mrs. Ken-
nady was qualified according to law

On application permission was granted to Ulyses Rogers to
keep tavern securities Peter Chastain & Henry Ware 30/
paid in full

306 Henery McMurdy vs Lewis Watson. Attmt. Ezekiel Hudnell
being summoned as garnishee made default on a siri facias
being ordered against him made a second default its ordered
that judgment be entered against him for the Ŀ 15 and cost
of suit

On application permission is granted to John Gorman to keep
a tavern securities William Abney and Thomas Spraggins

In the matter of Mcerness Minter a minor of 15 years of age

The above minor came into court and chose Peter Morgan his
guardian who being approved of by the court it is ordered
that the said Peter Morgan be appointed guardian as aforesaid to the person estate and effects of the said minor whereupon the said Peter Morgan came into court and entered into
bond for Ł 500 sterling with William Terry and Jesse Scruggs
securities jointly and severally for the due execution of
the said duty & trust

Mr. Jesse Scruggs being cited agreeable to an order of last
court he being presented by the grand jury for default was
excused as an overseer of that part of the road leading
from Turkey Creek opposite this Court HOuse & Dan Bud appointed in his room

307   Joseph Wood a minor of the age of 13 years. The said Wood
appeared in court and made choice of Samuel Scott as his
guardian who approved of by the court as the guardian of
the person and estate of the said Joseph Wood whereupon the
said Samuel Scott entered into a bond for the sum of Ł 2000
sterling with Drury Pace and William Reynolds as securities
for the due execution of the said duty & trust

Thomas Key being presented as an overseer of the road made
an excuse to the court and was excused

Ordered that Aron Herrin be appointed overseer from Horns
Creek to Mill Creek   William Watson from Mill Creek to Peter
Days Mill Creek and that all hands that was formerly under
Capt. Key above Mill Creek to work under Aron Herrin and
those below with William Watson

Capt. James Coursey was excused as an overseer of the road
from McCoys ferry that part from Turkey Creek near the
beaver dams & John McFatrick appd. in his room

308   John Coursey was excused as an overseer of Island ford road
to Augusta that part from Youngs place to Logg Creek and
John Stuart appointed in his room

Abraham Richardson was excused as an overseer of that part
of the road leading from Long Cane to Augusta that part from
Sweet Water to Pickens Ferry and the following persons were
appointed as commissioners Leroy Hammond Esqr John Handcock
& Wm. Covington

On petition of Sundry Inhabitants praying that a road be
opened from John Childs near Ninety Six the nearest and best
way to Goods ford on Stephens Creek from thence until it
intersects with the road leading from Fort Charlotte to
Charleston and also for a road from this Court House to Paces
Ferry on Savannah River and that Drury Pace, Elisha Robertson, James Harrison and John Childs view the ground for the
Ninety Six Road   Drury Mims, Nicholas Minor, Matt Martin
from this place to Paces ferry view and ground and report
next court

Capt. John Ryan was excused as an overseer of the road leading from the Island ford road to Augusta that part of road
from Hornes Creek to Chavous & Will Murphey appointed in his
room

309 William Nobles excused as an overseer of the road leading from
Andersons Ferry to Augusta that part Pinewood House to Cherokee
ponds and Drury Nipper appointed in his room

John Robert was excused as an overseer of the road from this
place to Barrentines and Jinkin Harris appointed in his room

William Howle was excused as an overseer of the road leading
from Hornes Creek to Gunnels Creek Peter Chastain appointed
in his room

McDowel & Co vs Joshua Miller. attachment. returned of
Sheriff levied on two mares ordered that the property be
sold and the money be put into the hands of the Clerk to
abide the event of the suit

George Farrar vs Thos. Bibb for 2000 Wt. Tobacco
Hickerson Barksdale being summoned as garnishee in this
cause made oath that he owed the said bill 1100 weight of
tobacco which was ordered to be condemned as the property of
the said Bibb to abide the event of the suit

Samuel Wright vs Isaac Wingate. Appeal from single magistrates Leroy Hammond Esq. Judgment of the magistrate confirmed

310 Present Leroy Hammond Esq.

George Farrar vs Thomas Bibb. Attmt. Ordered that the deposition of Hickerson Barksdale be taken in this case

Absolum Nipper Assignee of James Nipper vs Leonard Nobles &
John Herndon. Debt Judgment confessed for the balance of
the note with interest subject to instalments and subject
to any legal discounts & payments which can be proved

Edmond Boyd vs James Lyon. Debt Discount of Deft. cost

John Rainsford vs' Mathew Gayle Debt dismissed at Deft cost

Crookshanks & Speers vs David Zubley. Debt Abates by death
of the deft.

David Zubly vs William Evans. Debt abates by death of Pltf

The same vs The Same. Case same order

Ordered that a bench warrant issue agst. William Harris for
a contempt of Court & also for an assault on Capt. John Ryans
at the Court House Door on the oaths of George Metter &
Bazel Lowe

311 Thos Collins vs Benjamin Parker. Debt Dismissed at mutual
cost

Benjamin Parker vs Thomas Collins. Debt Dismissed at mutual
cost

Nathan Sims and Richard Pollard Exrs of Isaac Mitchel dec'd
adm. of Daniel Mitchel dec'd came into court and made a return upon oath respectively of all the bonds, notes, vouchers
& papers relating to Daniel Mitchel's estate ordered that the
Clerk do file the said papers

Ann Foreman, David Foreman, Isaac Foreman, Zelpha Foreman.
The children of Jacob Foreman minors. The said children
appeared in court and the court appointed Isaac Foreman guardian whereupon the said Foreman entered into bond of Ŀ 300
with Jonathan Whight and Benjamin Darby as securities

On application permission was granted to Shadrack Rozer to
keep tavern securities John Handcock and Sam Crafton fees
pd. 35/

Pickens & Co. vs John Herndon Pltf. judgment confessed according to note with stay of execution till next court

312   James Martin vs Sampson Griffin Abates by Death of Plaintiff

James Lauder vs Joel Chandler Abates by death of Plaintiff

John Saterwhite vs William Hardy   Abates by death of Deft.

John Kennady vs William Carson Continued by consent

James Jackson vs David Zubly Abates by death of Deft.

John Satterwhite vs William Hardy. Abates by death of the
Plaintiff

Peter Carnes vs Frances Little Judgment confessed for Ŀ 10
with stay of exn. 6 months

William Clack Junr vs James Coleman. Debt Ordered that a
commission issue to any three Justices in Wilkes County in
the state of Georgia to take the examination of William Clack
Junr. of the part of the deft. giving the Plaintiff ten days
notice of time and placeof such examination to be read in
evidence next court

James Martin vs Sampson Griffin. Daniel Parker proved his
attendance in this case four days @ 2/6

Ordered that this court be adjourned till tomorrow 9 o'clock.
Hugh Middleton, Benj. Tutt, Russell Wilson.

313   The court met according to adjournment on Wednesday the 13th
January 1790. Present the Worshipful. Leroy Hammond, Arthur
Simkins, Russell Wilson, Esq.

On application of Isaac Foreman ordered that the commissioners
who let a part of this building to him do view the same and
report to next court whether he has done his work according
to contract

Ordered that the Sheriff do furnish this Court House with a
lock out of the first money he has of the County before next
Court

On application of John Hammond permission was granted to him
to retail spiritous liquors, fees paid

Ordered that a dedimus issue to any two justices in the County
of Richmond Georgia to take the deposition of Thos. P. Carnes
Esq. in the cause of Nipper Assignee vs Leonard Nobles & John
Herndon he giving the legal notice of time and place

John Pursel vs John Handcock. Judgment entered by consent for Ł 24 s 2 subject ot the instalment law

314 Ordered that a siri facias issue against the securities of Robert Stark late Clerk of Edgefield County to shew cause why judgment should not go against them for the sum of Ł 20 s 19 d 8 & costs of suit

John Kennady vs Robert Bonner. Ordered that a dedimus issue to any three magistrates in the State of Georgia Richmond County to take deposition of George Hunt on the part of the plaintiff in this case giving the legal notice of time and place to the defendant

Joseph Cook vs Toliver Davis. Ordered that Leroy Hammond Esq. actual plaintiff in this suit be substituted in the room of Joseph Cook and that judgment be entered up as follows I do hereby confess judgment for the sum of Ł 40 sterling dischargeable on the delivery of 5000 pounds of merchantable tobacco at Hammonds ware house Campbelton on or before the 1st of Nov. next with stay of execution till that day and cost of suit

Charles Jenkins vs James Stuart Pltf. dismissed at Pltf cost. John Kennady proved his attendance two days and traveling 33 miles & s 1 for --- in this case

315 Present Benjamin Tutt Esqr.
Present John Purves Esqr.
Absent Leroy Hammond Esqr.

The State vs Robert Stark Clk. of Edgefield County. Judt. for illegal fees. The jury being sworn to wit, David Bowwell, Jonathan Myer, Henley Webb, Thomas Deloach, Michael Shaver, Robert Speer, William McCarty, Samuel Garner, Ogdon Cockeroff, Benj. Darby, Joseph Trotter, Joseph Nunn, who say we find the defendant guilty ordered that the verdict be recorded

Drury Mims vs Toliver Davis. Debt. Judgment confessed for Ł 28 s 11 d 8 with stay of execution until 1 Nov. next, subject be dischraged with 3500 weight of inspected tobacco if delivered at Cambels ware house by the said 1 Nov. next

Ebenezer Hill & Sarah his wife vs William Johnson. Slander referred to Elisha Roberson & Drury Pace with power of umprage to be related next court and made a judgment thereof by consent of parties

316 Ordered that this court be adjourned till tomorrow 9 o'clock Hugh Middleton,Benj. Tutt, Russell Wilson.

The Court met according to adjournment on Thursday the 14th January 1790. Present the worshipful. Hugh Middleton, Benjamin Tutt, Russell Wilson, Esqrs.

Thomas Adams vs John Walls. Pltf. dismisd. at Deft. cost stay of execution till next court

Thomas Collins vs Benjamin Parker. Pltf. Settled at mutual cost

James Munday vs James Hagwood. Pltf dismissed at Deft cost

Joseph Prince vs Benjamin Mock. Pltf. Settled at equal
cost pltf. pays 6/6 Thomas Howle proved his attendance in
this P & S four days @ 2/6

Teasdale & Co vs Richard Johnson Pltf. continued by consent

McLeavensworth vs Patrick Hays. Attmt. continued by consent

317 Samuel Wright vs John Herndon Pltf. Dismissed each party
pays his own cost

Ezekiel Harris vs David Zubly. Pltf'. Abates by death of
Deft.

John Glanton vs Morris Calliham Pltf. Dismissed at Deft.
cost

John Herndon vs Martha Talbert continued by consent

Jesse Lanier vs Frances Settle continued by consent

Mathew Duncan vs John Frederick Pltf. referred to Hartwell
Heart and John Thomas Fairchilds with power of umprage and
Robert to next court

John Buckelew vs William Robinson Pltf. continued by consent

Jacob Messer Smith vs Frederick Tilman. Pltf. Judgment according to note Ł 8 interest 1 year

Pickens & Co vs William Brooks Pltf. Dismissed at Deft.
cost

Pickens & Co vs John Herndon. Continued by consent

Ordered that the appearance dockett be called the second
time

318 Moody Burt vs Harvey & Harvey. Judt. attmt. Dismissed at
Pltf. Cost

Samuel Thornton vs Michael McCarty. Dismissed all cost paid
except the sheriffs fees

Benjamin Parker vs William Williams. Dismissed at Joseph
Dicks cost.

Benjamin Parker vs Thomas Collins. Dismd. at mutual cost

Pickens & Co. vs Thomas Lamar, R. M.   Debt judgment confessed for Ł 13 s 4 d 4 it being the balance due on the
note with interest

Charles Banks vs James Thomas. Judt. attmt. ordered in this
case

Reubin Beckum vs Robert Williams. Attmt. Dismissed at
Pltf. cost

Thomas Smith assnee vs Joseph Lewis. Attmt Ordered that
a sufficient quantity of the property attached be sold to
satisfy the Plaintiffs demands with three weeks, unless

137

sufficient security be given to the Sheriff to secure the plaintiffs debt & cost which security shall be approved of by the sheriff provided also that the said Lewis or any person for him give security for the said debt agreeable to the instalment law as the note is subject to instalments

319 The State agt. Robert Stark Esq. Extortion at the instance of William Dobey & Richardson Bartlett, It is ordered that judgment be given for Ƚ 10 s 17 sterling being three times that amount of the Extorted fees in the inditment and cost of the prosecution

Joshua Thorn & wife vs Allen Hinton. Referred to Abram Richardson & Charles Rhodes with power of umpirage and their award to be a rule of this court

M. C. Leavesnworth vs Patrick Hayes. Attmt. Ordered that two dedimus issue directed to any three Justices in Richmond County State of Georgia to take the examination of Nathan Hill --- Barkley -- Exum & to any three Justices in Chatham to take the examination of James Merilus in the above action on the part of the Plaintiff giving 15 days notice of time and place of such examination Witnesses to be sworn of this voir doir

320 The State ads Tobt. Stark late C. E. C. Illegal fees. On motion of Charles Goodwin Esq. on behalf of Suckey Coody Widow who presecuted as well on the part of the County as of herself and on hearing evidence Ordered that judgment be entered up for s 24 being 4 times the amount of the exhorted fees one moity to the County and the other to the widow Cody

Thomas Smith ads Joseph Lewis. Attmt. ordered that a dedimus issue to any two justices in Liberty County in the State of Georgia to take the deposition of Thomas Sheppard, giving the Defendant 15 days notice of time & place

Joshua Thorn vs Allen Hinton. James Martin produced his attendance in this case 8 days @ 2/6 and John Currey 11 days @ 2/6

On application of Mr. John Blocker ordered that letters of admn. be granted the estate of John Lofton to him on his giving bond in the sum of Ƚ 150 with Henry Ware & Solomon Bird securities & the following persons were appd. appraisers to the said estate viz. Thos Hagins, N. Dillard, Lewis Youngblood & John Oliphant. John Blocker sworn as adm. accd. to law

321 Thomas Dozer was sworn in open court as a constable for this county

Ordered that Henry Ware undertaker of this receive Ƚ 5 of the first Money that comes to the Clerks hand for tavern license and the abllance of his account by paid him notes of hand due for estrays Ordered that the clerk pay Mr. H. Ware s 20 for a table in this house out of the money rec'd for tavern lisence

Ordered that this court be adjourned until the second Monday in April next. Hugh Middleton, Benj. Tutt, Russell Wilson.

The court met according to adjournment on Monday the 12th of
April 1790. Present the worshipful Arthur Simkins, Hugh
Middleton, Aquila Miles, John Sturzenegger, Esq.

322 Ordered that the grand jury be drawn to serve October term
when the following persons were drawn

1. James Anderson	11. Solomon Pope
2. Samuel Walker	12. George Cowan
3. Drury Mims	13. Richard Johnson
4. Robert Samuel	14. John Gorman
5. James Brooks	15. John Handcock
6. Right Nicholson	16. Thomas Galphin
7. George Martin	17. Robert Lamar
8. William Abney	18. Thomas Anderson
9. Philip Lamar	19. Caleb Holloway
10. Arthur Watson	20. Morrice Guin

Ordered that Petit Jurors be drawn to serve at July Term
next when the following persons were drawn accordingly.

1. William Howle Junr.	16. Thomas Freeman
2. James Heart	17. William Bolton
3. Samuel Mays	18. Reubin Holloway
4. Alxr. Oden	19. John Adams
5. John Clackler Junr.	20. John Wallace
6. James Henderson	21. Robert Lowe
7. James Buckelew	22. Mathew Barrott
8. William Cockran	23. John Jackson
9. Joseph Collier	24. James Martin
10. William Carson	25. George Miller
11. Nicholas Minors	26. Thomas Butler
12. David Thomson	27. William Dean
13. George Abney	28. Joseph Hightower
14. Edward Bussey	29. John Herndon
15. John Savage	30. Josiah Stephens

(N. B. There is no page numbered 323)

324 The papers relating to the estate of Charity Anderson were
produced to the court by John Watson adm. which papers con-
tain an account of receipts and payments made by the said
admr. ordered that they be received and filed in clerks office

Mathew Duncan vs John Frederick. referred to Hartwell Hart
& John Thomas Fairchilds who returned their award into court
which is hereby made the judgment of this court

Ordered that the Sheriff return the writ of venire for the
grand Jurors, when the following persons appeared

John Lowe, foreman	Jacob Smith
Nathl. Howel	Lud Williams
Thomas Key	William Glover
William Spraggins	John Childs
Caleb Holloway	William Childs
Robert Lang	Samuel Burges
James McMillian	Isham Green
Thomas Mauberry	William Butler
Jones Rivers	John Myer
William Longmire	

William Shinholster having resigned his guardianship obtained
in July term   On application of Abraham Ardis Ordered that

the said Abraham Ardis be appointed guardian to William Shinholster Junr. on his giving bond in the sum of Ł 100 with
Isaac Ardis and Jacob Zinn securities, and that said Abraham
be improved to take into his possession the person and estate
of said William Shinholster Junr. which bond was accordingly
given

On application of Mary Green widow to Isham Green deceased
ordered that letters of admn. be granted to her on her giving bond in the sum of Ł 600 with John Moore Esq. and James
McMillian securities which was accordingly done and she qualified according to law

Ordered that the Sheriff return the writ of venire for the
Petit Jurors, when the following persons appeared
  1. Nathanel Bacon   14. Henry Zimmerman
  2. Hezekiah Gentry   15. Richard Henderson
  3. Edward Couch   16. John Stuart
  4. Matt Martin   17. Christian Gomillian
  5. Frederick Williams   18. William Murphey
  6. Edmond Pursell   19. Robert Russell
  7. William Clark   20. Absolom Roberts
  8. Henry Parkman   21. Edward Vann
  9. William Hill   22. David Lyles
 10. Seth Howard   23. John Caroley (Corley?)
 11. Jesse Jernagen   24. Shadrack Henderson
 12. Isaac Foreman   25. Evan Morgan
 13. Philip Shipes

326 On petition of sundry inhabitants ordered that John Stuart,
     Thomas McGinnis, John Blocker, John Hill and Henery Zimmer-
     man view the ground from John Hills mill on Mountain Creek
     the nearest and best way to Harlins old place on Turkey
     Creek from thence running aptd. creek to a ford just below
     McGinnis and from thence to the Island ford road where Mc-
     Ginnis path intersects near John Simkins & report to court
     house

     Lydia Leech an infant above the age of 14 years came into
     court and made choice of Thomas McGinnis and John Blocker as
     her guardians who are hereby appointed on their giving bond
     and security as the law directs, whereupon John Stuart and
     John Hill came into court and agreed to be their securities
     in the sum of Ł 200 and were approved of by the court

     James McDonald being appointed constable appeared and took
     the oath accordingly

     Dennett Abney and James Tonlin were both qualified as con-
     stables for this county

     On application of Robert Gillam & with the consent of Amos
     Mitchel Ordered that letters of admn. be granted to the said
     Robert Gillam on his giving bond in the sum of Ł 500

327 On the estate of Daniel Mitchel deceased not administered
     upon, Hugh Middleton & John Moore esq. were securities for
     the said admn. qualified according to law

     On application permission was granted to Enock Grigsby to
     keep tavern securities Barkley Martin and John Ryan fees
     paid

The State vs John Ryan. Judmt. Assault the Deft. came into court and pleads guilty

On application of Mr. Samuel Mays for letters of admn. on the estate of George Mee ordered that the said letters be granted to him on his giving bond in the sum of Ƚ 200 with William Anderson and William Hill as securities.

Ordered that this court be adjourned till tomorrow 9 o'clock Arthur Simkins, Hugh Middleton, John Sturzenegger.

The court met according to adjournment on Tuesday 13th April 1790. Present the worshipful Arthur Simkins, Hugh Middleton, John Moore, Esquires.

328 Ordered that the grand jurors be impannelled & sowrn which was accordingly done and Mr. John Lowe appointed foreman, received their charge and return to their room

Leroy Hammond Esq. ads George Cowan. Jeremiah Roberts came into court and acknowledged himself special bail in discharge of the common bail

Ordered that William Green, Toliver Bostick, Thomas Edwards and Joel Lipscomb or any three of them do appraise the estate of Isham Green deceased

On application of Capt. George Cowan, ordered that Jones Rivers be overseer of the road from Martins meeting house to Wares ford on Stevens Creek

On motion of Sarah Cockran stating that her husband Benjamin Cockran made a will of the 28th August last which will or testament, James Gray was a subscribing witness, that the said Gray hath been applied to and will not attend court to prove the aforesaid will, whereupon it is ordered that Hugh Middleton Esq. oblige the said James Gray by attachment or other legal means to come before him and give such evidence as he may be able respecting the execution of the said will by Benj. Cockran and return the testimentary so taken to the next court.

329 Henery McMurdy agt. Ezekiel Hudnel. By consent of both parties the execution issued in this cause is suspended until the first day of June next & then a new execution to Issue

Robert Mosely vs John Rainsford. Ordered that David Burke be allowed for his attendance as a witness for Mosely to be paid by the said Rainsford on the said Burks proving his attendance according to law and the said Rainsford be allowed only for the attendance of three witnesses the term the said suit was continued at the said Moseleys cost

James Frazier vs Joseph Cook. Dismissed at Pltf. cost

James Hargrove vs M. M. Reynolds. dismissed at Deft. cost

Burges White vs James Coursey & Jas. Lyon. Settled at the Deft cost

Jesse Lott assignee vs Bullock & Elisha Brooks. By consent of parties ordered that this suit be referred to John Fairchilds & John Moore Esq. with power of umpirage their award to be returned to me next court & to be the judgment thereof

330 LeRoy Hammond ads Randal Griffin & Geo. Dooly. Dismissed at Deft. cost

Charles Goodwin vs George Dooly. Same order

LeRoy Hammond vs George Dooly. Same order

The State vs William Nichols. Judt. for assault on a constable True Bill, John Lowe, foreman

Ordered that a capias issue to take Wm. Nichols.

The State vs Christian Gomelian. Inditet. for tavern keeping without a license. Pleads not guilty and traverses to next court

The State vs William Harris & James Harris. Inditement assault. True bill. John Lowe, foreman

Andrew Pickens & Co. vs Jonathan Myers. Judgment confessed for the sum due on the note with interest subject to the instalment law with stay of execution six months

The Same vs Thos. Lamar, H. Creek. Judgment confessed for the sum due on the note with interest subject to the instalment law with stay of execution 6 months.

James Sheppard entered himself as security for cost in the interpleader of George Pearson on the attachment Abner Hammond against William Bellamy.

331 The State vs Moses Carter No bill John Lowe, foreman

George Tankersley vs John McCoy. Ordered that a dedimus issue John, Wm. Gilber & David Creswill or any two of them to take deposition of Oliver Jeter in the above cause giving the plaintiff 10 days notice of time and place

Ordered that the last will and testament of Henry Key deceased be admitted to the record the same having been legally proved before John Purves Esquire in the year 1777 by the subscribing witness to the said will.

Hugh Middleton vs Amos Mitchel. Pltf. Judgment confessed for Ł 4 s 1 d 4 with stay of execution one month

The State vs Christian Gomillian. Indt. for keeping tavern without license Thomas,Fredk. Swearingen came into court and ackd. themselves to the County;Christian Gomillian Ł 50 Thos & Fredk. Swearingen Ł 25 each for the appearance of the said Gomilian at the next court & to abide the order of the court   his
                                  Christian X Gomillian
                                          mark
                                  Thos Swearingen
                                  Fredk. Swearingen

332 William Clack Senr vs James Coleman. continued by consent and that the deposition of George Dooly be taken by consent the parties being present to cross examine him

William Key ads Will Huggins. from the judgment of John Moore
Esq. a single magistrate of this county judgment reversed
with cost

John Haregrove ads William Brown. Pltf. dismissed at Conrade
Galman cost by consent of said Galman

Joseph Bryant vs George Heart. Attmt. Ordered that the
property attached be sold and that the money be lodged in
the hands of the Clerk to abide the event of suit

William Key vs William Huggins. Appeal Joseph Tucker and
James Coursey proved their attendance in this case two days
each @ 2/6

Thomas Conel & Co. vs Philip Johnson. Judgment confessed
for Ł 14 s 18 d 11 with stay of execution 6 months waving
all benefits of the instalment law

Ordered that the lands of Robert Garrett dec'd be sold agreeable to his will on the second Thursday in May next at the
house of Jones Rivers in four equal division, the terms of
the sale to be Ł 3 cash payed at the day of sale for each
division and the rest of the purchase money to be paid, ½ at
the next Christmas and the other ½ at the Christmas after
bond and approved security be taken by said Jones Rivers who
is impowered together with his wife Mary Rivers executrix
to the last will of the deceased be made titles to the purchasers

333 Ordered that a lycence be granted to Thomas Butler to retail
spirituous liquors William Butler & Edmond Martin agree to
be his securites   fees paid

Thomas Handcock sworn constable for this County

Robert Flore vs Hugh Middleton Dismissed at Plaintiff cost

Ordered that the court be adjourned till tomorrow morning
9 o'clock. Arthur Simkins, Hugh Middleton, Aquila Miles.

The Court met according to adjournment the 14th of April
1790. Present the Worshipful Arthur Simkins, Russell Wilson,
Aquila Miles, John Swearingen, Esqs.

334 West Cook came into court and acknowledged his lease and release to Peter Carnes for ¼ acres lott No. 4 Campbelton
which was ordered to be recorded

John Hammond vs Leonard Marbury. Ordered that a commission
do issue to William Freeman and Dalziel Hunter Esq. of Richmond County to take the examination of Horatio Marbury and
George Hull to be read in evidence in this cause

Ordered that Arthur Simkins Esq. be and is hereby appointed
Treasurer for this county and that he given bond with approved security in the sum of Ł 1000 for the faithful discharge of the said trust, and that he keep fare and proper
receipts and expenditures of the County Money and of all
fines levied and tavern licenses accounts of strays and all
accounts in specialties owing to the County & that he render
an account upon oath to the said justices ever thereunto
required

143

Ordered that the Clerk of the County and others having any
money or other specialties in their hands immediately pay
and deliver the same into the hands of the said treasurer

335 Ordered that all monies hereafter to be collected by the
Sheriff or other officers for the use of the County be immediately paid into the hands of the Treasurer and that all
bonds or notes for money made payable to the Justices of the
County be immediately put into his hands and that the
treasurer be allowed 4 pr. cent on all monies by him paid
away by order of the said court

The last will and testament of David Zubly deceased was proved
by the oaths of John Sturzennegger and Ann Zubly which was
ordered to be recorded Ordered that John Myer, Jonathn.
Myer, Lud Williams, and Samuel Burges do appraise the estate
of the said deceased. Mrs. Ann Zubly qualified as Executrix
according to law.

The last will and testament of Thomas Kirkland deceased was
proved by the oaths of Arthur & Abner Watson & ordered to be
recorded and that Arthur Watson, James Harrison, Samuel Satcher & Hez. Watson do appraise the estate of said deceased.
Mrs. Lucy Kirkland was qualified according to law as exr.

The commissioners John Gray, Edward Mitchel and John Cheney
who let a part of this House to Isaac Foreman having returned
that the work was done accd. to contract were discharged
from this office

336 George Pearson vs Abner Hammond Trover on an interpleader a
Jury being impannelled & sworn (viz) Isaac Foreman, Hezekiah
Gentry, Edward Couch, Matt Martin, Frederick Williams, Ed-
mond Pursell, William Clark Senr., Jesse Jernigan, Philip
Shipes, Henry Timmerman, Richard Henderson, Seth Howard...
agree the the negro cook that is now in dispute is the right
of Mr. George Pearson and also that the cost fall on Mr.
Hammond.   Isaac Foreman, foreman

Ordered that Rowland Williams, Jacob Odom, Arthur Watson &
Hezekiah Watson or any three of them do appraise the estate
of George Mee deceased.

Leroy Hammond Esq. vs Isaac Luker. I do hereby confess
judgment for the sum of Ł 15 s 16 d 6 sterling with interest
from 1 Jan 1786 and cost of suit with stay of execution
3 months

Edward Keating vs George Cowan. Attmt. The defendant came
into court and confessed judgment for the sum of Ł 53 with
interest from this day payable in equal payments in one two
& three years from this date the plaintiff to pay the cost
of suit to this time

337 The State agt. JohnTurner Inditment No prosecution appearing, its ordered that the said Turner be discharged

Alex McGregger vs David Zubly. Fifi facias in debt, ordered
that the Exon. in this case issued be set aside with costs

On motion of the County attorney to have Robert McCombs constable removed from his office, tis ordered that the said
Robert McCombs be removed from his said office for misbehav-

ior and mal practices in his office accordingly

The State vs James Harris.   Inditement for an assault John
Carter & Benjamin Darby ackd. themselves bound to the County
Court of Edgefield in the sum of Ł 25 each and the said James
Harris in the sum of Ł 50 to be levied on their several goods
& chattels: Provided that the said James Harris does not ap-
pear at the next court to answer the said bill of inditement

Charles Banks agt. James Thomas.   Juditial attmt.   On a
writ of enquity the same Jury as before do say we find for
the Plaintiff Ł 18 sterling & cost of suit

338   On motion of the County attorney it is ordered that he do
apply to the Treasurers of the State for the Bond of Robert
Stark Esqr. & His securities for his good and faithful discharge of his late office of Clerk of this County and this
Court do thereby authorise and empower the County Attorney
to receive the same and give such receipt therefore as may
be necessary.   and it is further ordered that the County
Attorney do put the same in suit for the purpose of making
satisfaction to those persons who have been aggreived by the
late Clerks conduct

The State vs John Ryan.   Inditement for an assault the defendant came into court and pleads guilty whereupon the court
fined him s 1 ordered that he be dischraged on payment of
costs

Lud Williams vs James Sheppard   Continued by consent

339   John Kennedy vs William Carson   Continued by consent

Whereas the legislature in the year 1784 passed an act that
the road leading from the Island Saluda to the Cherokee Ponds
between Turkey and the said ponds be altered by leaving the
other road near Turkey Creek and running by the plantation
of Arthur Simkins and from thence to the plantation of John
Frazier from thence the nearest way to Marshals old place
from thence to the nearest way to Marshals old place thence
to Leonard Nobles old place near the Head of Cheveres Creek
from thence to James Jernagins old place on said creek and
from thence intersecting the said road leading from the
Island Ford of Saluda to Augusta at Davis's grave It is ordered that Samuel Walker, Nathan Whight, Bazel Lowe, Ulyses
Rogers and John Ryan be appointed to view the ground for the
said road and to report thereon at the next court preparatory
to its being laid off

Benj. Tutt vs James Sheppard.   discontinued at mutual cost

Ordered that this court be adjourned till tomorrow morning
9 o'clock.   Arthur Simkins, Aquila Miles, John Sturzenegger.

340   The court met according to adjournment on Thursday the 15th
of April 1790.   Present the worshipful Arthur Simkins, Aquila Mils, John Sturzenegger.

The court proceeded to call over the appearance dockett the
second and last time in order that issues be made up and
stand ready for trial at the next court whereupon the following orders were made

Charles Martin vs John Allen. contd.

Same vs Same   Contd.

Wm. Moseley vs John Herndon   Contd.

Leroy Hammond vs George Cowan   Contd.

Joel Thacker vs Kenedy & McMurdy.   Contd.

William Stafford vs Edwards & Co.   contd.

Leroy Hammond vs James King   Contd.

Leroy Hammond vs Alexn. Oden.   Deft. at Pltfs cost

Same vs Isaac LUker. Judt confd.

Leroy Hammond Junr. vs Lott & Jernigan.   Contd.

Joseph Butler vs Alexn. Downer   Contd.

Thomas Taylor vs William Terry.   Contd.

341   Matt Gayle vs Jno. P. Wagnon   Settled deft. cost

Conel & Co. vs Richd. Johnson   Contd.

John Barton vs Jno. Cureton   Contd.

James Tutt vs Jinkin Harris   Contd.

Richardson Bartlett vs John Cheney.   contd.

William Jeter Junr. vs Joel Chandler   contd.

Pickens & Co. vs Richd. Johnson   contd.

Jno. Hammond vs Isaac Lewis & Securities of Stark.   Contd.

Solomon Bird & Co. vs John Purves.   Contd.

James Johnson vs Leonard Marbury   Attmt   default.

Wm. Mathews assignee vs Ulysses Rogers   contd.

Martha Talbert vs John McCoy.   Contd.

P. Carnes came into court as Garnishee and made oath in
what sum he was indebted to Leonard Marbury as will appear
by his deposition filed in the Clerks office of this County

John Hammond atty in fact for Mary Taggert. vs Leonard
Marbury. Attmt. Judgment by default. Peter Carnes came
into court as garnishee and made oath in what sum he was indebted to Leonard Marbury as will appear by his dispostion
filed in the Clerks Office of this County

342   John Hammond vs Leonard Marbury. Attmt. Judgment by default
Peter Carnes Esq. came into court as garnishee and made oath
in what sum he was indebted to Leonard Marbury as will by
his deposition filed in the Clerks office of this county

M. C. Leavensworth vs Patrick Hays. Attmt. Continued by
consent

Joseph Bryant vs George Heart. Attmt. Judgment by default

Alexn. Oden vs Charles Franklin Attmt. Edmond Franklin
being summoned as garnishee came into court and on his oath
it appears that there is Ł 6 in his hands which was to await
the event of suit

Benjamin Tutt vs George Tankersley. Attmt. contd.

Abraham Richardson vs Richard Call. Judgment by default.

M. C. Leavensworth vs Patrick Hays. Attmt. Ordered that a
dedimus issue to Dalziel Hunter, William Freeman, and Godfrey Zimmerman or any two of them to take the deposition of
Nathan Hills, William Evans & Littleberry Stone giving 10
days notice of time & place to the defendant

343 Benjamin Tutt vs Alexander Oden. Discontinued at Defendants
cost and charges

Fields Pardue & Co vs Isaac Norrel. Case Judgment confessed
for Ł 10 s 14 d 9 with interest from 1 Jany 1785 subject to
the instalment law and stay of execution 2 months

John Waistcoat vs Robert Stark. Debt Abates by death of
plaintiff

The State vs William & James Harris. Ind. for an assault
William Harris came into court and ackd. himself to owe the
County of Edgefield in the sum of Ł100 and John Harris,
Jinkin Harris in the sum of Ł 50 each to be levied on their
several lands, tenements, goods and chattles to be void on
condition that said William Harris shall appear in his proper person at the next court to answer the above inditment

John Herndon assignee of Thos. Beckum vs Martha Talbert.
The parties by their attys. and after debating the case tis
ordered that judgment be entered for the plaintiff for the
sum of Ł 6 s 6 d 8 with interest from the 1st January 1786
subject to instalment law

344 Lyon Henery vs Vincent Powel. Attachment ordered that a
dedimus issue to the state of Georgia Burk County directed
to William Little and -- Bradgley Esqrs. to take the deposition of John Gross, Thomas Lewis and Bole Right on the
part and behalf of the dft. he giving the plaintiff 10 days
notice of time and place

Isaac Teasdale & Co. vs Richard Johnson. Plaintiff Judgment
for Ł 3 s 5 d 6 with interest from 7th February 1787 & cost
of suit

Ordered that the Treasurer of the county do pay unto LeRoy
Hammond Esq. all such debts as may be due to him by an assignment of Isaac Foreman for undertaking & building part of the
Court House out of the monies that he may receive for the
use of the County.

Wm. Freeman & Murrey vs Frederick Glover. Case referred to
William Moore and James Gowdy with power of umpirage their

award to be returned to the next court and made the judgment thereof

William Freeman & Hodgens vs Frederick Glover. Case ordered that this cause be referred to Wm. Moore & James Gowdy with trover óf umpirage their award to be returned to the next court and be made the judgment thereof

345 The presentments of the Grand Jury were taken under consideration when the following orders were made thereon

1st & 2nd Ordered that the overseers be cited to appear at the next court and shew cause why an inditement should not be preferred agt. them

3rd Ordered that a certified copy of this present. be transmitted by the clerk to the comissioner of location of this District and that another order be transmitted to his excellency the Governor

4th Ordered that a citation issue to the Commissioners to shew causey why they have not carried the law into effect

5th. Ordered that a capias issue against Charles Jinkins to compel his appearance at the next court

George Farrar vs Thomas Bibb. Attmt. on writ of enquiry The verdict of the same Jury as before say that Thos. Bibb pay ℔ 12 with interest & cost.

John Hammond vs Leonard Marbury. Attmt. on writ of inquiry The same jury...Leonard Marbury do pay to John Hammond ℔ 126 s 19 d 2 with interest & cost of suit

346 John Hammond vs Leonard Marbury. Att. on a writ of inquiry The same jury...we find for the Plaintiff ℔ 48 s 6 d 4 sterling with interest from 1 July 1779 & cost of suit.

Jacob Messer Smith ads Isaac Hill. Trover John Hill proved his attendance on the part of the Plaintiff 8 days in this cause @ 2/6

Solomon Edwards vs Hugh Carson. Frederick Williams proved his attendance 4 days in this case

Seth Howard vs Frances Little. William Tarrence proved his attendance 6 days as a witness in this cause

Ordered that the court be adjourned till the second Monday in July next   Arthur Simkins
                                                Aquila Miles
                                                John Sturzenegger

END OF VOLUME

148

1   The Court met according to adjournment on the 10th of Oct
1794. Present the Hon. Arthur Simkins and Thomas Bacon,
Esquires.

Ordered that the Grand Jurors be drawn to serve next March
term when the following persons were accordingly drawn Viz:

1.	Edmund Martin	11.	Haley Johnson
2.	Seth Howard	12.	Edward Mitchel
3.	Solomon Pope	13.	Samuel Savage
4.	James Haregrove	14.	William Simkins
5.	Keland Smith	15.	John Lucas
6.	George Ken	16.	Walter Taylor
7.	William Shinholster	17.	John Griffiths, Sr.
8.	William Boaroam	18.	Andrew Lee
9.	Abner Perrin	19.	Lewis Tillman
10.	Thomas Galphin	20.	Joseph Dawson

Ordered that the Petit Jurors be drawn to serve next March
term when the following persons were drawn:

1.	James Whitehead	16.	Right Nicholson
2.	Mordacae McKinney	17.	Lewis Clark
3.	Thomas Warren	18.	Rd. Cawley
4.	David Meyer	19.	Drury Adams
5.	John Cawley Junr.	20.	Joseph Cunningham
6.	Thomas Butler	21.	Robert Allen
7.	John Vardell	22.	Thomas Scott
8.	John Shiveley	23.	John Mobley, Sr.
9.	Mark Nobles	24.	Benjamin Dosby
10.	Samuel Abney	25.	Robert Melton
11.	Nathan Melton	26.	Edward Holmes
12.	David Bazemore	27.	John Elam
13.	Aaron Ethridge	28.	Wm. Green
14.	Abner Cawley	29.	John Finley
15.	John Ethridge	30.	Thos Murrah

2   Ordered that the Sheriff return the Writ Vinire for Grand
Jury which was read and the following persons appeared
to wit:

1.	James Cobbs Junr.	8.	George Martin
2.	James Courrey	9.	David Boswell
3.	Daniel Barksdale	10.	John Savage
4.	Jonathan Meyer	11.	Drury Mathews
5.	John T. Lowe	12.	John McFatrick
6.	John Cheney	13.	William Jeter Jr.
7.	William Key	14.	Robert Long

Who were sworn and rec'd their charge and returned to their
room

George B. Moore vs Daniel Varksdale. Judgment confessed for
Ł 7 starling d 7 with interest and to November.

Absent the Hon. Thos Bacon, Esq.

Duncan Campbell vs Alex Edmunds Plffs. Judgment confessed
for Ł 7 13 with interest added to note stay Execution till
25th Dec next

Present the Hon. Wm. Anderson, Esq.

Duncan Campbell vs George Moseley. Plffs. Judgment confessed
for Ł 4 s 10 interest from this day till 25th dec next Execution to stay till then

Duncan Campbell vs Edmund Whatley Plffs. Judgment confessed for 17 & d 8 with interest from this day till 25th dec. next Execution to stay till then

3   Richard Gant, Esq. produced his admission as an attorney at law, Ordered that his name be enrolled as an attorney of this court.

James Adams resigned his office as Constable which was re'cd

On the appearance dockett being called

John Hill vs Mark Nobles. Slander Dismissed at Petit Costs

Vashte Vann vs John Mitchel Case. Dismissed at Deft. cost

David Moore vs Henry Parkman. Case Dismissed at Deft cost

Issue Docket

Duncan Campbell vs Joseph Barksdale Debt. Judgment confessed according to note stay Exon till the 25th Dec next

McCallum & Gardner vs Samuel Willison. Plffs. Judgment confeseed for Ƚ 6 s 2 d 2 stay exon till six months

Samuel Willison vs John Cheney. Debt. Judgment Confessed for Ƚ 25 with interest according to Note stay Levy 12 months

Duncan Campbell & Co. vs William Fudge. Judgment confessed agree to specialty stay Exon till the 25th Dec next

4   Ordered that this Court be adjourned till tomorrow 10 o'clock Arthur Simkins, W. Anderson, Thos Bacon.

The Court met according to adjournment 11th Oct 1794 Present the Hon. Arthur Simkins, William Anderson & Thomas Bacon, Esquires.

On application of Jacob Hebbler permission was granted to him to keep tavern securities John Hill & Joseph Tucker.

Ordered that the Sheriff return the writ of Vinire for the Petit Jury

The State vs John Mallett & Jesse Lott. Recognizance Stand over on Arnold Berry's producing an account against the estate of Henry Boalting, Dec'd for boarding and cloathing the children of the said Decd. the court allowed him Ƚ 5 a year for each.

Samuel Carter came into court and was qualified as constable for this county

On application of James Walker for letters of admn. on the estate of Joseph Walker Ordered that the same be granted him on his entering into bond in the sum of Ƚ 50 with William Harden and John Day as his security bond executed

5   James Walker quallified and the following persons or any three of them do appraise the said estate To wit: Robert Samuel, Phill May & Phil May Jr. & William Griffin.

an inventory of the estate of William Williams was retd. by
Robt Owen, Wms. Adm. & ordered to be recorded.

An inventory of the estate of Mathew Burt was returned by
Frank Burt one of the Exors and ordered to be recorded

The Grand Jurors returned the following bills.

The State vs Joseph Burcham.   Ind   Petit Larceny   True Bill,
James Cobbs Jr., foreman

The State vs Mathew Brazeel Ind. Assaulting constable in
Exor. of his office. No bill; James Cobb Jr., foreman

Francis Burt adm. of Moody Burt, decd. returned an account
of sales of the crop of the said estate on oath Ordered to
be recorded

On the Newmarkett road that part leading from Gunnels Creek
to Horse Ordered that Timothy Cooper to be over in the room
of Danl Macus Exd.

6   The State vs John Reynolds. John Reynolds came into Court
and acknowledged to owe the State Ł 25 to be made and --- of
his goods and chattles, lands & tenements provided he fail
to appear to this court to answer to all such matters and
things as shall be prefered against him and shall not depart
without leave of the court, then this recognizance to be void
Fielding Reynolds acknowledged himself as security in the
above   his
                              John N Reynolds
                                   mark
                              Fielding Ryenolds

The State vs. James Cheney & John Cheney Jr.   Ind.   Assault
& Battery. James Cobbs Jr., Foreman.

The State vs George Cheney, James Cheney, John Cheney Jr.
Ind. Assault & Battery. True Bill, James Cobbs Jr., foreman

Henry Manley vs Barkly Martin Debt. Judgment confessed for
Ł 25 and d 5 with interest from 6 June 1793 with stay Exon
till first of August next

Ordered that David Sandige be overseer of the road Campbell
to the Augusta Road in the room of Barkley Martin excused

7   On the Charleston Road leading from Cambridge that part from
Burton's old place to Amos Richardson, ordered that Young
Allen be overseer in the room of John Pool excused.

Assa Wade a Minor came into Court being of full age to choose
his guardian made choice of David Boswell which choice was
approved of, Ordered that the said D. Boswell give bond in
the sum of Ł 50 with R. Johnson Jr. and Jerimiah Hatcher
as his securities which was done.

Ordered that the person and Estate of the said Assa Wade be
in the hands & possession of the said David Boswell.

Davis Moore vs Philip Johnson Plffs. Durn for the Plff.
for Ł 5 s 10 and costs of suit

On Martin Road from this place to Coody's old mill, Ordered
that Britton Mims be overseer in the room of Lewis Tillman,
excused, and that Richard Christmass be overseer of the same
road from Coody old Mill to Mat Martins.

Ordered that this court be adjourned till Monday 10 O'clock.
Arthur Simkins, W. Anderson.

The Court met according to adjournment on the 13th of Oct.
1794. Present the Hon. Arthur Simkins & William Anderson,
Esquires.

8   The last will and testament of William Strother was proved
by the oaths of David Pets and Henry King Esq. Joycey
Strother qualified as Ex. of the said Ind. will and John
Strother & Solomon Pope was quallified as executors and the
following persons or any three of them to appraise the said
estate. To wit: Amos Richardson, Wright Nicholson, Lodwick
Hill & Bartlet Bledsoe.

An Inventory of the estate of Stephen Glover was recd and
ordered to be recorded. Ordered that all the personal estate of Stephen Glover be sold at the Rev. Charles Bussby's
house on the first Thursday in November next on a credit of
12 months the purchasers to give bond and security.

On application for Hezekiah Gentry for letters of admn. on
Pleasant Burnetts estate, Ordered that the same be granted
on his entering into bond in the sum of Ł 100 with Daniel
Bullock and Dennett Abney as his surities which was done
and that Hezekaih Gentry quallified as adm. and the following
persons or any three of them to appraise the said estate
To wit: Ejah Weatherington, James Nichols, Valentine Cawley,
& Anthony Leach.

The State vs Lidia Parker. Lydia Parker and Rice Swearingen
came into court and acknowledged themselves to owe the state
this is to say the sd. Lydia in the sum of Ł 25 and the said
Rice in the sum of Ł 12 s 10 to be made and levied of their
several goods and chattels lands & tenements provided

9   the said Lydia shall fail to appear to this court and shall
not depart without leave of court till she is discharged by
the court as a witness on the part of the state against
George Randle. Witness our hands and seals.

her
Lydia+ Parker
mark

his
Rice W Sweaingen
mark

Miss Mary Bowers a daughter of Benjamin Bowerscame into court
being of age to choose her guardian, made choice of Isaac
Ardis which choice was approved. Ordered that the said
Ardis give bond in the sum of Ł 200 for the faithful discharge
of his trust which was done.
Also the court appointed Isaac Ardis as guardian to Nancy
Bowers and ordered that he give security in the sum of Ł 200
and then the court adjourned untill 10 o'clock tomorrow
morning. Arthur Simkins, W. Anderson.

152

The court met according to adjournment on the 14th of October 1794. Present the Honbl. Arthur Simkins, William Anderson, Thomas Bacon, Esquires.

10 An inventory of the Estate of John Bedingfield was returned by Cradock Burnell Adm. of said estate was received and ordered to be recorded

The last will and testament of John Williams (S.D.) deces'd was proved in open court by the oath of John Hamilton and ordered to be recorded. Wm. Caldwell and Joseph Williams were qualified as Exors and the following persons or any three of them to appraise the said estate. To wit: John Bullock, Wm. Robinson, Leonard Walter & Nathan Lesscomb.

Paul Abney admr. of John Hamilton returned an acct. against the said estate on oath which approved of by the court. Ordered that all bills of Indictment & papers relating thereto traversed to the present court and all recognizances returnable to this court be continued over until the next court and that in cases where the parties & witnesses have not attended or been bound over that the clerk issue copies for their appearance at next court

John Steele asigne vs William Vann. Plffs. William Vann came into court and confessed Judgment for 5 guineas with interest according to note.

11 Ordered that all the personal estate of John Bedingfield which was this day returned be sold at the house of Alexander Downer on first Monday in Nov. next on a credit of seven months the purchasers to give bond and security

Duncan Campbell & Co. vs Winfrey Whitlock. Plffs. Judgment confessed for ₺ 4 seven-fifths with costs of suit stay ex. 25th Dec. next

Duncan Campbell & Co. vs Michael Blocker. Judgment confessed for ₺ 3 s 11 d 7 with costs of suit. Stay 25th Dec next

Duncan Campbell vs John Carter. Att. Nathan White garnishee in this case confessed judgment for ₺ 19 s 13 d 5 & costs of suit stay Exon 25th Dec next

John G. Cook came into court and was qualified as a constable

Ordered that Mrs. Mary Haregrove adm. of William Hargrove dec'd be authorized to sell a bay mare belonging to the estate of the said William on the credit of 7 months at the house of Robert Meltons on the first Monday in Nov. next

12 Mrs. Ann Zubly Ex. of the estate of David Zubly returned an acct. against the said estate on oath which was lodged with clerk for his inspection to report to next court.

The Court requests that John Clark, Esq. do advertise & sell a cow and two calves which were tolled before him by Nathaniel Howel at the plantation of the said Nath. Howel on a credit of 6 months take note and security and transmit the same to the treasurer of this county as soon as possible

Cranshaw Parkman vs Robert Melton. Plffs. Durn for plff.

Ł 7 s 15 d 10 & costs of suit.

James Hagood vs Reuben Frazier. Award returned for Ł 15 s d 7 subject to any legal setts off that the deft. can make judgment accordingly.

Henry Wilson vs Dan Bullock. Judgment confessed for Ł 8 s 18 d 8 with costs of suit stay Exon. 2 months.

On application of John Kelly permission was granted him to keep Tavern securities William Terry & Thomas Riddle

Drury Mims vsUlyses Rogers & Peter Chasturn. Judgment by default.

13   David Glover vs Richard Quarles Case. Dismissed at Deft costs.

On the Petit Jury being called the following persons appeared
1. Joshua Thorne   10. William Martin
2. John Fudge   11. Joseph Nunn
3. John Killcrese   12. Thomas Davis
4. Toliver Cox   13. Benjamin Franklin
5. John Frederick   14. Isaac Brunson
6. Robert White   15. William Spraggin
7. John Griffiths Jr.   16. John Day
8. Nathan Trotter   17. John Playlock

14   Drury Mims vs Ulysses Rogers. Debt. Judgment by Default. on a writ of enquiry a Jury being Impannelled and sworn to wit: Jno Griffiths, foreman; Joshua Thorn, John Fudge, John Killcrease, Toliver Cox, John Frederick, Robt White, Nathan Trotter, Zachariah Lunday, William Martin, Joseph Nunn & Benjamin Franklin...find for pltff.

The Grand Jurors Returned their Presents. Rec.d the thank of the Court and were Dischraged.
Ordered that the Clerk file the same Presentments

Ordered that the Exors of John Thurmond have power to Sell of the Personall property of that said dd. as will raise Ł 20 for payment of Debts due from the said Estate

John Steele assignee of Shaw vs William Brooks & Terry. P & S. Judgment confessed for 5 guineas with interest accd to Note & Costs

Hugh OKeefe vs Wm L Jno Parker. Debt Contd.

Gabl. Ragsdale vs Jno Riply & Others. Dismissed.

15   John Steele assignee vs Alexander Frazer. P & S Judgment confessed for 5 guineas with interest according to Note

David Moore vs Richard Johnson Junr. Case Judgmt. Confess'd for Ł 14 5/9 & costs of suit Stay Exon till 1st Sept next

Duncan Campbell & Co vs John Carter Colo. Case Judgmt. Confess'd for Ł 14 14/6 and costs of suit Stay Exon till 1st Jany next

Richard Johnson Junr vs John Williams. Case. Judgment confessed for Two Thousand Weight of Tobacco @ 11/8 pr Hundred With Interest and Costs of Suit Stay of Exon till 1st Sept next

Isaac Polock & Judith Mimms admn. of Lyon Haney vs Vincent Rowall. Judgment Revived

David Moore & Julius admn. of William Moore vs Caleb Holloway Deft. Judgment by Default. The same Jury as before Verdict Ŀ 15 Int. acc to Note.

16   John Hill vs Chisley Farrar, Stephen Garrett, James Coursey. Case. Judgment confessed by James Coursey and Stephen Garrett for Ŀ 18 with interest according to note Stay Execution 8 months.

John Steel assignee vs Wm. Newsome. plffs. Judgment confessed according to note. Stay 6 months.

McCawlye & Davies vs George Chaney. Plffs. Decree for the plff. for Ŀ 6 s 6 d 1½ with interest accd. to note

Edmund Holliman,Isham Mitchel & Peter Chastain. On writ of Judg. the same Jury as before verdict for Ŀ 5 & costs of suit. Judgment accordingly.

Ordered that this court be adjourned till tomorrow nine o'clock. Arthur Simkins, W. Anderson.

17   The Court met according to adjournment on 15 Oct 1794. Present the Honble Arthur Simkins, William Anderson, Thomas Bacon, Esquires.

Saml. Wright vs George G. Tankersley. Judgment by default. Saml. Garnisher on his oath saith he has no property in his hands nor had he at the time of giving the attachment.

John Arledge vs Isaac Hughs. Judgment by default.

John Wait vs Joseph Dew. Alt. Judgment by default.

William Stewart vs Eliza Sturzenagger. Dismt. Deft. cost.

Henry Wilson vs Robert Hatcher. Decree for Ŀ 6 s 2 d8½ with interest according to note   stay Exon. 3 months.

Russel Wilson Esq. vs Joshua Deen. Dismd. Deft. costs

18   McCallum & Gardner vs James Talbert & Bartlett Martin. Judgment confessed by <u>Barkley</u> Martin as security for James Talbert for Ŀ 18 s 14 & costs of suit with stay Exon till first August next.

Richard & John Moore vs George & Samuel Abney. Plffs. Decree for the plffs. for Ŀ 6 s 12 with interest from 16th Nov 1792 & costs of suit.

Young Allen vs Wiley Glover. Plffs. Decree for plff for Ŀ 7 s 19 d 8 and costs of suit.

Frances & Henry Wilson vs Jacob Hibler. The same Jury as yesterday was sworn and say we find for plff. according to

note with interest & costs allowing the credit for the rect.
John Griffith, foreman.

Andrew Pickens & Co. vs John Carter & Seth Howard. Sci fa
Judgment accordingly. Order that the Judgment obtained
against John Herndon be renewed against the said John Carter
& Seth Howard as securities for said Herndon.

John Bell vs James Penny. Judgment by default the same Jury
Verdict Ł 19 s 10 with interest and costs. Judgment accordingly. John Griffiths, foreman.

19   Eugene Brenan & Co. vs Burrel Johnson. Plffs. Stay exon 3
mo.   Judgment confessed according to note

Absent Arthur Simkins, Esq.

John Rainsford vs William Jeter Jr. Slander on issue joined
the same jury as before on their oaths do say we find the
plaintiff Ł 2 s 10 and costs of suit. Judgment accordingly
John Griffiths, Foreman.

Garrett & Hollimon vs Benjamin Ryan Jr. Plffs. Judgment
confessed for Ł 7 s 1 d 1½ and costs of suit Stay of levy
till the 25th Dec next

John Suite Assignee of Shaw vs Abraham Richardson. Plffs.
Judgment confessed for Ł 5 s 8 d 9 with interest accr. to
note with costs of suit

Benjamin Glover vs John & Edmond Martin. Debt. Judgment
confessed for Ł 10 with interest accordg to note Stay Exon
6 months.

The last will and Testament of Mary Fuqua was proved in open
court by oath of Wm. Weems and ordered to be recorded and
that James Baker one of the Exors mentioned in the said will
was quallified as such and the following persons to appraise
her estate. John Covington, John Hardy, Richard Hardy, John
Curry.

20   Rue Clevaling Admr. of James Cleavling returned an amount
of note due to the said estate of said Cleavland on oath

John Glover vs Thomas Lamar Debt. Judgment confessed according to note for Ł 100 sterling with interest and costs
of suit.

Patrick Hayes vs Samuel Willison. P & S. Dismissed Plff.
costs Joseph Hightower came into court and acknowledged himself security for costs in this amt all the actions at present on the Dockett where the said Hayes is Plaintiff

Miss Sally Dalby in court the court appointed John Simkins
give bond in this sum of Ł 500 with Robert Button and Britton Mims as his security which was done

Owen Williams, son of Williams, being of age to choose his
guardian appointed of by the court Ordered that the said
Robert give bond in the sum of Ł 500 which with James Baker
and Robert Yeer as his securities which was done

21   the Court appointed the said Robert Owen Williams as guardian
      for Miss Valinda Williams.

      Ordered that this Court be adjourned till tomorrow 9 o'clock
      Arthur Simkins, W. Anderson, Thos Bacon.

      The Court met according to adjournment on 16 Oct 1794.
      Present the Hon. Arthur Simkins & William Anderson.

      Duncan Campbell & Co. vs Alexander Oden. P & S. Decree for
      the Plff for Ł 3 s 12 d 5 & costs

      Charnal Hightower Thorne vs Christopher Hall & Abm. Richard-
      son. Plffs Judgment confessed for Ł 10 annl. costs of suit

22   James James vs Jacob Hibbler. Debt. Dismd Defts. costs

      Jacob Hibbler vs John Hammond. Debt. Dismd. Judge Bacon's
      costs.

      Eugene Brenan & Co. vs John Cheney. P & S. Judgment confessed
      accd. to note. Stay exon three Mo.

      Eliza King vs William Blackley & Thomas Ellis. P & S.
      Decree for plff Ł 7 s 3 & costs interest accd. to note

      Eliz. King vs Thos Ellis & Wm. Blackley. Plffs. Decree for
      plff Ł 7 s 3 interest & costs

      Eugene Brenan & Co. vs John Wright P & S . Judgment con-
      fessed according to note with costs of suit.

      The Exors Adam Hyles vs The Exors of Wallison. Case writ
23   of inquiry the same Jury as yesterday. we find for the plff
      Ł 12 with interest thereon from 1 March 1784.

      John Steele assignee of share of Geo Cowan vs Elenor Cowan
      Adm. in her own wrong decree for plff for Ł 8 s 8 d 9 with
      interest according to note

      Davis Moore vs Thomas Lamar Debt. Judgment confessed Ł 8
      d 7 d8½ interest & costs

      Davis Moore indorsee W. Glover indorsee Thomas Butler vs
      Thomas Lamar H. C. Debt. Judgment confessed for Ł 55 with
      interest according to note Stay of levy till 1st Oct next

      Davis Moore Ind. of Ben Ryan Jr. vs Thomas Lamar H. C.
      Judgment confessed for Ł 35 and costs with interest according
      to note same Stay as above

      Kevin Taylor & Murren Vs. Thomas Lamar H. C. Ordered that
      the summary process on the tryal dockett be consollidated
      at the plaintiffs costs except the expense of one Writ Judg-
      ment confessed for Ł 29 s 7 d 4 Stay levy six mo.

24   James James vs William Eavans. Debt. On a writ the same
      Jury as before on their oaths do say we find for the plain-
      tiff Ł 17 s 7 d 3 according to note with costs of suit.

      Solomon Pope vs Thomas Lamar Debt. Judgment confessed ac-
      cording to note Ł 32 s 16 d 6 with interest and costs of suit.

Allen Glover vs William Nichols, Thomas Lamar. **Debt**. Judgment confessed for Ƚ 14 s 4 d 11 with interest accd. to note Stay levy six months.

Davis Moore & Chastain vs Daniel Gunnels. Dismd Deft. Costs.

Davis Moore vs Michael Blocker. Judgment confessed accd. to note

Davis Moore vs William Coursey Case. The same Jury as before on a writ of inquiry on their oaths do say we find for the plff. Ƚ 10 s 7 d 6 3/4 with costs of suit.

25 Arthur Harper vs Joshua Hammond. Three appeals from the Judgment of Hightower Judgment confessed for Ƚ 14 s 4 d 9 3/4 and costs Stay six mo.

Saml. Mays Esq. came into court & signified his resignation as sheriff of this county whereupon the court proceeded to the appointment of a sheriff and upon casting up the ballott it appeared that Jeremiah Hatcher was unanimously elected.

Eugene Brenan & Co. vs Davis Moore & Peter Chastain. Debt. Judgment confessed according to note with costs of suit.

John Ryan Indorsee of Peter Carvas vs West Cook. Debt. The same Jury as before on their oaths do say we find for the plffs $400 and costs of suit.

Mr. Shaw under the direction of the court on the part of the Plff. argues that the Deft. have a stay of Levy 6 months and if he the deft. has any legal defense it shall be allowed.

James Stewart vs James Wilson. Dismd Deft.

Benja. Glover vs John Moore. Two suits dismd. Plff costs.

26 Eugene Brenan & Co. vs Truman Wight. Judgment confessed for Ƚ 12 s 3 d 7¼ stay levy 3 months with interest according to note.

E. Brenan & Co. vs Peter Chastain. Judgment confessed for Ƚ 57 s 5 d 3 & costs Stay 6 months with interest according to note.

Richard Johnson Jr. vs John Williams. Case. The same Jury as before on their oaths do say we find for the plff. 3000 weight of tobacco at 10/6 per 100 with interest according to note

Arge Garner vs James Pukett. Nonsuit.

Wm. Pitman vs John Pitman. Slander. Nonsuit.

Wm. Pitman vs John Pitman. Case. Nonsuit.

Duncan Campbell & Co. vs Henry Ware Jr. Judgment confessed according to note stay Exon till the 1st Oct next

27 Jacob Hebbler vs William Blackley & Thomas Ellis. Debt on Judgment by defts special bail Ordered in this case an affidavit filed in the clerks office.

Davis Moore vs Henry Parkman Senr. Case Dismissed Deft costs

Wm. Shaw vs Abraham Richardson. Debt. Judgment by default.

John Ryan vs Joseph Reed. Alt. Dismd Deft. costs

Toliver Bostick assignee James Hawkins vs William Moore son
of Rd. Debt. The same Jury as before on their oaths do say
we find for the plaintiff according to note.

Francis Lightfood vs Wm. Moore son of Rd. Debt. The same
Jury as before on their oaths do say we find for the plff
according to note with interest and costs.

William Shaw vs Abraham Richardson. Debt. The same Jury as
before say we find for the plff 2000 weight of tobacco at
11/ with interest & costs.

28   Henry & Frances Wilson vs John Moore, Esq. Debt. Judgment
confessed for Ƚ 35 s 11 d 2½ with costs of suit   stay of levy
till 1 Jan next

The court taking into consideration the presentments of the
Grand Jurors and made the following Orders to wit.
1. Presentments   Ordered to be laid before the legislature
2. Do---

James McQueen vs Barkley Martin. Appeal Judgment Confirmed
for Ƚ 2 s 13 d 5 and costs.

James McQueen vs Barkley Martin. Appeal Judgment confirmed
for Ƚ 2 s 6 d 8 and costs

29   On application of Mims & Moore permission was granted them
to keep tavern security Henry Ware Jr. & Lileston Pardue

Samuel Willison vs Absolom Napper. Appeal Judgment reversed

Philip Lamar vs George B. Moore. Appeal Judgment Reversed

Philip Lamar vs George B. Moore. The same order

(above repeated four more times)

30   On the application of Stephen Norris for a distributive
share of his fathers estate Ordered by the court that one
third part thereof be allotted to Rebecca White Relic of
Thomas Norris, Accd. and that the remainder of said estate
be distributed in equal proportions among the several children and their representatives of the said Thomas Norris,
and that Richard Tutt, John Gray, John Addison and Samuel
Walker or any three of them be and are hereby appointed commissioner to distribute the same and to take bonds from the
several representatives to refund, in case it should --
afterwards appear that they had received more than their
distributive shares of said estate.

Arthur Simkins Esq. absented himself.

Ordered that this court be adjourned till tomorrow morning
nine o'clock. W. Anderson, Thos Bacon.

31   The court met according to adjournment 17 Oct 1794. Present Honble Arthur Simkins, Thomas Bacon, Esquires.

Joakim Bulow vs Thomas Harrison P & S. Decree for the plff for Ƚ 5 d 4 and costs of suit.

Hunt & Stallings vs Joseph Reed. Plffs Judgment default. Decree for plff Ƚ 6 s 1 d 1 costs of suit

David Sandige vs John Cheney. Plffs. Judgment confessed accd. to note Stay Exon 2 months.

Ordered that Benjamin Lewis be overseer of the Blandford Road that part from West Harris' to Ephram's branch & Drury Mathews from thence to Burton's old place.

In addition to an Order entered fifteenth Ordered that the persons and estate of Salley Dalby be in the hands & possession of John Simkins as guardian.

The court taking into consideration the regulation of Tavern Rate.
Ordered that the following Rates & no others be received by all Tavern Keepers for the ensuing year.
Jamacca or good West India Rum or French Brandy per pint 1/6
Peach Brandy one and two pence per pint
Continent distilled Rum or Taffie per pint 10
Whiskey per pint one shilling
Ginn one and six pence per pint 1/6
Madaria Wine per quart or bottle 4/8
Ordinary wine per do. 2/4
Porter per quart or bottle 2/4
32 Cyder per quart 6 pence
Hott Dinner 1/6 cold do. 1/
Supper or Breakfast one shilling
Clean Lodging a night four pence
Stabling & fodder for a horse a night 1.0
Corn per quart two pence
Oats

Willie Eavans vs Samuel Carter Dismissed

William Covington vs Allen Hinton. Abated by death of Deft.

Duncan Campbell vs George Cheney. Settled Defts costs

John Williams & wife vs Henry Ware Sr. Sur. Dismissed

James Hagood vs Ezekiel Hudnal. Judgment by default

Abimileck Hawkins vs Moses Carter Nonsuit

Thomas Bacon Esq. vs Pleasant Thurmond Settled at Defts. except the plff Alt. fee

William Wilson vs Richard Jones. Sci fa Dismd.

Mark Nobles vs John Hill. Slander Dismd. defendants costs

William Pardue vs Richard Pardue. Deft.

160

33 Duncan Campbell & Co vs Henry Ware Jr. Deft. Judgment con-
    fessed according to note stay Exon till 1st Oct next

    The court taking into consideration the presentment of the
    Grand Jury and made the following Order to wit:
    On the petition of Sundry inhabitants of Beech island and
    places adjacent Ordered that Abram Ardis, George Ringland,
    Craddock Burnell, Phillip Lemar & Robert Cochran or a major-
    ity of them be commissioners to build a bridge over Horse
    Creek at a place known by the name of Bevan's Bridge said
    bridge to extend as far as the Commissioners or a majority of
    them shall think it necessary so as to render the swamp of
    said creek safe and passable and that they advertise 20 days
    notice of the same and let the building of said bridge to the
    lowest bidder and that the undertaker give hard and approved
    security to build the same in three months and keep it in good
    repair for seven years and also leave it in good repair at the
    end of that time, that the undertaker be paid in the following
    manner Viz: one fourth part when shall undertake another fourth
    part at the raising of the bridges and the remaining half when
    the bridge shall be finished said money to be paid part in
    cash and part in notes on citizens of this county and the un-
    dertaker to have a choice of said notes and that the commis-
    sioners be impowered to draw on the county treasurer for the
    above sums of money respectively.

34 The court request that Henry King Esq. do sell two head of
    cattle Tolled before him by James O'hara three head of cattle
    toll'd before him by Benjamin Wages and one by Jonathan Wea-
    ver the above estrays to be advertized and sold on a credit
    of six months take note and transmit the same to the treasurer
    of this county as soon as possible.

    On motion and complaint of Burgess White, John Frazier, Saml
    Landrum, Jeremiah Hatcher, Esq. Ordered James Burke and Wil-
    liam Burk two orphan boys be bound (as apprentices) to some
    good tradesman if any to be had if not to some planter under
    the directed of some Justices of the Peace in this county.

    Ordered that this court be adjourned till in Course. Arthur
    Simkins, Thos. Bacon.

    The Court met according to adjournment on the 5th day Jan
    1795. Present the Hon. Arthur Simkins, Esq.

    The last will and testament of John Pursel was further proven
    by the oath of Ebenezer Hill.

    An inventory of the estate of Pleasant Burnett was returned.
    Ordered to be recorded

    Ordered that all the personal estate of Pleasant Burnett dec'd
    be sold at the house of Hezekiah Gentry on the fourth Monday
35 in January instant on a credit of 12 months the purchasers
    to give bond and security

    The last will and testament of Mary Foreman was proved by the
    oath of John Perry which was ordered to be recorded Isaac
    Foreman executor of the said last will was quallified as
    such. Ordered that Samuel Walker, John Gray, William Harden
    & John Addison or any three of them do appraise and inventory
    the said estate.

Ordered that all the personal estate of William Brown be sold
on the fourth Saturday of this instant (Jany.) at the house
of John Abney on a credit of 12 months the purchasers to give
bond and approved security.

The last will and testament of Lewis Clark was proved by the
oaths of Ben Clark and Joseph Walker and Ordered to be recorded. Bukner Blalock & Zilpha Clark was quallified as exors
and excutrix to the said Will. Ordered that Shadrack Deas,
John Blalock, Isaac Foreman & V. Swearingen or any three of
them do appraise the said estate.

An inventory of the estate of William STrother was returned
and ordered to be recorded

On application of Ezekiel McClendon permission was granted
to him to keep tavern securities Van Swearingen & Isaac Kirkland.

36 On the application of Abraham Jones executor of William Glascock who was surviving executor of John Beddingfield, to be
quallified as executor on the estate of said Beddingfield
its ordered by the court that Dradock Burnette be cited to
appear at Edgefield Courthouse on the 11day day of March
next then and there to show cause if any he has why the administration granted to him on the estate of said Beddingfield
should not be set aside & administration of the same committed
to said Abraham Jones according to law.

On application of Anjalicha Jernagen, widow of Jesse Jernagen
and William Burdet for letters of administration on the said
Jesse Jernagen estate. Ordered that the same be granted them
on their entering into bond in the sum of Ł 150 with Henry
King and Samuel Deloach as securities which was done and the
said Anjalicha and William quallified as admors. Ordered
that Henry King, Thomas Dozier, Samuel Deloach, John Smidley
or any three of them do appraise and inventory the said estate.

37 On application of Mary Berry for letters of administration
on her dec'd husband Arnold Berry's estate. Ordered that the
same be granted on her entering into bond in the sum of Ł 200
with Agden Cockeroft and Nathl. Bolton as securities which
was done and the said Mary quallified as an Admrx. Ordered
that the following persons or any three of them do appraise
the said estate (to wit) Henry King, Sam. Deloach, Wm. Burdit,
& Wm. Rotten.

On application of Mrs. Cumfort Brunson widow of Josiah Brunson
decd for letters of administration on the said estate. Ordered
that the same be granted her on her entering into bond in the
sum of Ł 700 with which was done and the said Cumfort Brunson
quallified as admx. Ordered that the following persons or
any three of them do appraise the said estate to wit: Jesse
Roundtree, McC. Leavenworth, Nathl. Barr & Philip Lamar.

Miss Salley Dallby came into Court being of full age to choose
her guardian made choice of Eugene Brenan as suit which was
approved of by the court. Ordered the said guardian give Bond
in the sum of Ł 500 with John Simkins and Francis Burt as his
securities which was done. Ordered that the person and estate
of the said Salley Dalby be in the hands and possession of the
38 said Eugene Brenan as guardian.

Mrs. Celia Martin wife of Simon Martin came into Court and acknowledged her right of Dower and third of 100 acres of land known by the name of Poverty Hill conveyed by her said husband to William Covington which was ordered to be recorded

The last will and testament of Solomon Pope was proved by the oath of Demsey Wever & William Cain and Ordered to be recorded John Pope and Wiley Pope were quallified as Exors to the said will. Ordered that the following persons or any three of them do appraise the estate (to wit) John Duglas, John Salter, William Little & Lodwick Hill.

Joseph Hightower Esq. came into court and was qualified as a Justice of the Peace for this County by taking the oath for that purpose appointed and Russell Wilson Esq. did so likewise.

On application of Elijah Rogers for letters of admn. on the estate of Alexander Wilson deceased Ordered that the same be granted him on his entering into Bond in the sum of Ł 200 with John Hill and John Anderson as securities which was done and the said Elijah Rogers qualified as an administrator.

Ordered that Robert Roebuck be overseer of the road leading from Hatchers Pond to the old Wells in the Room of Thomas Moseley Excused.

39 Ordered that Benjamin Adams be excused as an overseer of the road from New Market to Horns Creek on the Hatchers Pond Road and that Fielding Runnels be appointed in his room.

Ordered that Rue Swearingen be overseer of the road from Countyline to the Head of Horns Creek in the room of William Day bound on the same road as above.

Ordered that Arben Moore be overseer of the New road from Turkey Creek to where the path from John Blocker's to Olivers Place crosses the road in the room of John Blocker excused

Ordered that William Simkins be Overseer of the road from Blocker's Path crosses to the Court House in the room of Elias Blackburn excused.

Ordered that John Addison be overseer of the Road from Edgefield Court House to Horn's Creek in the room of Casper Gallman excused.

Jesse Griffin produced his account against the estate of Aaron Booth amounting to Ł 160 s 11 d 5 which was allowed of by the court

On application of Benjamin Hightower permission was granted to him to keep tavern sureties: Joseph Hightower Esq. & Jerimiah Hatcher Esq.

40 Joseph Hightower Esq. & Joshua Harrison commissioner to view & report upon a road leading from Cherokee Pond to Day's old Meeting House having returned their report ordered that said road be opened agreeable to said report & that Hightower Thorne be overseer over said road

Ordered that Joshua Hammond be overseer over the road leading

163

Campbelton to the Pinewood House from the fork of the five
knotched road to the first Hill above the fork above John
Halls in the room of William Tarrance excused.

On appiication of William Yarborough permission was granted
to him to keep tavern securities John Gorman and Jesse
Griffin.

On application permission was give to John Gorman to keep
Tavern securities William Yarborough & William Covington

Van Swearingen Esq. came into court and was quallified as a
Justice of the Peace for this county by taking the oath for
that purpose appointed

41 The last will and testament of Charles Hammond was proved by
the oath of William Covington and ordered to be recorded Miss
Catherine Hammond was quallified as an Executrix of the said
will. Ordered that the following persons or any three of
them to appraise said estate (to wit) Joshua Hammond, William
Tarrence, Leroy Hammond and William Covington.

John Cheney lodged an account on Oath with his vouchers against
the Estate of James Cheney.
Ordered that the clerks file the same and report fully thereon
next court.

Ordered that this Court be adjourned till tomorrow morning
ten o'clock. Arthur Simkins.

The Court met according to adjournment on 6 January 1795.
Present the Honorable Arthur Simkins, Esq.

The Clerk having examined the account of Arthur Watson Executor of Michael Watson deceased and reports that there is
the sum of Ł 27 s 7 d 6 due him which is allowed of by the
42 Court Arthur Watson exor of Michael Watson decd. returned a
further account against the estate of Michael dec'd on oath
together with his vouchers ordered that the clerk do file
the same examine and report to next court

On applications of Alexander Edmunds for letters of administration on Samuel Edmunds Estate Ordered that the same be
granted him on his bring into bond in the sum of Ł 70 with
John Bloack & John Cogburn as his sureties which was done
and the said Alexander qualified as an administrator.
Ordered that the following persons or any three of them do
appraise the said estate To wit: Drury Adams, Penia Howles,
William and Russell Bukum.

On application of William Moore by Colonel Samuel May, permission was granted to him to keep Tavern Securities Samuel
Mays and William Butler, Esq.

On petition of Sundry inhabitants for a road from Gorman's
to the new road Ordered that William Moore, Thomas Spragins,
and Nathaniel Abney do view the ground and report to next
court.

Present the Hon. William Anderson.

John Blocker Esq. produced a certificate of his quallification

as a justice of   peace for this county under the hands of
the Hon. Arthur Simkins. Ordered to be filed with the Clerk
of Court.

Mrs. Buffinton widow of Peter Buffington came into court and
relinquished her right of admn. to her said husband Peter
43 Buffington in favors of Samuel Mays & Rydon Grigsby. Ordered
that the same be granted them on their entering into Bond in
the sum ₺ 150 with Russell Wilson & William Butler as their
sureties which was done and the said Samuel Mays and Rhydon
Grigsby was qualified as admr. and the following persons or
any three of them to appraise the said Estate (to wit) John
& Joseph Moseley, Simon Brooks and Dannett Abney.

John Ryan Esq. produced a certificate of his qualification
as a Justice of the Peace for this county under the hand of
the Hon. Arthur Simkins. Ordered that the same be lodged
with the clerk.

On application of Mary Grigsby, widow of Enoch Grigsby,
Samuel Mays and Rhydon Grigsby for letters of admn. with the
will annexed on the estate of the said Enoch Grigsby. Ordered that the same be granted them ontheir entering into
Bond in the sum of ₺ 1000 with William Butler and Russell
Wilson, Esq. as their secureties which was done and the following persons or any three of them to appraise the said estate William Butler, Jacob Smith, Russell Wilson and William
Dozer. Mrs. Mary Grigsby, Rydon Grigsby & Samuel Mays
qualified as admrs.

John Blocker Esq. came into court and took the oath of an
Executor to the said Will and Testament of John Jacob Messer
Smith. Ordered that the following persons or any three of
them do appraise the said Estate   (to wit) Thomas McGinnis,
John Stewart, Michael Shaver & Henry Zimmerman.

44 The last will and testament of Enoch Grigsby by way proved
by oath of William Butler, William Simkins and Sampson Butler
and ordered to be recorded

Presley Bland came into court and was qualified as a constable
for this county

An inventory of the estate Hazekiah Walker was returned and
ordered to be recorded. Ordered that all the personal estate
of Hezekiah Walker be sold at the house of Samuel Walker on
Friday the 13th of this instant (Jan.) on a credit of 12
months the purchaser to give bond and surety.

Present the Hon. Thomas Bacon.

The last will and testament of Allen Hinton was proved by the
oath of John Lee and ordered to be recorded and Wm. Covington
qualified as an administrator with the will annexed on the
resignation of Hightower Thorn, the sole Executor to the said
will.

William Daniel, Esq. produced a certificate of his qualification as a Justice of Peace for this county under the hand of
Arthur Simkins, Esq.

Ordered that the following persons or any three of them do

165

appraise the Estate of Allen Hinton, decd. to wit: Leroy
Hammond, John Hammond, Charles Old & Joseph Fuqua. Ordered
that all the personal Estate of the said Hinton be sold on
the 4th Saturday in this instant, January, the whole of the
estate being first inventory said returned to the clerk office

45 Jeremiah Hatcher, Esq. produced his commission as sheriff
for this county which was read. Ordered that the said Jeremiah be sworn as such which was done and Bond given in the
sum of Ⱡ 1500 with John Ryan and Samuel Mays as sureties.
Jeremiah Hatcher, Esq. was qualified as sheriff by taking the
oaths of office and the constitution for that purpose appointed.

Jeremiah Hatcher Esq. produced Sampson Butler as his under
sheriff for the County who was approved of by the court and
he sworn accordingly.

Samuel May admr. returned an account against the estate of
George. Dec'd. Ordered that the same be lodged with the clerk.

Mrs. Rachael Brazil came into court and relinquished her
right of admn. on the estate of her former Husband Benjamin
McKinny Estate in favor of his son John McKinney. Ordered
that the same be granted him on his entering into Bond in
the sum of Ⱡ 150 with Frederick Swearingen and Thomas Adams
as his secureties which was done and the said John McKinney
was qualified as an admr. and the following persons appointed
to appraise the said estate (to wit) Bibby Bush, Arthur Watson Esq. and John Salter.

On application of William Longmire permission was granted him
to keep Tavern sureties Edmund Whatley and John Sillivant

46 On application of Bibby Bush permission was granted him to
keep Tavern Sureties Frederick Swearingen & John Williams

John Addison was qualified as constable for this county by
taking the oath of office and Constitution.

On Petition of Sundry Inhabitants of Horns Creek and others
Ordered that Col. John Martin, Thomas Key, Aquilla Miles,
Shurley Whatley Sr., Absolom Roberts or a majority of them
be and they are hereby appointed commissioners to build a
bridge over Horns Creek at a place near where the Martin Town
Road now crosses the bridge to extend so far as the commissioners shall think proper to make it safe and passable and
that they advertise the same 30 days, and let it to the lowest
bidder and the undertaker give bond and security to keep the
same in good repair seven years and also to leave it in good
repair at the end of that term. One fourth part to be paid
the undertaker when he undertakes the other fourth at the
raising the bridge and the remaining half when the bridge is
finished.

Ordered that Richard Tutt be and is hereby appointed commissioner for the purpose of regulating and stamping and marking
47 all weights and measures belonging to the County of Edgefield
and that he provide at the expense of the County a strong box
with a good lock and key to hold the said Measures which is
to be kept in the Court house and that the commissioner hereby
appointed shall obey the call of the Commissioners of any of

the tobacco inspection in this county once in every year to
regulate the weights at their respective Ware Houses.

Ordered that all the personal Estate of Peter Buffington
be sold on Thursday 29th of this instant at his late dwelling
house on a credit of 12 months the whole Estate being first
inventoryed and returned to the clerks office.

Ordered that this court be adjourned till the court in course.
Arthur Simkins, W. Anderson, Thos Bacon.

The Court met according to adjournment on the 11th day of
March 1795. Present the Hon. Arthur Simkins, Esq.

Ordered that Samuel Center be overseer of the road from the
Widow Wests to the Intersection of the Charleston Road from
Lees Bridge to Clouds Creek in Room of William Ethridge excu-
sed.

48   Lodwick Hill return list of defaulters for not working on
the road from Amos Richardson to Barry Travis' (to wit) William
Nicholson, John Rogers, Wm. Gains, Samuel Humphries, Charles
Partin, Wormly Bland, John Bledsoe, John Strother, James
Buckalew, Joseph Brown, Josiah Howel, Alexander Wilson, Jeremiah Strother, Joel Brown & Presley Bland. Ordered that they
be cited to appear to that intermediate Court to show cause
if any they can why they fail to work on the said road &
that Joseph Lewis the warner be summoned as a witness.

An inventory of the Estate of Jesse Jernagen was returned and
ordered to be recorded. also an inventory of party of the
said Jesse Jernagan's Estate given to his son, Henry Jernagan.

Mrs. Angelicah Jernagan Admr. to the said Jesse Jernagan returned an account of the debts due the said estate on oath
which was ordered to be recorded

An inventory of the Estate of Joseph Walker's was returned by
James Walker admr. & ordered to be recorded. Ordered that all
the personal estate of Joseph Walker dec'd be sold on the
first Monday in April next at the home of James Walker in a
credit of 12 months the purchaser to give bond and security.

On inventory of Arnold Berry Estate was received and ordered
to be recorded. Ordered that all the personal estate of Arnold Berry be sold on the last Monday in March instant at the
House of Nathaniel Bolton on a credit of 12 months the pur-
49   chasers to give bond and security. The amount of sale of
Morris Gwinn was returned on oath by John Gwinn Admr.

An Inventory of the estate of Benjamin McKinney was ordered
to be recorded. Ordered that all the personal estate of
Benjamin McKinney be sold on the last Thursday in March instant
at the House of Rachael Brazil on a credit of 12 months the
purchaser to give bond and security.

Edmund Whatley having applied formerly for letters of admn. on
the estate of George Cowan dec'd and no person appearing to
oppose him ordered that the same be granted to him on his
entering bond in the sum of Ƚ 200 with John Sullivin & Daniel
Marcus which was done and the said Edmund Whatley qualified
as an admr. Ordered that the following persons or any three

of them do appraise the said estate. To wit: John Martin,
Samuel Doolittle, Shearly Whatley Sr., Absolom Roberts.

An amount of sale of the estate of William Brown was returned
on oath of John Abney admr. and ordered to be recorded

Ordered that all the personal estate of George Cowan be sold
on the last Tuesday in March (instant) on a crd. of 12 months
at the house of Leroy Roberts the purchaser to give bond and
security the whole estate to be first inventory'd and returned
to the clerks office.

Elkanah Sawyers Esq. came into court and was qualified as a
Justice of Peace for the County of Edgefield by taking oath
of office and constitution for that purpose

50 Ordered that James O'Harrow be overseer of the Road in the
room of Amos Richardson Excused that pay from Amos Richardson
one half from there to Chappells Ferry.

An amount of sale of the Estate of Hezekiah Walker was rec'd
on oath of Samuel Walker and ordered to be recorded

An amount of sale of the Estate of Stephen Glover deceased
was returned on oath of Charles Bussey and ordered to be recorded

On application of John Terry permission was granted him to
keep tavern securities James Coursey and John Spratt

Mrs. Ann Zubly, Executrix of David Zubly returned an amount
of money recieved for the estate on oath the amount being
Ł 10 s 18 d 11.

On application of John Tarrance for letters of administration
on the estate of his father, William Tarrance's estate,
Ordered that the same be granted him on his entering into bond
in the sum of Ł 300 with Joseph Hightower and Charnal Hightower Thorne as security which was done and the said John
Tarrance qualified as admr. Ordered that the following person
or any three of them do appraise the said Estate (to wit)
Joshua Hammond, C. Hightower Thorne, John Carter, John Hall.

Present the Hon. Wm. Anderson, Esq.

51 James Harrison Esq. produced a certificate of his qualification as a Justice of Peace for the County of Edgefield under
the hand of Thos Bacon, Esq. which was filed by the clerk.

Ordered that the grand Jurors be drawn to serve as grand
Jurors at next October Term the following persons were drawn
(to wit)
1. Thomas Lamar H. C.   11. Nathaniel Bacon
2. Isaac Ardis   12. Joseph Hammond Jr.
3. John Searles   13. Joseph Hightower
4. John Bostick   14. Richard Moore
5. George Perrin   15. Thomas Carter
6. George Bussey, Sr.   16. Michael McKie
7. Marshall Martin   17. Arthur Watson
8. Robert Lamuel   18. Meshack Wright
9. Amos Richardson   19. Philip Lamar
10. Benjamin Ryan   20. John Covington

Ordered that the Petit Jurors be drawn to serve next October
term when the following persons were drawn to wit:

1.	Henry Webb	16.	William Glover
2.	John McDonald	17.	Frederick Tillman Jr.
3.	Moses Mathews	18.	Hezekiah Oden
4.	William Nobles	19.	Joseph Summerall
5.	James King	20.	William Marsh
6.	Samuel Hall	21.	Russell Beckum
7.	Charles Broadwater	22.	Thomas Wilson
8.	Lewis Ethridge	23.	Daniel Bird
9.	Richard Tate	24.	William Pardue
10.	John Hester	25.	William Howle
11.	George Boulware	26.	Charles Jones
12.	Constant Oglesby	27.	David Rowe
13.	Anthony Cooper	28.	Samuel Wilson
14.	Mathew Caps	29.	William Carley
15.	Tire Fike	30.	William Cochran

52 Ordered that the Sheriff return the writ of Venire for the
Grand Jury which was read

The last Will and testament of Bryant Green was proved by the
oath of John Hall & Jacob Parrish and ordered to be recorded
Thos. Carter and Edward Green came into court and were qualified as Executors to the said Will and the following persons
were appointed to appraise the said estate to wit: John Carter, John Hall, John Tarrance, John Howard.

Present the Hon. Thos. Bacon, Esq.

John Hall vs Charles Lavender & David Glover. Case.
Judgment confessed for Ŀ 13 s 11 d 4 stay of exon 7 months
without interest

Robert Milton vs John Carter. P & S Dism'd Deft. cost.

Philip Burt one of the Exors of Mathew Burt came into Court
& was qualified as such by taking the oath for that purpose
appointed.

Patrick Hays vs Mary Meyer Admx. P & S. abate by Death of
Deft.

George Ker vs Alexander Oden. P & S Judgment confessed according to note stay Execution 3 months.

53 John Steele assignee vs William Yarborough P & S Dismissed
Deft.

George Ker vs David Thompson Case. Judgment confessed for
Ŀ 13 s 2 d 1 with interest from this day till paid stay exn.
9 months

Saml. Marsh vs Daniel Gunnels P & S. Judgment confessed
for 1500 weight tobacco at 13 per hundred stay Execution 9
months.

Jacob Hibbler vs Joseph Wallace P & S Dismissed plff cost.

An inventory of the Estate of Solomon Pope was rec'd and ordered to be recorded

John Herndon son to William a minor of full age to choose his guardian came into court and made choice of Thomas Adams as his guardian which was appointed by the court. Ordered that 54 the person and Estate of the said John Herndon be in the hand and possession of the said Thomas Adams as guardian

On application permission was granted to Alexander Downer to keep Tavern securities Joseph Fuller, Richard Quarles.

An amount of the sale of Estate of Alex'd McMillian was recd on oath of James McMillian Admr. and ordered to be recorded

On application of David Richardson permission was granted him to keep Tavern securities Davis Williams & William Moore

Ordered that this court be adjourned till tomorrow nine o'-clock. Arthur Simkins, W. Anderson. The court met according to adjournment on 12 March 1795. Present the Hon. Arthur Simkins, William Anderson & Thomas Bacon, Esquires.

Ordered that Jacob Hibbler be overseer of the road from Cuffertown Creek to Cyper in the room of James Sanders excused.

55 On application of Capt. A. Perrin for Stephen Mantz permission was granted to the said Mantz to keep Tavern securities Abner Perrin.

Ordered that the sheriff return the writ venire for the Petit Jury which was read and on calling over the Pannels the following persons appeared (to wit)

1. Mordacar McKinney
2. John Shurley
3. Mark Nobles
4. Nathan Melton, Exd.
5. David Bazemoore
6. Aaron Ethridge
7. Abner Corley
9. John Ethridge
10. Wright Nicholson
11. Richard Corley
12. Drury Adams
13. Joseph Cunningham
14. Robert Allen
15. Thomas Scott ex'd
16. John Mobley
17. Robert Melton
18. Edward Holmes
19. John Ealam
20. Thomas Murrah

[There was no number "8"]

The last will and testament of Angus McDaniel was proved by the oath of Richard Tutt, Lewis Youngblood and Stephen Norris and ordered to be recorded. Mrs. Ann McDaniel and Elias Blackburn was qualified as Extx & Exr. to the said will ordered that the following persons or any three of them do appraise the said Estate John Cogburn, Moses Harris, Lewis and John Youngblood.

56 Melines Conklin Leavenworth vs Patrick Hayes. Attorney Dismissed Plffs. cost.

An inventory of the Estate of Alexander Edmunds was rec'd and ordered to be recorded

The writ of venire for Grand Jurors having been read yesterday & on calling over the Pannells the following person appeared and were empannelled & sworn (to wit)

1. Edmund Martin, foreman
2. Seth Howard
3. James Hargrove
8. William Simkins
9. John Lucas
10. John Griffith, Sen.

4. William Shinholster
5. George Ker
6. Abner Perrin
7. Haley Johnson

11. Lewis Tillman
12. Joseph Dawson
13. Edward Mitchell

John Steele Assinee of Shaw vs John Phillips. P & S Judgment confessed according to note with costs stay levy 6 mos.

An inventory of the estate of John Pursel was rec'd and ordered to be recorded

An Inventory of Allen Hintons estate being returned by William Covington Admr. into the clerks office agreeable to an order of last court.

57 Ordered that the same be recorded.

An Inventory of the Estate of Peter Buffington, dec'd was returned into the clerks office S. May admr. agreeable to an order of last court ordered that the same be recorded

The grand jurors returned the following Bill.

The State vs James Boothe Jr. Indictment Hog Stealing No Bill. Edmund Martin, Foreman.

Silas Green vs William Fudge. Appeal from the Judgment of Jas. Hightower Esq. Judgment confessed for s 50 & costs

Craddock Burnett admr. with the will annexed of John Beddingfields Estate returned an amt. of sale of the sales of the said Estate on oath which was rec'd and ordered to be recorded

The last Will and testament of Marckerness Goode was proved in open court by the oath of Paul Holloway & ordered to be recorded

An Inventory of Lewis Clarks Estate was received and ordered to be recorded

John Hammond vs Michael Blocker. Alt. Judgment confessed for Ł 4 s 13 d 2 and costs stay execution 2 months.

58 John Hammond vs John G. Cook. Alt. John G. Cook came into Court and confessed Judgment as surety for James Pukett for the sum of Ł 7 s 18 stay of levy 3 months.

On Petition of Sundry Inhabitants ordered that William Anderson, Oswell Eave, Thomas Wilson, James Robert Mayson & William White or a majority of them be and they are hereby appointed commissioners to build a bridge over Wilsons Creek at a place known by Eves Ford or at the nearest and most advantageous place adjacent thereto the Bridge to extend so far as the said Commissioenrs or a majority shall think proper to make it safe and passible and to advertise the letting the Bridge 15 days and let it to the lowerst bidder the undertaker to give bond and security to keep the same in good repair for the term of 7 years and to leave it in good repair at the end of that term, one fourth part to be paid to the undertaker when he undertakes the other fourth at the raising the bridge and the remaining half when the bridge finished.

Batte Eavans vs Zachariah Ray   Appeal Judgment confirmed with costs   stay Exon 6 Mo.

Eugene Brenan & Co. vs Joel Chandler.   P & S   Judgment confessed according to note stay execution 3 mos.

59   Francis Pukett vs John Cock   Alt.   John Searles being summoned as guarnishee in this alt. came into court and after being sworn on his oath saith that gave his note for Ł 30 payable to John Cock.   Ordered that the same be condemned in the hands of the said garnishee provided that the said note was not assigend before the levying of the attachment for the payment of the Plaintiff debt when established

John Wimberly vs Thomas Lamar.   Appeal Judgment confirmed

James Robertson vs Robert Stark Sr.   Alt.   Judgment by default on a writ of inquiry a jury being empanneled & sworn to wit: Robert Milton foreman, Mordica McKinney, John Shurly, Mark Nobles, David Bazemore, Aaron Ethridge, Abner Corley, Richard Corley, Robert Allen, Edward Holmes, John Ealam & Thomas Murrah on their oaths do say we find for the Plaintiff Ł 12 with interest from July 1790 & costs of suit.

60   Phil May Jr. vs John Fudge.   Debt.   Judgment confessed according to note Stay Execution levy six months.

James Robinson vs Robert Stark Sr.   Alt.   William Covington on being sworn as garnishee in this attachment on his oath saith that he cannot say whether he is indebted to the absent Dibton Stark until he has had a settlement with Stark or his representatives.   it is ordered that if it appears after settlement that if there is any money in his hands it is condemned for the plaintiffs use.

Ordered that this court be adjourned till tomorrow 9 o'clock. Arthur Simkins, W. Anderson, Thos. Bacon.

The court met according to adjournment on 13th March 1795. Present the Hon. Arthur Simkins, Thomas Bacon, William Anderson, Esquires.

On application of Abiah Morgan yesterday for letters of admn. on Onias Morgan decd.   Ordered that the same be granted on his entering into bond in the sum Ł 20 with Hugh Middleton
61   Esq. and William Covington as his sureties which was done. Ordered that Chas. Blackwell, James Thomas, William Reynolds & Samuel Scott or any three of them do appraise the said Est. and the said Abiah Morgan was qualified as an admr.

On application of Joseph Dick permission was granted to him to keep tavern Securities. Isaac Ardis & Jacob Zinn.

The last will and testament of Featherstone Cross was proved in open court by the oath of Samuel Boyd and ordered to be recorded   Peter Malone one of the Exors mentioned in the said was qualified as an Exor. by taking the oath for that purpose appointed.   Ordered that the following persons or any three of them do appraise the said Estate.   To wit: Samuel Scott, James Thomas, Daniel Barksdale & Henry Ware.

Pressley Bland Indorsee vs Joshua Deen & Richard Lewis. P & S

Judgment confessed by Joshua Deen according to note Stay
Execution 1 month

The last will and testament of Mary Meyer was proved in open
court by the oath of Joseph Fuller and ordered to be recorded.
Jesse Rountree one of the Executors mentioned in the said Will
was qualified as such by taking the oath for that purpose
appointed. Ordered that the following persons or any three
of them do appraise the said Estate. To wit: Lud Williams,
George Bender, John Savage & William Shinholster.

62 The State vs John Watson. Ind. Assalting Constable in the
    Execution of his office...Jury Robert Melton, foreman;
    (same as before)...Not guilty.

    William Shaw vs John Watson P & S Judgmt Confess'd according
    to 2 Notes.

    Eugene Brenan vs Marshall Martin P & S Judgment confessed
    according to Note. Stay of levy till 20th April next

    The Grand Jurors Returnd the following Bills (to wit)

    The State vs Fields Pardue. Indictmt Assault True bill,
    Edmd Martin, forem.

    The State vs Andrew Glover. Indt. Assault. True bill.

    The State vs John Hatcher Indt. Assault. True bill.

63 The State vs John Reynolds. Assault & Battry. True Bill.

    Duncan Campbell & Co. vs Richard Johnson Junr. Case. Judg-
    ment confess'd for L 11 17.11 Stay Exon till 1st of July

    The State vs John Davis Assault Dft. Discharged

    Reuben Frazer vs Benjamin Green. Attm. Ordered that a De-
    dimus Potestatum Issue directed to any Two Justices of the
    Peace in Chatham County in the State of Georgia to take the
    Examination of Richard Wayne as a witness on the part of the
    Defendant....

    John Randle vs Jessee Roundtree. Assault. On issue joined.
    (same jury as State vs John Watson) find for Plaintiff L 2
    s 5 with costs of suit.

64 The State vs Richard Burton Indictment Assault & Battery.
    True Bill.

    The State vs George Randle Indictment Cattle Stealing.
    True Bill.

    The State vs Aaron Kite. Indictment Petit Larceny, True Bill.

    The State vs Noah lias Nart Wimberly. Indictment. Giving
    a negro a Pass. No Bill.

    Joseph Hightower, Treas. vs James Barronton & Rob White. P &
    S. Judgment confessed by James Barronton according to note
    Stay execution till 1st of May next

Rachael Mallett vs Richard Johnson. Appeal Judgment confirmed.

On application of Col. John Martin & West Cook for letters of
admn. on the Estate of Col. James Martin, decd. Ordered that
the same be granted to them on their entering into bond in
the sum of Ł 800 with Robert Samuel & George Ker as sureties
which was done & the said John Martin & West Cook were quali-
65 fied as admrs. by taking the oath for that purpose appointed.
Ordered that the following persons or any three of them were
appointed to appraise the said Estate. To wit: William Howle
Jr., Drury Adams, George Martin & John Ealam.

Jos. Hightower, Tr., vs West Cook & E. Ferrell. Case. Same
indictment.

On application of John Hall permission was granted to him to
keep tavern surities Seth Howard & John G. Cook

Ordered that all the personal Estate of Col. James Martin decd
be sold at House of William Newson on Thursday the 9th of
April next on a credit of 12 months the purchaser to give
bond and approved security the whole estate to be inventoryed
and returned into the clerks office previous to the issue the
order for sale.

Ordered that this court be adjourned till tomorrow morning 9
o'clock. Arthur Simkins, W. Anderson.

66 The court met according to adjournment on the 14th March
1795. Present the Hon. Arthur Simkins,William Anderson, Esq.

Thomas Butler vs Jonathan Richardson Contd. Plaintiffs cost

The State vs James Cheney, John Cheney Junr. Tavern Indictment assault and Battery on issue joined whereupon came a
jury to wit: Robert Melton foreman and the same of the other
yesterday who say...not guilty.

John Steele assignee of Wm. Shaw vs Vachel Clary. Debt.
Judgment confessed for Ł 10 and interest according to note
with costs with stay of sale till 1st August next paid to
Wm. Shaw Ł 6 s 17 d 7 this day.

Daniel Griffin vs James Robert Mayson. P & S. Ordered than
an -- issue against the body of Jonathan Chiles for a witness
this action on the part of the Defendant for contempt

Samuel Wright vs George Tankersly. Altm. Dismissed.
Ordered that Robert Burt surety for John Williams as guardian
for James Coody be discharged therefrom.

George Ker vs James Coursey. Debt. Judgment confessed according to note with interest & cost with stay of sale till
1st Jan. next.

Benjamin Glover Indee. vs William Eavans. P & S Decree
added to note with cost of suit.

John Cheney vs Melenes C. Leavensworth Case. Judgmt. Confess'd for the amt. of the Note discharged in Tobacco at
13/6 pr Hundred with Stay Exon two months.

Benjamin Glover vs Rufus Inman. P & S Decree acd. to Note with Costs of suit.

John Callett vs Daniel Barksdale. P & S. Barkley Martin & Malines C. Leavenworth surety for costs.

68 John Steele assignee vs Littleberry Bostick. P & S. Decree according to note with costs of suit stay till 1st Aug next

An inventory of the Estate of Mary Foreman was returned by Isaac Foreman executor.

Nicholas Lowe vs Robert Melton & Frederick Tillman Jr. P & S. Dismissed

Absent Arthur Simkins, Esq.

John Simkins vs Benjamin Ryan & Peter Chastain. P & S. In-dm't by Default. Decree for ₺ 8 with interest according to note.

John Hammond vs Thomas Ellis. P & S. Judgment by default Decree for ₺ 6 s 13 d 11 with cost.

Present Arthur Simkins, Esq.

Christian Roundtree vs Melines C. Leavenworth. Debt. An -- issue.
Ordered that David Whitmoore a material witness in this case for contempt.

Ordered that this court be adjourned till Monday morning 9 o'clock. Arthur Simkins, W. Anderson.

The Court met according to adjournment on 16th March 1795. Present the Hon. Arthur Simkins, Esq.

69 On application of Jesse Scruggs security for Peter Morgan as guardian to Mackeness Minter, a minor, son to William Minter, decd., ordered that the said Peter Morgan be cited to appear at the next intermediate court to give counter securtiy for the relief of the said Jesse Scruggs.

On application of Butler Williams permission was granted to him to keep Tavern Securities Britton Mims & Littleberry Adams

Ordered that all the personal estate of Jesse Jernagan be sold on the first Thursday in April next at the late dwelling of the said dec'd on a credit of 12 months the purchaser to give bond and approved security

The Clerk having reported fully that the acct of Mrs. John Cheney admr. of James Chaney lodged last intermediate court on oath of said John Cheney ordered that the same be allowed of.

John Cattlett vs Daniel Barksdale. P & S. Judgment confessed for ₺ 9 s 19 d 10 with costs stay execution 3 months.

Present the Hon. Thomas Bacon.

Melines C. Leavenworth vs Patrick Hayes. Alt. Reinstated.

Charles Martin vs Samuel Landrum. Debt. Judgment confessed according to note stay Execution till June 'next.

The state vs James Crissup. Ordered that his recognance be forfeited.

70 The State vs John & Audry Glover. Ordered that a Bench Warrant issue against William Harper a witness on the part of the State to compell his attendance as a witness to next juditary court.

The State vs Thomas Gray. Ordered that a issue against John Coursey as security to show cause why his recognizance should not be forfeited.

The State vs Hannah Brooks. Bastardy. Ordered that a issue against her to show cause why her recognizance should not be forfeited.

The following Bill which were returned on Saturday by the Grand Jury were omitted to be entered on the minutes to wit:

The State vs William Harper Indictment for Assaulting a constable. True Bill.

The State vs John Atwood. Indictment Purgery No bill.

The state vs Rufus Inman. Indictment assault a Deputy Sheriff. no bill

71 Philip May Jr. vs Ann & Alex Rayburn. P & S Decree for the plff for Ł 4 s 10 and d 1 & cost stay execution 4 months.

Richard Lanier vs John Philips. P & S. Decree for the Plaintiff for Ł 8 with interest from 1st of Sept. last, Stay exn. 3 months.

The State vs JosephJeter & William Jeter Jun. Indictment assault the same Jurors as before on their oaths do say we find Joseph Jeter guilty, George Manly & William Jeter Jr. not guilty.

An inventory of the Estate of Jones Rivers was rec'd and ordered to be recorded.

William Killcrease vs William Blackley. P & S. Judgment confessed for 1000 weight of tobacco to be settled at s 11 per hundred and costs of suit stay levy 3 mo.

72 John Mallett vs Benjamin Melton. Debt. Ordered that a dedimus Potestatum issue directed to any two Justice of the Peace in the State of Georgia Green County to take the examination of Benjamin Crooze as a witness for the defendant be given the plaintiff 10 days notice of the time and place of such examination.

Ordered that this court be adjourned till tomorrow morning 9 o'clock. Arthur Simkins, Thos Bacon.

The court met according to adjournment on 17th March 1795. Present the Hon. Arthur Simkins, Thomas Bacon.

Eugene Brenan & Co. vs George Cheney. P & S. Dismissed at Deft. cost

Isaac Kirkland vs Peter Hillard. P & S. Judgment confessed for $14 each party paying his own costs.

Samuel Wright vs George Tankersley. Alt. P & S. Dismissal

73   Samuel Ramsay vs John Philip. P & S. Judgment confessed according to note

Eugene Brenan & Co vs George Cheney. P & S. Dismissal Plffs costs.

Patrick & Alex McDowall vs Thomas Lamar H. C. Debt. Judgment confessed for Ł 10 s 17 d 6 with interest and costs of suit on two notes of hand stay of levy untill 1st Nov. next

John Hatcher vs Thomas Adams. Slander on issue joined whereupon came a jury to wit: (same as before)...we find for the plaintiff Ł 10 and costs of suit.

Hunt and Stallings vs Samuel Wright & Jas. Day. P & S. Dismissal for want of security for costs.

John Hill vs Robert Clary. Att. P & S Dismissed pltffs costs.

74   Daniel Griffin vs James Robert Mayson. P & S. Decree for the plaintiff for Ł 4 s 9 with interest according to note & costs of suit.

Seth Howard vs Robert Clary. Attm. Dismissed each party paying Amt. and Seth Howard the Clerks costs.

Daniel Griffin vs James Robert Mayson. Case and all matters in dispute Ordered that this cuase be referred to Toliva Bostick & Thomas Gary with power of umpirage and report to next court to be made a rule thereof. Approved of by the Court.

Johnathan Weaver vs James West. Case approved Dockett Judgmetn confessed for 2000 weight tobacco to be Estimated at s 13 d 6 pr. hundred with costs of suit. stay exen. till 20th Dec. next without int.

Crookshank & Co. vs John Garrett. Case Dismissed Plff cost.

John Leach vs John Monk. Case Dismissed Plff costs.

Joseph Hightower Tr. vs John Herndon & Seth Howard. P & S Dismissed

75   Seth Howard vs Thomas Lamar Case. Judgment confessed for 3000 weight Tobacco at s 11 per hundred with interest from 13th Nov 1794 till paid Stay of levy 6 months.

John Clark vs William Brown. Case Judgment by default.

William Moore Vs John Spragins Gorman. Plffs. Dismissed default costs.

John Steele asignee vs Thomas Spraggins. P & S Continued.

John Jolly vs John Gorman. P & S. Dismissed Default costs.

The same vs the same. P & S. Same order.

The State vs Joseph Jeter Assault.
On the jury finding him guilty whereupon the court proceeded
and fined him Ł 5 and costs.

Ordered that this court be adjourned till tomorrow morning
nine o'clock. Arthur Simkins, Thomas Bacon.

76 The Court met according to adjournment on 18th March 1795.
Present the Hon. Arthur Simkins & Thomas Bacon, Esquires.

Daniel Ritchey vs Robert Samuel. Case on issue joined
whereupon came a jury (same as before) we find for the plaintiff Ł 10 s 10 & costs of suit.

Frances Burt vs Richard Johnson & J. Hatcher P & S Stand
over.

Jesse Roundtree vs Thomas Lamar. Debt. Ordered that the
defendant give special bail in this action.

Thomas Handcock vs Joab Glover. P & S. Judgment confessed
for 1050 weight of tobacco to be settled at 13 sh. per hundred and costs stay of levy 1 month.

77 Charles Goodwin vs William Breoks. P & S Judg by default
dismis'd

John Beckum vs Reuben Beckum. P & S Judgment by default
Decree for 1100 wieght of tobacco to settle 12/6 per hundred
& costs of suit.

James Willson vs Thomas Lamar. Appeal from the indictment of
Acquilla Miles, Esq. judgment confirmed for Ł 2 s 10 & costs.

Charles Cooper vs Thomas Lamar. Appeal from the Judgmt. of
Aquila Miles, Esqr. Judgt. confirmed for Ł 2 s 1 & costs

The Admors. Tutt dec'd vs Abner Perrin. Judgment according
to bond Stay execution 3 months.

The Admors. Tutt vs William Dawson & William Eavans. Debt.
Judgment confessed according to bond and costs of suit.

George Ker vs Ulysses Rogers. Alt. it appearing to the
court that in this case there was a verdict for Ł 16 s 18 with
costs. Ordered that the same be recorded. Judgment accordingly.

78 John Todd vs James Cobb. Debt on issue joined wherefore came
a jury (same as before)...we find for the plaintiff Ł 14 s
2 d 10 with interest from April 3rd 1792 & costs of suit.

Philip Lamar vs James Hargrove. Appeal from the Judgment of
Joseph Hightower, Esq. Judgment confirmed.

The Same vs Benjamin Hightower. Appeal from the Judgment of
Joseph Hightower, Esq. Judgment confirmed.

178

The Same vs Robert Farish Esq. Appeal from the Judgment of
Joseph Hightower. Judgment confirmed.

The Same vs George Hogarth. Appeal from the Judgment of Joseph Hightower, Esq. Judgment confirmed.

79 Philip Lamar vs William F. Taylor. Appeal from the Judgment
    of Joseph Hightower, Esq. Judgment confirmed.

Ordered that Ricahrd Tutt Esq, John Simkins and Eugene Brenan
or a majority of them be commissioned to advertise immediately at the several public houses in the vicinity of the Court
House and let on the first Saturday in April next to the lowest Bidder. The Tarring well, with clean good Tar not boiled
more than well made hot and put on in that order, the whole
outside of the goal as well as the roof as the whole sides &
ends. Also the roof of the Courthouse and shall at the same
time fix close under both eaves of the Court House Roof,
trough or gutters which shall prevent the tar from dropping
or lodging on the weatherboarding which is painted. The
said work to be done over before the last day of June next.
Which shall be paid out of the County fund. Ordered that
the commission be served with a copy of the above order.

80 Hugh O'keefe Indm. vs Wm. & John Parker. Debt on issue joined
    the same Jurors as before. We find for the plaintiff ₺12
    with lawful interest from 16 Oct 1792 with cost of suit.

P. & A. McDowall vs Richard Newman. P & S Judgment according
to note.

Eugene Brenan & Co. vs Henry Swearingen. P & S Judgment for
₺ 5 s 13 d 7½

Peter Chastain vs Jesse Rountree. Nonsuit.

Same vs Same Nonsuit.

Ann Banks vs Joshua Hammond Nonsuit.

P. & A. McDowall vs Frances Lightfoot & James Wilson. Debt
Judgment by default. Verdict of the same Jury as before
according note and costs of suit.

81 John McKinney vs Vallentine Brazil. Issue Continued.

John Hammond vs Nathaniel Shearly Issue continued.

Angus Dallas & Walker vs Samuel Burgess Do Do

The Exors of Hammond vs Moses & Jenkins Harris. Judgment
confessed according to note.

The same vs William Reynolds. Stand over issue joined.

William Shinholster vs Mary Meyer. Abated by D. of Deft.

Thomas Butler vs Marshall Martin. Debt. Judgment confessed
acc to note stay 3 months.

James Vessels & wife vs Edmund Martin. Stand over issue

Robert Gardner vs Angus Cunningham. Stand over issue.

Garird Banks & Napper vs William Evanas. Stand over Issue.
C. Goodwin Security.

82 Young Gains vs David Gains. Stand Over Issue

Ann Rowan vs Wm. & James Coursey Stands Over Issue

Eliza Ann Pruvis Exx. vs Samuel Burges. Stands Over Issue

Drury Mims vs John Hammond Stands Over Issue

Rue Cleaveland Admr. vs Richard Johnson Junr. Stands Over
Issue.

William Covington vs Nicholas Shaffer. Jud by Default Issue

George Ker vs J. T. Lowe Stands Over Issue.

George Ker vs Charles Wells. Stands Over Issue

Richard Quarles vs James McQueen. Stands Over Issue.

John Steele assignee vs Timothy Haver. Judmt by Default
Issue.

James Shepperd vs Jonas Griffin. Judmt by Deft. Issue.

83 Jesse Roundtree vs Thomas Lamar Stands Over Issue

Andrew Pickens vs James Lyon. Att Stands Over issue

P & A McDowall vs Jno Norwood. Stands Over issue

E. Brenan & Co. vs John Williams. Stands Over Issue.

P. & A. McDowall vs Saml Landrum. Stands Over Issue.

Eugene Brenan & Co. vs John Mims Senr. Stands Over Issue.

John Hammond vs Marshall Martin Stands Over Issue.

John Spraggins Gorman vs Vachel Clary. Stands Over Issue

Adam Bruner vs Christopher Hammel. Stands Over Issue.

Adam Bruner vs Christopher Long. Stands Over Issue.

84 William Humphries vs Jesse Gains. Attm Non suit.

Isaac Teasdale vs Andrew Burney Alt. Stand over as issue

Richard Johnson Jr. vs John Williams. Alt. Stand over issue

On application of John Simkins permission was granted him to
keep Tavern sureties, David Thompson & Sampson Butler

On application of Arge Gann permission was granted to him to
keep Tavern securities David Huff and Robert White.

Edward Court vs Alex. Bland. Appeal from Judgment reversed.

Ordered that this court be adjourned till the court in course.
Arthur Simkins, Thos. Bacon.

The court met according to adjournment on 6th July 1795.
Present the Hon. Arthur Simkins Esq.

On application of Paul Abney permission was granted him to
keep Tavern securities Joshua Dean & John Cadle.

85 An amount of the sale of Arnold Berry was returned on oath
of Mary Berry Admrx. which was rec'd and ordered to be recorded.

On application of Maj. B. Martin permission was granted
to Matt Martin to keep Tavern Securities Barkley Martin &
Sampson Butler.

Ordered that Thomas Warren be overseer of the road leading
from Anderson Ferry to the Waking plan from Clouds Creek to
the District line.

On application of Thomas Banks permission was granted to him
to keep Tavern securities John Cadle & Ogden Cockeroft.

On application permission of William Dozer (Rd. M. Dozer)
permission was granted to him to keep Tavern securities
Russell Willson & Sampson Butler.

On application of Thomas Taylor permission was granted to
him to keep Tavern Moses Taylor and Jesse Cox.

On application of John Swillivan for letters of Admn. on the
Estate Jonathan Swillivan ordered that the same be granted
him on his entering into bond in the sum of Ł 200 with Littleberry Adams & John Curry as his securities which was done
and the said John Swillivan was qualified as administrator
to the said estate. Ordered that the following persons or
any three of them being first sworn do appraise & inventory
the same: Absolum Roberts, Shearly Whatley Sr., Aaron
Herrin and Edmund Whatley.

86 On application of Barrott Travis permission was granted him
to keep tavern securities John Bledsoe and Alexr. Wilson.

Elisha Palmer came into court and acknowledged his deed of
100 acres of land more or less to John Huffman which was
ordered to be recorded.

On application of Joseph Summerall permission was granted
him to keep Tavern, Ebenezer Hill and Jiles Letcher.

Ordered that John Swillivan be overseer of the road from
Horns Creek in the room of Aaron Harrison excused.

Ordered that William Holmes be overseer of the road leading
from Cambridge to the Ridge that part from Barrott Travis'
to Indian Creek in the room of Philip Ikner excused.

Ordered that Jeremiah Mobley be overseer of the road from
John Jones to James Buckelew in the room of Ogden Cockeroft
excused.

An amount of sale of the estate of Joseph Walker was returned
on oath of James Walker admr. and ordered to be recorded.

An inventory of the Estate of Onias Morgan was returned and
ordered to be recorded

87 Ordered that all the personal Estate of Onias Morgan be sold
at the home of Abiah Morgan on the last Monday in July (inst.)
on a credit of 12 months the purchaser to give bond and
security

An inventory of the estate of William Torrence was returned
and ordered to be recorded

On application of John Adams permission was granted to him
to keep Tavern security Samuel Carter and John Hill.

Ordered that Bibby Bush be overseer of the road leading from
Lees Bridge to the Pine house that part from his house to
Christian Gomillion in the room of Elisha Barronton excused.

An amount of the sale of the estate of Frederick Sisson dec'd
was returned on oath of William Humprhies exr.   and ordered
to be recorded.

Robert O Williams being heretofore appointed Guardian to
Olinda Williams came into court and entered into bond in the
sum of Ŀ 200 with John Swillivan and Robert Lang as his sec.

The court requests that James Harrison Esq. advertise and sell
an estray cow yearling in the possession of Thomas Stallsworth
on a credit of 6 months take note with good security and transmit the same to the Treasurer of this county as soon as possible.

An inventory of the estate of Bryant Green was returned and
ordered to be recorded

88 An inventory of the estate of Josiah Brunson was received and
ordered to be recorded

On application of John Clark Esq. for letters of admn. of
David Zubly with the will annexed Ordered that the same
be granted him on his entering into bond of Ŀ 500 with
Casper Nail Jr. & Nathaniel Howel as securities which was
done and the said John Clark was qualified as an admr. with
the will annexed.

Present the Honbl. Thos Bacon.

On application of John Clark, Esq. & Walter Taylor for letters
of adm.n on the estate of Ann Zubly decd., Ordered that the
same be granted on their entering into bond for Ŀ 500 with
Nathaniel Howell, Joseph Fuller as their securities which was
done and the said John Clarke Esq. & Walter was qualified
as admr. to the said Ann Zubly.   Ordered that the following
persons or any three of them do appraise the said estate
Lud Williams, John Savage, William Shinholster, & William
Tobler.

An inventory of the Estate of Mary Meyer was returned and
ordered to be recorded. Ordered that all the personal estate

of Mary Meyer, except one bed and furniture and three small chairs be sold on a credit of 12 months at the late dwelling of the said dec'd the purchaser to give bond and security sale on Friday the 31st of this instant.

89 On application of Jesse Roundtree for letters of admn. on the estate of John Meyer dec'd. Ordered that the same be granted him on his entering into bond in the sum of Ł 500 with JohnClark & William Fudge as her securities which was done and the said Jesse Roundtree qualified as an admr. Ordered that the following persons or any three of them being first sworn do appraise and inventory the said estate to wit: Lud Williams, George Bender, William Shinholster & John Savage.

An inventory of the estate of Angus McDaniel was recd. and ordered to be recorded

On application of Mrs. Mary Moore, Thomas Bacon, Andrew Pickens for letters of admn. on the estate of James Moore dec'd ordered that the same be granted on their entering into bond in the sum of Ł 1000 with Thomas Key, Barkley Martin & William Key as securities which was done and the said Mary Moore, Thomas Bacon and Andrew Pickens was qualified as admrs. to the said estate. Ordered that the following persons or any three of them do appraise the said estate to wit: Philip Lamar, Harley Johnson, Jesse Rountree & Fields Pardue, Nath'l Bacon.

On application of William Newsom permission was granted him to keep Tavern securities Butler Williams & Daniel Huff

90 The court appointed Joseph Hightower Esq. Coroner for this County.

The last will and Testament of Benjamin Mosely was proved by The Oath of Littleberry Adams & Ordered to be recorded. Priscilla Moseley, George Moseley & Thos Adams qualified as Executrix. Ordered that the following persons or any three of them being first sworn to appraise the said estate: Lewis Tillman, Daniel Huff, Littleberry Adams & Butler Williams

An amount of sales of the Estate of George Cowan was returned on oath of Edmund Whatley Admr. and ordered to be Recorded.

Thomas Williams a minor son to William Williams being of age to choose his guardian came into Court and made choice of John Sullivan which choice was approved of. Ordered that the said John Swillivan enter into bond in the sum of Ł 150 which was done. Ordered that the person & Estate of the said Thomas Williams be in the hands and possession of the said John Swillivan as guardian.

Ordered that William Griffin be overseer from the old Wells to Hightower Tavern in room of William Fudge excused.

Ordered that Fields Pardue be overseer of the road leading from Savannah River near Campbell's Ware house lot from thence to a direct line in the room of Barkley Martin excused as per the order

On petition of Sundry Inhabitants for a road leading from

183

Abbeville County line near Murry of old store to intersect
the Martintown road near Joseph Colliers.

Ordered that James Frazier, Absolum Williams and Abner Perrin
be and they are hereby appointed commissioner to view the
ground from the county line to Stephens Creek and from thence
to Turkey Creek, James Sanders, John Talbert & William Eavans
from thence to Jos. Colliers on the Martintown road near
Colliers Jno Martin, Jas. Collier, Davis Thompson. Ordered
that the above appointed Commissioners view the ground &
report to next intermediate court.

Ordered that Joseph Fuller be overseer of the road leading
from John Hammond Ferry to Pretty run bridge and from this
place where the said road comes into the road from Cherokee
Pond to the said Ferry which leads to Maj. Pardue's in the
Room of John Hammond excused.

92   Ordered that John Glover be overseer of the road leading from
Cloud's to Adams Ferry that part from Roundtrees old Mills
to said Ferry.

Ordered that Benjamin Milton be overseer of the road leading
from Lees Bridges to the Pine House that part Bibby Bushes
to the Mine Hole in the room of James Brum, excused.

Ordered that William Bush be overseer of the road leading
from E. Court House to the Ridge that part from Brazels to
Jas. Barrentines in the room of Adam Stalnaker, excused.

Ordered that John Miller be overseer of the road called the
Old Long Cain Road that part from John Jones's to Little
Stevens Creek in the room of West Harris, excused.

Permission was granted to West Harris to keep Tavern Securities Samuel Landrum, Joel Chandler.

Ordered that his court be adjourned till tomorrow ten o'clock.
Arthur Simkins.
Ended the 6th July 1795. R. Tutt, O. E. C.

END OF VOLUME.

187

188

Rydon 165(2)
Grimke, John J. F. 123
Gross, John 147
Guin see also Gwin
Guin, Morrice 110, 117, 120, 139
  Morris 76
Gunnels, Daniel 2, 108, 113, 158, 169
  Dicy 2
  James 14, 30, 82(3), 100(4), 125
  Moses 2
  Rosannah 2
  Sarah 2
  Saunders 2
Gunnels branch 3(2), 19, 75, 108, 134, 151
Gwin, Morris 7, 33, 36, 40
  Norris 12
Gwinn, John 167
  Morris 167

Hagin, Thomas 9, 22, 25, 27, 38, 132, 138
Hagoo(d), James 37, 154, 160
  William 73
Halfway swamp 4
Hall, Christopher 157
  John 131, 164, 168, 169(2), 174
  Samuel 169
Hamilton see also Hammelton
Hamilton, John 153(2)
Hammel, Christopher 180
Hammilton, William 62, 85, 94, 103
Hammond, 179
  Abner 119, 142, 144
  Ann 70, 85, 95, 104
  Col. 60, 61
  Catherine 164
  Charles 58, 102, 164
  Elizabeth 115(2)
  John 9, 15, 16, 22, 47, 48, 54, 60, 64, 73, 80, 81, 82, 83, 94, 96, 109(2), 115(3), 116(3), 121, 132, 135, 143, 146(3), 148(2), 157, 166, 171(2), 175, 179, 180(2), 184
  John Jr. 23
  John Sr. 19, 24, 62
  Joshua 2, 11, 27, 32, 45, 62, 63, 71(2), 72(2), 97, 158, 163, 164, 168, 179
  Joseph Jr. 168
  Leroy 1(2), 6(3), 7, 13, 15, 17, 20(2), 22, 24, 28(4), 30(2), 31(2), 33, 41(2), 42, 44, 45, 48, 49, 51(2), 53(3), 55, 57(2), 58, 61, 63, 65, 66(2), 67(2), 68(2), 71, 74(2), 75, 81, 82(2), 84, 86, 90, 91, 92(7), 94, 96(3), 98(3), 99(2), 100(2), 102(3), 103(3), 111, 114, 115(4), 116(2), 119, 121, 124(2), 125, 127(3), 129(2), 133, 134(2), 135, 136(2), 141, 142(2), 144, 146(3), 147, 164, 166
  Leroy Jr. 146
  Samuel 32, 60, 78, 104, 119
Hammonds warehouse 136
Hampthon, Henry Allison 85
Hampton, Edward 18
  Henry 78, 85
  John 85, 91, 94, 122
Hamton, John 78
Hancock, John 3, 10, 12(4), 13(2), 19(2), 20, 28, 29, 40(2), 42, 55(3), 56, 68, 71, 75
Handcock, Frances 61, 93

John 98, 101, 103, 109, 124, 133, 135, 136, 139
  Thomas 143, 178
Haney, Lyon 155
Hard Labor Creek 22, 43, 75
Harden, William 161
Hardin, Margaret 50(2)
  William 50(2), 59, 62, 150
Hardiss, Isaac 78
Hardy, John 12, 26, 34, 47(2), 156
  Richard 156
  William 34, 70, 93, 126(2), 135(2)
Har(e)grove, James 18, 39, 41, 51, 53, 83, 98, 106, 111, 112, 141, 149, 170, 178
  John 143
  Mary 153
  William 38(2), 39, 63, 106, 112, 153
Hargins, John 47, 75
  Thomas 47
Harkins, James 41, 54
  John 9, 70, 105
Harlin, Ezekiel 11, 13, 16, 25
Harlens Ferry 37, 38, 43, 87, 109
Harlins place 140
Harper, Mr. 93, 102
  Arthur 158
  Robert 18, 84
  William 176(2)
Harrel, Abner 16
Harrell, Philip 42
Harris, 2
  Benjamin 20, 33, 34, 43, 126
  Elizabeth 51
  Ezekiel 88, 90, 100(2), 116, 118, 124, 127, 128, 129, 137
  Isaac 34
  James 6, 7, 10, 24, 100, 108, 123, 142, 145, 147
  Jenkin 4, 13, 24, 34, 49, 51, 58, 66, 68, 69, 70, 106, 131, 134, 146, 147, 179
  Jesse 10, 43, 87
  John 4, 7(2), 13, 16, 17, 23, 25, 26, 36(2), 46, 100, 147
  Mary 46
  Moses 7, 26, 34, 52, 68(2), 70(2), 107, 131, 170, 179
  Sarah 15, 25, 33, 38, 59, 65, 83, 92
  Thed. 50
  Thomas 110
  West 160, 184
  William 23, 134, 142, 147
Harris Plantation 37
Harrison, 95
  Aaron 181
  James 9, 34, 35, 40(2), 41, 43, 47, 50, 51(2), 63, 67(2), 70, 91, 94(2), 105, 106, 110, 111, 117, 118, 120, 128, 133, 144, 168, 182
  James, C.T. 33
  James, R.B. 40
  John 6, 15
  Joshua 163
  Thomas 30, 160
Hart see also Heart
Hart, Hartwell 139
  James 77, 82
  Robert 126
Hartley, Daniel 30
Harveland, Jacob 97
Harvey, 137
  Blassingame Jr. 127
  Elizabeth 76
  Joel 118

Littleberry 118
  William 72(2), 76
  William B. 32(2), 45
  William Baker 45, 59, 66
  Zepheniah 72
Hatcher, J. 178
  Jeremiah 119, 151, 158, 161, 163, 166(2)
  John 173, 177
  Robert 155
Hatchers pond 37, 163(2)
Hater, John 11
Haters pond 37
Haver, Timothy 180
Hawkins, Abemeleck 16, 60, 80, 83, 93, 160
  James 159
Hays, Patrick 119, 137, 138, 147(2), 156, 169, 170, 176
Hayne, William 33
Heart, George 143, 147
  Hartwell 137
  James 67, 139
Heath, Abraham 5, 14
Hebbler see also Hibbler
Hebbler, Jacob 150, 158
Henan, James 39
Henderson, James 10, 20, 25, 40, 47, 50, 139
  John 21, 105, 111
  Nathaniel 10, 76, 86
  Obadiah 9
  Richard 40, 47, 130, 140, 144
  Shadrick 10, 20, 25, 47, 50, 87, 130, 140
Hendon see also Herndon
Hendon, Ephriam 116
  John 68, 71
Hendren, Ephraim 116
Hendricks, Jabish 27, 72
Henry, Lyon 107, 115, 121, 125, 126, 147
Henton, Allen 32
Hern, Daniel 41, 42
  Drury 132
Herndon, John 1, 4, 13, 26, 31, 32, 34, 39, 43, 59, 60, 61, 68(2), 73(2), 78(2), 80, 85, 93, 97, 98, 101, 106, 109, 110, 112, 118, 124, 125, 126, 131(2), 134, 135(2), 137(3), 139, 146, 147, 156, 170, 177
  William 39, 170
Herrin, Aron 133, 181
  James 50
  William 64
Herrin Plantation 64
Hester, 119
  John 169
Hibbler, Jacob 155, 157(2), 169, 170
Hicks, Christopher 22
  Edmond Bugg 115
  John 39, 45, 95
Hightower see also Hitower
Hightower, 158
  Benjamin 163, 178
  Christopher 2
  James 171
  John 24, 60, 93, 93, 102
  Joseph 2, 23, 34, 73, 76(2), 81, 82, 87, 90, 94, 106(2), 131, 139, 156, 163(2), 168(2), 173, 174, 178(2), 179(3)
  Joseph Jr. 177, 183
  Martha 102
  Sterling 88
  William 24, 52, 82
Hightowers Tavern 183
Hill, Ebenezer 102, 136, 161, 181
  Isaac 126, 148

190

196

Richard 89
Wingate, Isaac 134
Wise, Jacob 37
Witherton, Richard 43, 69, 77,
   91
  Thomas 69
Witzel, Eleanor 11, 20
  John 11(2), 20
Wms, John 70
Wommack, John 122
Wonack, John 91
Woods, 118
  Joseph 133
Wooten, Thomas 33, 63, 93
Wright, John 157
  Jonathan 118
  Mishack 19, 27, 43, 168
  Samuel 78, 98, 102, 124, 134,
    137, 155, 174, 177(2)
Wullivan, Patrick 64

Yancey, 25
  James 20
Yarborough, William 164(2), 169
Yates, Abraham 73
  Thomas 73
Yeer, Robert 156
Youngblood, Henry 54
  James 70
  John 170
  Lewis 132, 138, 170
  Thomas 10, 20, 25, 47, 54(2),
    64, 66, 113, 118, 121, 124
Youngs place 133

Zegler see also Zigler
Zigler, David 40, 47(2)
Zimmerman, Godfrey 147
  Henry 105, 130, 140(2), 165
  Peter 76, 87
Zin, Voluntine 76, 87, 89
Zinn, Jacob 66, 89, 109, 140,
  172
Zubly, Ann 144, 153, 168, 182
  David 9, 19, 21, 23, 30(2),
    31, 40, 44, 49(2), 51, 52,
    88, 90, 97, 100, 101, 102,
    103, 110, 112, 118, 121,
    124, 127, 128, 129, 134(2),
    135, 137, 144(2), 153, 168,
    182

Philemon--76
Shaderick--40

www.ingramcontent.com/pod-product-compliance
Lightning Source LLC
Chambersburg PA
CBHW021045210326
41598CB00016B/1106